Stalin's Armour, 1941–1945

Stalin's Armour, 1941–1945

Soviet Tanks at War

Anthony Tucker-Jones

Pen & Sword
MILITARY

First published in Great Britain in 2021 by
Pen & Sword Military
An imprint of
Pen & Sword Books Ltd
Yorkshire – Philadelphia

ISBN 978 1 52677 793 5

A CIP catalogue record for this book is
available from the British Library.

Typeset by Mac Style
Printed and bound in the UK by TJ Books Limited,
Padstow, Cornwall.

Pen & Sword Books Limited incorporates the imprints of Atlas,
Archaeology, Aviation, Discovery, Family History, Fiction, History,
Maritime, Military, Military Classics, Politics, Select, Transport,
True Crime, Air World, Frontline Publishing, Leo Cooper, Remember
When, Seaforth Publishing, The Praetorian Press, Wharncliffe
Local History, Wharncliffe Transport, Wharncliffe True Crime
and White Owl.

For a complete list of Pen & Sword titles please contact

PEN & SWORD BOOKS LIMITED
47 Church Street, Barnsley, South Yorkshire, S70 2AS, England
E-mail: enquiries@pen-and-sword.co.uk
Website: www.pen-and-sword.co.uk

Or

PEN AND SWORD BOOKS
1950 Lawrence Rd, Havertown, PA 19083, USA
E-mail: Uspen-and-sword@casematepublishers.com
Website: www.penandswordbooks.com

Contents

List of Illustrations

1. In 1941 Soviet dictator Joseph Stalin had the largest tank fleet in the world, but he and his generals did not know how to deploy it effectively. (All images sourced by author)
2. Georgi Zhukov, future Hero of the Soviet Union, gained valuable experience in tank combat fighting the Japanese in 1939 and ended up Stalin's deputy commander.
3. Konstantin Rokossovsky started the war as a mechanized corps commander and went on to take part in all the major battles on the Eastern Front, including Moscow, Stalingrad, Kursk and Operation Bagration.
4. The T-34/76 medium tank first came off the Kharkov factory production line in January 1940. The Model 1940 (T-34/76A) is identifiable by the low-slung barrel of the 76.2mm L-11 anti-tank gun, below a distinctive bulge in the mantlet housing the recoil mechanism.
5. Similarly, the KV-1 heavy tank had first gone into production in February 1940 at Leningrad's Kirov works and was available only in limited numbers.
6. The first production version of the KV-1 was designated the Model 1939. It is easily recognizable by the rounded recuperator above the 76.2mm L-11 tank gun barrel. The Model 1940 T-34 had a similar arrangement.
7. Model 1940 KV-1 uparmoured with 35mm plates which were bolted on. The Germans dubbed this version the KV-1E.
8. Abandoned KV-1 with added turret applique armour.
9. German soldiers examine the remains of a KV-1. It has the uparmoured turret which has done nothing to save the tank from destruction.

10. The KV-2 with its enormous turret housing the 152mm M1938/40 howitzer. This could not be traversed unless the tank was on level ground, which severely restricted its ability to fight off-road.

11. It is not clear if this KV-2 was in a hull-down position to guard an airfield, or whether it simply sank under its own weight.

12. Horse-drawn German baggage wagons pass a KV-2 left on the roadside.

13. Two KV-2s left derelict on the road by their unit. The nearest has 'I Kompanie' scrawled on the side of the turret, the victors having already laid claim to it.

14. This side view shows an impact hole between the first and second return rollers. It was this that severed the track. The gun suffered damage as it has been holed.

15. This KV-2 put up a fight before succumbing. Three impact marks can be seen just to the right of the hull machine gun and on the right-hand side of the main gun mantlet.

16. The bulk of the Soviet fast tanks consisted of the BT-5's uparmoured successor the BT-7, seen here with the newer conical turret, which went into production in 1935.

17. Overturned BT-7 Model 1935 with the rounded hull nose and early cylindrical T-26-style turret.

18. One of hundreds, if not thousands, of BT drivers who died with their machines.

19. German troops examine captured BT-7s caught in an ambush.

20. BT-7 fast tanks abandoned at the roadside. Up to 5,000 of these were built at the Kharkov Locomotive Factory along with the T-34 medium tank.

21. The single-turret T-26B light tank appeared in 1933 (the earlier T-26 had twin turrets) and was armed with a 45mm or 37mm gun. Its low speed and poor mobility compared to the BT-5 resulted in production being abandoned in the mid-1930s.

22. The T-26 was obsolete even in 1940; while its 45mm gun could destroy all German armoured vehicles except the Panzer IV,

Introduction

At the moment Adolf Hitler's panzers struck the Soviet Union in mid-1941, the Red Army was in the middle of a major restructuring and redeployment. Joseph Stalin's generals, in a bid to counter the growing Nazi threat, were in the process of slowly moving numerous reinforcements westward. Stalin had at his disposal the largest tank fleet in the world, but many of his tanks were obsolete and spread across the country. His commanders struggled to agree how best to use them; should they support the infantry divisions or be massed as a dedicated mobile reserve? On the eve of war, it was belatedly decided to form dedicated mechanized corps, that would gather the tanks together in armoured divisions, but these were far from ready.

Nonetheless, how did Hitler, with around 3,500 panzers, overwhelm Stalin's fleet of almost 20,000 tanks? The truth of the matter is that by the time of Operation Barbarossa most of the Red Army's poorly-armed and under-armoured tank fleet was completely out of date. To compound matters, the Red Army was still in disarray thanks to Stalin's bloody purges and the resulting ongoing reorganization. Its training was poor as was the supply chain and logistical support. This of course was aggravated by the enormous size of the Soviet Union, which required units and supplies to travel great distances to get to the front. Soviet ineptitude ensured that the panzers only had to contend with a fraction of Stalin's total force.

In some areas Stalin's tank designs were technically superior to those of Hitler's panzers. For example, the T-26 light tank and BT-7 fast tank were both armed with a 45mm gun, which was larger than the standard German 37mm tank gun. However, both tanks had very thin armour and their tracks were too narrow to handle excessive off-road conditions. Some 75 per cent of the Soviet tank force consisted of these and most of them were swiftly lost trying to defend the approaches to the Soviet Union's major cities.

Although the formidable KV-1 heavy and T-34 medium tanks were armed with a 76.2mm gun, it was of an inferior velocity than originally intended thanks to the obstructive political machinations of the Red Army's Artillery Directorate. Both tanks though, which were just coming into service, had thick sloped armour and wide tracks that spread the ground pressure, giving them better cross-country capabilities than their opponents.

While the KV-1 and T-34 were very progressive designs, with good armament-armour-mobility ratios, both were let down by serious clutch and transmission problems. While the T-34 was eventually fine-tuned into a war-winning tank, the KV-1's automotive problems were never fully rectified and it was eventually dropped from production in favour of newer designs and self-propelled guns. Although well-armed compared to the panzers, when the war broke out neither the KV-1 or T-34 were available in large numbers. Those in service were quickly lost thanks to incompetent crews.

Most of Stalin's tankers lacked adequate training at the tactical level and their tanks were often short of ammunition and fuel. Maintenance was also very poor. Reports indicate that around 30 per cent of Soviet tanks needed repairs before the war even started. Once the initial fighting commenced up to 50 per cent of the Red Army's tank fleet was lost simply to breakdowns and a lack of fuel. In other words, gross mismanagement and incompetence. The Red Army's high command saw it as such and many generals were executed for their poor conduct.

Designing a tank is always a compromise between speed, weight, armour and armament. Get the combination right and it gives you a winning edge, get it wrong and it ends in disaster. Most early Soviet tanks opted for speed, as they were seen as little more than armoured cavalry designed to charge through the enemy's lines in support of the infantry. The dominance of cavalry officers in the Red Army after the Russian Civil War was responsible for this mindset. At the same time, the Red Army was struggling to get to grips with how it should employ its ever-growing number of tanks. In the summer of 1941 all of Russia's light, medium and heavy tanks proved complete disasters against Hitler's panzers and superior German strategy. Only after a very shaky start did the T-34 catch the eye of the Red Army's beleaguered generals.

While the T-34 had a number of innovative advantages over its competitors, one in particular stands out. The main problem faced by the British Churchill and Cromwell, the American Sherman and the German Panzer IV and the Panther was that they could not be upgunned beyond a 76mm/77mm calibre gun. The hulls of these tanks simply did not permit a larger turret and therefore a larger calibre anti-tank gun. This greatly limited their tank-killing capabilities. The Allies never really overcame this shortcoming until the advent of the American Pershing tank armed with a powerful 90mm gun but by then the war was all but over. The Germans only got round this limitation by producing higher-velocity 75mm guns plus the Tiger I and II armed with an 88mm gun, but the latter were only built in limited numbers.

The squat hull of the initial T-34/76 enabled the Soviets to conduct a very significant enhancement. They were able to fit a larger cast turret that could house a much bigger gun – namely an 85mm high-velocity anti-aircraft gun redesigned as an anti-tank weapon. The resulting T-34/85, while it may have not given the Red Army battlefield dominance, certainly gave them much-needed parity with the later panzers. This, and the T-34's vast numbers, were a war-winning combination. The T-34's design ensured that it was easy to build and just as importantly easy to maintain on the battlefield regardless of the weather.

In contrast, while the Allies and the Germans enjoyed success with a range of tank destroyers and assault guns, those T-34s converted to an assault gun role proved far less satisfactory. The British and Americans armed some Shermans with 76mm and 77mm guns, but these were very few in number and did not make up for the Sherman's poor armour. Likewise, the Sherman-based Achilles/Wolverine tank destroyer faced the same problem. It was in trying to replicate the German Sturmgeschütz or assault gun concept that the T-34 came a cropper: its tank destroyer variants were little more than a stopgap, until the heavy KV tank chassis married to a 152mm howitzer produced a really invincible tank killer. Only the T-34-based SU-100 tank destroyer, armed with a 100mm gun, provided additional punch that the T-34/85 could not.

It was Soviet experience in Spain during the 1930s that led indirectly to the T-34's development, which gave them an important technological edge over the Germans. In the wake of the Spanish Civil War many Soviet experts concluded that the towed anti-tank gun was a far more effective weapon than the tank, and that the rudimentary armoured combat in Spain refuted the new theories about mechanized warfare. However, they failed to take into account the unsuitable Spanish terrain, the poorly-trained crews and the relatively small numbers of tanks employed.

The Soviet tank specialist General Dimitri Pavlov, who served in Spain and was one of the innovators of Soviet mechanization during the early 1930s, observed first-hand the increased use and accuracy of anti-tank weapons. Both the BT-5 and T-26 suffered a gradual reduction in armour effectiveness and this lead the Soviet Union to ensure that its tanks were not only splinter and small-arms proof, but could also withstand direct hits by small-calibre artillery. Ironically Pavlov's experiences in Spain were to ultimately cost him his life, for he also drew the wrong conclusions about the deployment of armour. He advocated the French doctrine whereby tanks were deployed in direct support of the infantry. He felt that the emerging German doctrine of Blitzkrieg by mass armour was not sound. On returning to Russia in 1939 he argued in favour of disbanding the unwieldy Soviet tank corps.

Just five months before Hitler's attack, during December 1940 and January 1941, senior Soviet commanders attended a key conference followed by war games. There was then a gathering in the Kremlin, the last of its sort before the German invasion. The aim was to assess the progress made by the armed forces following the war with Finland and Hitler's Blitzkrieg victories in Europe. Some commanders still advocated the horse over the tank and crucially Stalin, while he defended the tank, made no executive decision about the future of the Soviet armoured forces.

General Ia N. Fedorenko warned that there were 'too few modern tanks and that a number of tanks which were standard equipment in the Red Army were already obsolete'. He argued that no time should be lost in increasing production of the new KV and T-34 tanks and that funding should be redirected to this end. Marshal G.I. Kulik, who favoured the cavalry and artillery, was completely dismissive of this advice. Crucially Stalin stood up and said that the balance was right. The chance to increase T-34 production was lost. Nonetheless, about 55,000 T-34s were eventually built, representing 68 per cent of Soviet tanks built during the Second World War.

Countdown to War
Along the boulevards and in the parks of the Soviet Union's major cities in the summer of 1941 talk amongst the citizens was of war. Much of Europe was either allied to Hitler, subjugated by him or in open conflict. With the Nazis now so firmly ensconced in western Poland, the question on everyone's lips was what were Hitler's intentions toward Russia? The Soviet Union's cultural elite, its artists, writers and filmmakers, had been harnessed to support Stalin's delusional propaganda; Berlin was Moscow's friend. Nevertheless, while the Soviet press was heavily censored, there was no hiding what the Nazis had been up to in Western Europe, Scandinavia and the Balkans. Hitler's incredibly successful panzer-led Blitzkrieg could not be easily ignored.

From the old men playing chess on park benches to the babushkas in the bustling markets, talk was never very far from war. Sons had seen fighting in the Far East and in Finland or were on 'liberation' duties in the Baltic States. For the average Russian, Byelorussian and

Ukrainian it was hard to conceive that Nazi Germany would be so foolish as to invade the well-armed Soviet Union. Besides, Stalin and his coterie of sycophants in the Kremlin had made sure that Mother Russia was safe from attack by creating a buffer zone stretching through southern Finland, the Baltic States and eastern Poland. The Red Army's doctrine of forward defence was assured – or so the public thought. If there were to be war, Poland would be where the panzers would be stopped by a concerted armoured counter-attack.

The Soviet public's perception of the Red Army was that it was a well-equipped force that the Nazis would be mad to attack. The Soviet press had been full of its heroic exploits in Spain, Mongolia and neighbouring Finland. Only the upper echelons of the Soviet leadership knew the truth, that despite all the impressive window dressing in the shape of military hardware, the Red Army was not a competent fighting force. There is no denying that in 1941 it was a far from a modern army; its treatment at the hands of Stalin and its performance on the battlefield in recent years meant Hitler had a low opinion of it, which was to have disastrous results.

The German-Soviet Second Treaty of Rapallo in 1922 helped Germany sidestep the military restrictions of the Versailles Treaty, which had limited its army to 100,000 men, and banned conscription, tanks, military aircraft and submarines. In return for diplomatic recognition the Soviet government granted Germany access to much-needed raw materials and food. The fledgling Red Army also granted the Germans training facilities where they could try out prohibited equipment. A tank school was set up at Kazan and a flying school at Lipetsk, sowing the seeds for the Panzerwaffe and the Luftwaffe. Future generals who attended included Heinz Guderian, the father of Germany's Panzerwaffe. This relationship ended abruptly in 1933 when Hitler came to power. Within two years, he had torn up the Versailles Treaty, reintroducing conscription, building panzers and other military hardware, and reoccupying the demilitarized Rhineland.

Stalin was not blind to Hitler's stated aim of carving out living space, or Lebensraum, in the East and turned to Britain and France for help. As far as they were concerned he was worse than Hitler, who seemed to be working wonders with the German economy; besides the Soviets made no secret of their desire to regain lost imperial possessions. Stalin watched as Hitler annexed Austria and partitioned Czechoslovakia with impunity. Indeed, the final straw was not being invited to the Munich Conference, which let Hitler have his way with Czechoslovakia. Stalin was left with little option but deal directly with the Nazis. The West was completely caught out on 21 August 1939, when it was announced that Joachim von Ribbentrop, Hitler's foreign minister, was flying to Moscow to sign a nonaggression pact with Stalin. The pact, signed two days later, granted Hitler a free hand to invade Poland the following month. This action finally brought him into direct conflict with Britain and France.

What nobody knew at the time was that that the pact included a secret agreement. Signed just two days after the pact itself, this called for the partition of Poland between Germany and the Soviet Union. Estonia, Finland, Latvia and Lithuania were also recognized as being in the Soviet sphere of influence. Stalin was intent on regaining the tiny Baltic states as well as the Karelian Isthmus from Finland (in order to protect Leningrad) to safeguard his western borders. Hitler's Wehrmacht began their onslaught on Poland, a nation that both Britain and France were pledged to support in the event of a threat to her independence or territorial integrity, at dawn on 1 September 1939. Sixteen days later the Red Army rolled into eastern Poland along an 800-mile front to link up with the victorious Wehrmacht, which in the preceding weeks had systematically crushed the Polish Army. Just ten days later Warsaw surrendered and by 6 October the fighting was over.

Two weeks after moving into Poland, Stalin ordered the Finns to hand over the Karelian Isthmus. When they refused once more, the Red Army rolled in only to receive an unexpected beating. Alarmingly, Britain and France almost found themselves at war with Germany and the Soviet Union as they were poised to help the beleaguered Finns; however, after dogged resistance, the Finns gave in to Stalin's demands in March 1940.

Stalin now felt secure in the knowledge that Hitler would never dare fight a two-front war, but in just three months during April to June 1940, Hitler overran Denmark, Norway, Luxembourg, Belgium, the Netherlands and France, leaving Britain alone and under threat of invasion. It soon became apparent that major German military preparations in occupied Poland, East Prussia, Romania and Finland indicated Hitler was planning to strike at the Soviet Union. Hitler reassured Stalin, claiming the troops movements east were simply designed to mislead Churchill into lowering his guard.

Soviet Defence Minister Marshal Semyon Konstantinovich Timoshenko and Chief of the General Staff General Georgi Zhukov were not convinced. In May 1941 they sought Stalin's permission for a pre-emptive attack, but he did not want to provoke Hitler's hardened Wehrmacht. Meanwhile Hitler moved into the Balkans, securing his southern flank ready to strike east. The war that followed on the Eastern Front was first and foremost a tank war. The Soviet Union witnessed some of the biggest and bloodiest armoured battles the world has ever seen.

While it is not too difficult to appreciate the vast scale of the tank battles fought on the Eastern Front, it is not so easy to grasp the myriad of factors that contributed to either victory or defeat. Essentially, armoured warfare on the Eastern Front was shaped by geography, technology and numbers. Soviet factories soon ensured that the Red Army enjoyed numerical superiority. While Byelorussia and Ukraine were on the whole suited to armoured warfare, the Pripyat Marshes helped shape the strategic options of the two sides. Much has been made of Russia's many rivers, which ironically did little to protect the Soviet Union from Hitler's Blitzkrieg, or indeed impede the Red Army's progress westward once it had eventually recovered from Hitler's initial onslaught.

The German and the Soviet armies took very differing views on how to combat the other's armour. The victories of 1941 in part lulled the Germans into a false sense of security when it came to tank production. Crucially the Germans proved incapable of standardization, producing a plethora of tanks, assault guns and self-propelled guns. Abandonment of the Panzer III in favour of assault guns, essentially a defensive weapon, soon signalled that Hitler had lost the strategic initiative. Subsequent German heavy tanks proved time-consuming to manufacture, were often unreliable and could not be built in decisive numbers.

The Soviets, on the other hand, were not slow to learn from the disasters of 1941; firstly, they rescued their vital tank factories, secondly to buy time they expended the remains of their tank fleet, and thirdly they then discarded those tank designs that had been found wanting and fine-tuned the T-34. Once this tank had been upgunned and produced in decisive numbers, the war largely became one of simple attrition. Soviet tank designers prudently opted to keep their tanks simple, robust and easy to build and repair. German tactical and even strategic capabilities ultimately counted for little against growing Soviet numbers.

Chapter 1

A Tank Aficionado

During the late 1920s the Red Army was slow to adopt the tank. The Russian T-27 tankette, based on a British design, was little more than a machine-gun carrier. However, it was to result in a long line of light tanks, which morphed into fast tanks and finally medium tanks – culminating in the T-34. One man in particular, General Georgi Konstantinovich Zhukov, proved to be a significant tank aficionado. He was to champion the Red Army's first tank brigades, divisions and armies. How did Zhukov, future hero of the Battles of Moscow, Kursk and Berlin, born to peasant stock in 1896, became Russia's most famous tank general? He was to achieve this largely through a combination of military aptitude and being in the right place at the right time. He also realized from the start that the future of warfare would be shaped by the tank.

Zhukov was conscripted in 1915 and subsequently joined the Red Army at the start of the Revolution. He first saw action during the Civil War against the Whites near Shipovo in 1919, when his unit was attacked by 800 Cossacks. A key lesson he learned was that cavalry must be supported by adequate firepower. His military career began to progress when he served as a squadron commander with the 1st Cavalry Army under future Marshal Semyon Mikhailovich Budenny; more importantly Zhukov's brigade commander was Semyon Konstantinovich Timoshenko.

After the war he soon rose to regimental and then brigade commander. Just over two decades later Timoshenko, by then a marshal and People's Commissar for Defence, ensured Zhukov became his principal assistant, Chief of the General Staff, in January 1941 at the age of 44. Notably Zhukov, prior to his appointment as Timoshenko's number two, served as Deputy Commander of the Byelorussian Military District. Neither Budenny nor Timoshenko would show the flare exhibited by Zhukov before or during the war. Budenny was a very old-school cavalryman, with a deep rooted scepticism of tanks, and was not considered very bright by some. Nonetheless, from 1937–9 he held the key posts of commander of the Moscow Military District, then the First Deputy People's Commissar of Defence and during the German invasion commanded the Southwestern Front.

Zhukov was appointed commander of the 3rd Cavalry Corps in 1937, but shortly after he was offered the 6th Cossack Corps. Zhukov was never a conservative cavalryman like Budenny, far from it. While commanding the 3rd and then the 6th Corps, Zhukov cooperated closely with the 21st Detached Tank Brigade, under M.I. Potapov, and the 3rd Detached Tank Brigade, under V.V. Novikov. Both commanders were, in Zhukov's own words, 'former mates of mine'. This experience was crucial.

Zhukov was offered the Byelorussian post at the end of 1938, commanding the cavalry and tank units, which were to comprise around five cavalry divisions, four detached tank brigades and other supporting units. Saying goodbye to the Cossack Corps, Zhukov travelled to Smolensk and during May 1939 conducted a series of exercises near Minsk, little realizing that this would soon be the scene of bitter battles with Hitler's marauding panzers. Of his time in Byelorussia, Zhukov recalled, 'It was clear that the future largely belonged to armour and mechanized units. Hence we gave undivided attention to questions of cavalry-armour cooperation, and the organization of anti-tank defences in combat and in executing manoeuvres.'

His next posting took him to the far-flung reaches of the Soviet Union. During the summer of 1939, Zhukov defeated the Japanese Army on the steppes of Mongolia so decisively that Japan never meddled in Soviet affairs again. It ensured that Stalin was free to fight on just one front rather than two when the time came. When Hitler's armies reached Moscow, Zhukov, with his wealth of experience, was there waiting for them along with his battle-hardened Siberian divisions. The Soviet-Japanese War could not have come at a better time for Zhukov and the Red Army. He would gain invaluable experience, developing his new armoured warfare tactics. He would also become familiar with the forces of the Transbaikal Military District, guarding the Chinese Manchuria-Manchukuo border. This district had come into being in the mid-1930s as a precautionary measure in response to Japan's invasion of China. It also helped create a very useful reserve for the Red Army.

The Soviet high command was understandably alarmed by Japan's conquest of huge areas of China and assessed that this constituted a very real threat to the Soviet border. Zhukov was ordered to see Marshal Voroshilov, the People's Commissar of Defence, in Moscow on 2 June 1939. Voroshilov told him, 'Japanese troops have made a surprise attack and crossed into friendly Mongolia which the Soviet Government is committed to defend from external aggression by the Treaty of 12 March 1936'. Zhukov jumped at the chance to show what he was capable of.

In effect the security of the whole of the Soviet Far East rested in Zhukov's hands. It was time to put into practice all his training in Byelorussia. Accompanied by a small team he flew east, landing first in Chita, headquarters of the Transbaikal Military District. Zhukov met with General V.F. Yakovlev, the military district commander, and his officers. Yakovlev appreciated Stalin was taking the Japanese incursion into the Mongolian People's Republic very seriously, especially if the People's Commissariat of Defence had sent a special envoy with the authority to take charge without recourse to any of the regional commands. In the first instance what Zhukov needed, to make a thorough assessment of the situation, was credible intelligence. He was informed that General N.V. Feklenko's 57th Special Corps was forward-deployed to the south-east in Mongolia, tasked with protecting the republic.

Just three days after his Moscow briefing, Zhukov arrived at 57th Special Corps' HQ at Tamtsak-Bulak in Mongolia and met with

Feklenko, Corps Commissar M.S. Nikishev and Brigade Commander A.M. Kushchev, Chief of Staff. To Zhukov's irritation the situation was a complete mess. The HQ had little appreciation of the situation, communication between the Soviet and Mongolian commands was non-existent and coordination lacking. Zhukov was very unhappy that none of the commanders, except for Nikishev, had even visited the front and therefore had little idea of what was happening on the ground. Grasping the situation, he travelled up to the front and found that local intelligence was equally poor. Zhukov quickly came to the assessment that in its present state, 57th Corps was not up to the job of directing operations nor stopping the Japanese.

He immediately sent his report to Voroshilov, stating he planned that Soviet-Mongolian troops should maintain the bridgehead on the right bank of the Khalkhin-Gol river, while preparing for a counteroffensive. Voroshilov agreed and the ineffectual Feklenko found himself immediately replaced by Zhukov. The latter's first move was to request reinforcements for the air force, plus three rifle divisions, and more significantly a tank brigade and artillery.

Zhukov, alert to the danger of his forces on the east bank being cut off, ordered a large-scale triple-pronged counter-attack with 450 tanks and armoured cars. Under his command was the 11th Tank Brigade, equipped with 150 tanks, the 7th Armoured Brigade with another 154 armoured vehicles and the Mongolian 8th Armoured Battalion, armed with 45mm guns. The 11th Tank Brigade, under its commander Yakovlev, was instructed to strike from the north, supported by the 24th Motorized Regiment, which pressed in from the north-west supported by artillery under Colonel Fedyuinsky. In addition, the 7th Armoured Brigade, under Colonel Lesovoi, was to attack from the south, supported by an armoured battalion from the Mongolian 8th Cavalry Division. Heavy guns from the 185th Artillery Regiment were moved up to support the attack on Bain-Tsagan and the 9th Armoured Brigade in the Khalkhin-Gol bridgehead.

At 0700 hours on 3 July 1939, Soviet aircraft and artillery commenced softening up Japanese positions. Two hours later tanks of the 11th Tank Brigade moved up with the full attack being launched at 1045 hours. Japanese defences and anti-tank guns were inadequate and Zhukov began to make ground. The Japanese response was to launch a counter-attack on the 4th, but it came to grief in the face of Soviet bombers and artillery. That night, the Japanese commander, General Komatsubara, gave the order to withdraw and his men were back over the river by the 5th. Their engineers blew the remaining bridges to prevent the Soviet tanks following, leaving many Japanese with little option but to swim for it. Those troops remaining on the eastern slopes of Bain-Tsagan were annihilated. Although Komatsubara and his HQ got back across the river, hundreds of his men drowned. He left much of his 10,000-strong force behind, strewn all over the mountain.

In the face of a Japanese counter-attack, the Soviets held their ground and by 25 July the Japanese, having suffered over 5,000 casualties, gave up. They counter-attacked again on 12 August and drove the Mongolian 22nd Cavalry Regiment from the Bolshiye Peski height to the south. At this point it would have been prudent for the Japanese to call it a day and summon the diplomats, but instead more anti-tank gun units were brought up ready for another counter-attack. They planned to attack along a 43-mile front on 24 August, but the dynamic Zhukov was to beat them to it by four days.

Zhukov's Soviet-Mongolian command prepared for a knockout counteroffensive. Reinforcements were brought up, including two rifle divisions, a tank brigade and two artillery regiments as well as supporting bomber and fighter units. Stalin, conscious that Hitler would be closely watching events in Central Asia, despatched further reinforcements to him. These included three infantry and two cavalry divisions, seven independent brigades, including five armoured, and additional artillery and air force units to create the 1st Army Group. Zhukov had everything that he needed.

By now Soviet reconnaissance aircraft had pieced together a good picture of the Japanese defences. Zhukov assessed that the Japanese were most vulnerable on their flanks. He knew that their greatest weakness was their lack of mobility, effective tank units and motorized infantry. This meant they would not be able to respond quickly to any Soviet breakthrough. Zhukov's armoured fist consisted of the 4th, 6th and 11th Tank Brigades and the 7th and 8th Mechanized Brigades. He planned to encircle the Japanese using his North, South and Central Groups, with his armour on the wings. The Soviets deployed 50,000 troops to defend the east bank and then Zhukov prepared to cross to the west, with three rifle divisions and his armoured forces. Waiting at their jump-off points were 35 infantry battalions, supported by a mobile force of 20 cavalry squadrons, 498 tanks, 346 armoured cars and 502 guns. At 0545 hours on 20 August Soviet aircraft blasted the Japanese forward positions, followed by a three-hour artillery and mortar bombardment.

Zhukov's tanks roared forward at 0845 hours. By the next day, to the south his forces had swung behind the Japanese, reaching the Khalkhin-Gol's east-west tributary, the Khailastyn-Gol. On the 23rd the Northern Group, backed by Zhukov's reserves, seized the Palet Heights and swung south. Although trapped, the Japanese resisted to the last. The two wings of Zhukov's attack linked up at Nomonhan on 25 August, trapping the Japanese 23rd Division. The following day Japanese forces outside the pocket tried to get through to them, but were met by Zhukov's 6th Tank Brigade. The Red Air Force also ensured that the Japanese could not bring up reinforcements, dropping 190 tons of bombs in 474 sorties during the first week alone. Having trapped the Japanese, Zhukov spent a week eradicating the survivors. By 31 August it was all over. His strategy had triumphed.

Zhukov's successful pincer operation at Khalkhin-Gol severely mauled the Japanese. He had passed his first major test of high-level command with flying colours. The Japanese claimed they lost 8,440 dead and suffered 8,766 wounded, while the Soviets claimed 9,284 casualties; however, losses for the Japanese have been put as high as 45,000 killed and Soviet casualties well over 17,000. Certainly, of the 60,000 Japanese troops trapped in Zhukov's cauldron, 50,000 were listed as killed, wounded or missing. The Japanese 23rd Division was all but wiped out.

Shortly afterwards, on 1 September 1939, Hitler invaded Poland and when the shooting stopped the Soviets occupied the eastern half of the country. Behind the scenes Stalin, alarmed by the ease with which the Wehrmacht had crushed Poland in just four weeks, feared that Finland and the Baltic States might provide a springboard for a Nazi invasion of the Soviet Union. He imposed a mutual defence agreement on Estonia, Latvia and Lithuania in October 1939. This involved allowing the Red Army to be based on their soil, and in July 1940 they were officially incorporated into the Soviet Union.

Then Stalin invaded Finland on 30 November 1939. Despite Timoshenko's overwhelming victory, the terrible performance of the Red Army greatly influenced Hitler's decision to invade the Soviet Union. Stalin mobilized half his regular divisions in Europe and western Siberia to fight his tiny neighbour. He relied on brute strength, but Soviet troops, whilst brave, had crucially lacked initiative. Nikita Khrushchev realized the wider ramifications, 'All of us – and Stalin first and foremost – sensed in our victory a defeat by the Finns. It was a dangerous defeat because it encouraged our enemies' conviction that the Soviet Union was a colossus with feet of clay.'

The ineptitude of the Red Army in Finland convinced Hitler that Operation Barbarossa would swiftly bring the Soviet Union to its knees. As a result, he chose to ignore Zhukov's resounding victory at Khalkhin-Gol. Unfortunately for the Soviet Union and the Red Army, the valuable experience gained by Zhukov in Mongolia, and during his earlier massed military exercises, was all but ignored. 'We relegated to oblivion the fundamentals of combat-in-depth tactics and of combined arms manoeuvres', recalled Marshal Biriuzov, 'which had been widespread before the Finnish campaign.'

After Khalkhin-Gol, Zhukov singled out his tank brigades, especially the 11th under Yakovlev, for praise, as well as the 36th Motorized Division under Petrov, and the 57th Rifle Division under Galanin. The 82nd Division, now under Fedyuninsky, was to distinguish itself fighting the Germans, while Fedyuninsky would command the 42nd

Army at beleaguered Leningrad. Potapov, who had acted as Zhukov's deputy, ended up commanding the 5th Army.

On the assumption that Operation Barbarossa went according to schedule, the German General Staff had to get their assessments of Soviet manpower, and indeed industrial capacity, right because it was vital they predict the Red Army's response. Accurate intelligence regarding Soviet front-line units and reserves was crucial to the success of the entire enterprise. It was these judgements that convinced Hitler to invade and secondly fight the Battle of Moscow in the winter of 1941/42, because he believed it would exhaust the depleted Red Army's reserves.

Crucially, thanks to his experiences in the Far East, Zhukov ensured that the Transbaikal Military District sowed the seeds for the Reserve Front, that would help defend the western Soviet Union. By the end of June 1941, Zhukov was anticipating being able to deploy just under 150 divisions running north to south in the Baltic, Western, Kiev and Odessa Military Districts. The manpower of these units was 50 per cent less than an average German division. The Wehrmacht would have to overcome these, plus at least another twenty regular army divisions being assembled.

Just before Barbarossa commenced, Timoshenko and Zhukov, who by then held the top posts of Commissar for Defence and Chief of Staff respectively, did all they could to warn Stalin of the growing threat of invasion. Zhukov was instructed to prepare State Defence Plan 1941. While this was based on the premise that Red Army operations would be in response to Nazi aggression, the idea was to take the fight to the enemy in an offensive rather than defensive manner. Zhukov's defence plan and Soviet mobilization plans envisaged nearly all the Red Army being deployed in the west.

This meant that of the Red Army's impressive order of battle, which comprised a total of 303 divisions, the bulk of them, some 237 divisions, would be deployed in the west facing the Nazi threat. However, of this impressive overall total, eighty-eight divisions were still in the process of being formed across the breadth and width of the Soviet Union.

Stalin's reluctance to mobilize and the logistics involved meant by the summer of 1941 only 171 divisions were in the field in the western Soviet Union, deployed in three belts. They were to be strengthened by Stalin's twenty-five new mechanized corps, fielding about 1,800 heavy and medium tanks plus thousands of inadequate light tanks. As a result, only a third of the Soviet divisions were actually in the crucial first defensive echelon. Under such circumstances it was clearly impossible for Zhukov to conduct a forward offensive defence.

Only in late April 1941 did Stalin acquiesce to Timoshenko and Zhukov's request to mobilize the reservists, as well as re-deploy troops from the Urals, Siberia and Far East to the west. This deployment could not be completed until 10 July – this was to prove three weeks too late. Fortunately for Stalin, when Hitler reached the very gates of Moscow, Zhukov knew what to do. He would save the Soviet capital and go on to defeat the Germans at Kursk and Minsk, then crown his remarkable career with the capture of Berlin.

Chapter 2

Lost Advantage

The panzer commander Major General Friedrich von Mellenthin acknowledged that the Red Army:

> began the war with the great advantage of possessing the T-34, a model far superior to any tank on the German side.... The Russian tank designers understood their job thoroughly; they cut out refinements and concentrated on the essentials – gun power, armour, and cross-country performance. During the war their system of suspension was well in advance of Germany and the West.

On the brink of war with Germany, Zhukov recalled that all was not well with the Soviet tank factories, thanks to the introduction of two new tank types:

> The Defence Committee studied the situation in the tank industry on the Central Committee's direction and reported that some of the plants did not fulfil production targets, had difficulties in adjusting production processes, and that the troops were getting the KV and T-34 tanks too slowly. The Government adopted appropriate measures. The Central Committee and the Council of People's Commissars passed exceptionally important decisions to organize mass production in the Volga area and in the Urals.

Zhukov appreciated that the T-34 was simply not ready in time:

We had failed to correctly estimate the capacity of our tank industry. We required 16,600 tanks of the latest types only, and altogether as many as 32,000 tanks to equip the new mechanized corps to full strength. Such numbers could not be produced in a year with the existing facilities ...

We managed to equip less than half the corps before the war broke out. And it was those very corps that essentially repelled the first enemy blows. The corps which at the outset of the war were still in the formative stage, were not ready until the time of the counteroffensive at Stalingrad, during which they proved decisive.

Besides Kharkov, the Soviet Union's other tank-building centre was Leningrad, with the Bolshevik, Kirov and Voroshilov factories, which were developing the KV heavy tank. Progress of the latter slowed up approval of the T-34 as it was Defence Commissar Marshal Klimenti Voroshilov's son-in-law Zhosif Kotin who was heading the heavy tank programme – hence KV. While Voroshilov dragged his feet over committing to the T-34, the KV-1 was approved for production in August 1939 at the Kirov factory (following the German siege of Leningrad the KV-1 programme was shifted to Chelyabinsk). Stalin fretted that the T-34 was too complex to build and the last thing he wanted was another T-28 medium tank or T-35 heavy tank, both of which could only be built in limited numbers. What was needed was something that could be built quickly to replace the T-26 and the BT-5/7.

Although it was intended that Kharkov would churn out 600 T-34s a month, Marshal Grigory Kulik, head of the Artillery Directorate, held up deliveries of the L-11 gun, while Voroshilov and General Pavlov argued the T-34 should be put on hold until a modernized version, the T-34M, was ready for mass production. This was to have a new turret, V5 diesel engine and torsion bar suspension but the reality was that this would not be ready until mid-1942.

Thanks in part to the dithering of Stalin, Voroshilov and Pavlov, by the time of the German invasion on 22 June 1941, the Kharkov and

Stalingrad tank factories had only built 1,226 T-34/76s, consisting of both the Model 1940 and Model 1941. This meant when Hitler's Operation Barbarossa opened just 5 per cent of the Red Army's tank force were T-34s and just 2 per cent were KV-1s. The rest of the Red Army's vast tank fleet were completely obsolescent. From January 1939 to 22 June 1941 the Red Army received over 7,000 new tanks, but the plants managed to put out only 1,861 KV and T-34 tanks before the war, which was clearly insufficient. The two principal tank types, the BT-7 and T-26, were simply not up to the job by 1941.

The Western Military District facing Eastern Europe had about 982 T-34/76s and 466 KV-1s. Key to the defence of Leningrad and the vital Kirov Tank Plant was the Baltic Military District, under Colonel General Kuznetsov. The bulk of the 1,045 tanks at Kuznetsov's disposal were old and only 105 were newer models. The 12th Mechanized Corps was able to muster 84 per cent of its tanks and the 3rd Mechanized Corps could only manage 55 per cent. The 7th Mechanized Corps had none of its authorized 420 T-34s and just 40 of its 120 KVs.

General Pavlov, in command of the Western Front, had at his disposal the powerful 6th Mechanized Corps, equipped with 238 T-34s, the only drawback being that they had not been issued with any armour-piercing rounds and each tank had only a single tank of fuel. Added to that, the 6th Mechanized's tank crews were far from proficiently trained. Within the space of a couple of weeks of Hitler's invasion half the T-34s and KV-1s had been wiped out, those that remained being caught in the Kiev Pocket. Once Pavlov's command had disappeared in the Minsk Pocket he was summoned back to Moscow and shot.

The Red Army's only other medium tank was the cumbersome-looking T-28. This had gone into production in 1932 and was fitted with three turrets, one mounting a 76.2mm and two with machine guns. Despite a crew of six and weighing almost 30 tons it could still manage almost 25mph. This tank was not used operationally until 1939, by which stage the T-34 was well on its way. The T-35 heavy tank, weighing in at 45 tons, which appeared in 1933 was a similar-looking tank though only about sixty were built. The Soviets also had thousands of light tanks that were not capable of taking on the panzers.

In the 1930s the bulk of the armour was made up of the BT light fast tank; the main model was the BT-5, a copy of the US Christie M-1931, equipped with a larger cylindrical turret, a 45mm gun, a coaxial machine gun and a larger engine than its predecessors. With a crew of three and a weight of 11.5 tons it could manage nearly 70mph on the road. The successor model, the BT-7, went into production in 1935. The single-turret T-26B light tank appeared in 1933 (the earlier T-26A had twin turrets) and was also armed with a 45mm or 37mm. Its weight of nine tons gave it a road speed of just 18mph. This low speed and poor mobility compared to the BT-5 resulted in production being abandoned in the mid-1930s.

Hitler had extensive intelligence on these tanks, having established a special department to survey Soviet industries, especially the weapons plants. In fact, his panzer troops already had experience of Soviet tanks thanks to Hitler's involvement in the Spanish Civil War. Although the Germans discovered that the Republicans' Soviet-supplied T-26 tank was superior to their Panzer I, the German 37mm PaK 35/36 anti-tank gun was found to penetrate 40mm of armour at 400 yards. The reality of the situation by the summer of 1941 was that the BT-5/7 and T-26 were obsolete and simply could not cope with the firepower of Panzer III and IV medium tanks or the Sturmgeschütz III assault gun, while the T-28 and heavy tanks like the T-35 and KV-1 were easily outmanoeuvred.

The brand-new T-34s first went onto action at Grondno in Byelorussia on the day of Hitler's invasion. Their appearance caught the Germans by surprise, but there were not enough of them nor did the Soviets know how to use them properly. The T-34 nearly never saw the light of day thanks to the infighting and political rivalries amongst the Soviet Union's generals, tank designers, factory managers and politicians. In an act of unprecedented bravado, the T-34's lead designer Mikhail Koshkin endangered his health and ultimately sacrificed his life to prove the tank's abilities. Ironically the T-34 was not even the official or proffered new medium tank design – it was Koshkin who went out on a professional limb and suggested an alternative to the prototype designs that were already under consideration. By personally presenting it to Stalin he sidestepped all the naysayers and a crucial decision was made.

At the same time, those overseeing the construction of the Red Army's latest KV-1 heavy tank along with the Soviet Artillery Directorate, responsible for producing anti-tank guns, did all they could to hinder and delay the birth of the T-34. The rivalry between the tank manufacturing plants in Leningrad and Kharkov ensured that there was an ugly tug of war over resources and priorities. Although everything was done to safeguard the future of the KV-1 after the opening months of the Nazi invasion, it was the T-34 that was kept in production. Both factories had to be relocated once Leningrad was besieged and Kharkov overrun by the Wehrmacht. The new home for the T-34 became aptly known as Tankograd.

Before all this happened, Stalin's move to secure his power base by purging his rivals almost robbed the Soviet Union of the T-34 altogether. Stalin was firmly in control by 1929 and had no intention of relinquishing power. Within two years, fearing the influence of his exiled arch rival Leon Trotsky (the number two figure, after Lenin, during the 1917 Bolshevik Revolution), he turned his attentions to the Red Army. This was one of the first minor bloodless purges of the armed forces. Those involved could count themselves extremely lucky for they were simply removed from their posts and in many cases dismissed. Relatively painlessly Stalin promoted his old Russian Civil War cronies.

Trying to haul the Soviet Union into the twentieth century by its bootstraps, Stalin launched his first 'Five Year Plan' in 1928. Its goal was to industrialize an agricultural economy largely trapped in the Middle Ages. The Red Army was also to be modernized. Mechanization required technical know-how and that posed a problem. There was a shortage of designers and to get round that in 1927 the Red Army cherry-picked young engineers from the Soviet automotive industry to be trained in tank design.

This was fortuitous, for just two years later the Red Army General Staff issued a special directive giving priority to the production of tanks. Under Marshal Mikhail Tukhachevsky's reform programme this called for tankettes to conduct reconnaissance, light tanks to act as cavalry, medium tanks for the breakthrough and heavy tanks for penetrating fortified areas. By that stage the Soviets only had the T-18 in production, based on the M-17 which had been produced during the Russian Civil War. Then in the summer of 1929 a series of tractor and car plants were set up in Chelyabinsk, Gorky, Moscow, Stalingrad and Yaroslavl. These would form the basis of the Soviet Union's wartime tank industry.

Tukhachevsky was a progressive thinker who appreciated the concepts of modern mechanized warfare. In the mid-1930s he had expanded his tactical concept of Deep Battle to a larger strategic concept known as Deep Operation. This bore a striking resemblance to the Nazi Blitzkrieg, as it envisaged multiple penetrations of the enemy's front lines, with exploitations of over 60 miles in depth using modern weapons such as tanks and aircraft.

Military vehicles were delivered to the Red Army at a rate previously unknown and it soon had approximately as many tanks as France – which was at that time the pre-eminent European military power. By 1935 Stalin had 10,000 tanks. At the same time, he began to fear that a revived and powerful Red Army would pose a threat to him. He turned to the Peoples' Commissariat of Internal Affairs – the dreaded NKVD, which came into being in 1934 as the forerunner of the KGB. Three years later the *Ezhovschina* (the Great Purge) fell upon the Red Army with a vengeance, leaving it in a state of almost total disarray. Amongst the victims was Tukhachevsky and his ideas were discredited by vengeful rivals. It was against this background that the T-34 was designed, developed and put into production – under such circumstances this was little short of a miracle.

West of Moscow, the Nazis discovered exactly what that miracle was. General Heinz Guderian reported:

On October 6th 1941 our headquarters was moved forward to Sevsk. 4th Panzer Division was attacked by Russian tanks to the south of Mzensk and went through some bad hours. This was the first occasion on which the vast superiority of the Russian T-34 to our tanks became plainly apparent. The division suffered grievous casualties.

Chapter 3

Stalin's Mechanized Corps

The initial grouping of the Red Army's tank units was very tentative and faltering. As early as March 1932 it created two mechanized corps, with the 11th in the Leningrad Military District and the 45th in the Ukranian Military District. These consisted of a mechanized brigade with three battalions of T-26 light tanks plus supporting arms, a tank brigade with BT fast tanks, and a rifle brigade. Two years later two additional mechanized corps, the 5th and 7th, were organized in the Moscow and Leningrad Military Districts respectively. At the same time separate mechanized brigades, tank regiments, mechanized regiments and mechanized divisions were being formed.

Exercises involving these early corps proved them to be very unwieldy and difficult to coordinate. Soviet newsreels of large-scale military manoeuvres conducted in Byelorussia and Ukraine showed tanks and planes acting in perfect concert with the artillery and infantry. Publicly it was all very impressive, but behind the scenes things were quite chaotic. This was in part due to a lack of tank radios, the mechanical unreliability of the tanks and the poor quality of the crews. This was not an ideal recipe for successful combined-arms operations, which needed above all to be highly mobile.

Soviet generals rightly deduced that the future lay with manoeuvre warfare, but they did not know how to implement it. Operations in depth were clearly the key. Their thinking coalesced around the concepts of direct and distant tank support for the infantry and cavalry as well as distant action. What they did not grasp was that for manoeuvre warfare, as well as good communications commanders also needed to be trained to be highly flexible in order to respond to developing battle conditions.

It was decided to give up on the corps concept and in 1935 the decision was taken not to form any more. Instead each rifle division was assigned a tank battalion with two companies equipped with T-26 light tanks and T-28 medium tanks. Each cavalry division was given a tank regiment with sixty-four BT fast tanks. For the Red Army's Five-Year Plan covering 1938–41, the number of tank formations was to remain static, with the four mechanized corps, twenty-one separate tank brigades and three separate armoured brigades.

However, eleven tank training regiments were to be established to improve crew proficiency. Also the combat element of the tank brigades was strengthened and in 1938 the mechanized corps were renamed tank corps. By this stage the corps were each supposed to have 560 tanks and 12,710 men. This seemed a step in the right direction, but then disaster struck. The following year, General Pavlov advised that the corps be disbanded rather than expanded. After commanding Soviet tank units in Spain, he had become Chief of the Main Directorate of Motorized and Mechanized Forces. He argued that the tank corps were too cumbersome.

A thorough review was conducted of the armoured forces' performance in Finland, Mongolia and Poland. The latter campaign involved the 15th Tank Corps from the Byelorussian Military District and the 25th Tank Corps from the Ukrainian Military District. Their commanders had struggled to coordinate the subordinate brigades, which embarrassingly resulted in the tanks falling behind the cavalry divisions. The Soviet Main Military Council, chaired by Stalin, agreed with Pavlov. This decision was one of the greatest blunders in Soviet military history. Ironically, Pavlov would end up in command of the key Western Special Military District.

Instead it was decided to form motorized divisions consisting of one tank regiment, two motor-rifle regiments and an artillery regiment. They would total 11,650 men with 258 BT tanks, 17 T-37/T-40 light amphibious tanks, 98 guns and mortars and 49 armoured cars. This effectively made them weak mechanized infantry divisions. The tank brigades were retained and it was planned to have thirty-two of them (plus ten tank regiments that would be expanded into brigades in wartime). The BT and T-26 brigades would have 258 tanks while the T-28 and T-35 brigades would have 156 tanks. All these formations lacked real punch and this reorganization simply served to dissipate the Red Army's striking force.

Stalin, Timoshenko and Zhukov watched with alarm as Hitler's Blitzkrieg, spearheaded by his panzers, swiftly crushed Europe's armies. The key to his success was undoubtedly rapid armoured mobility, supported by artillery and air cover. Worryingly, German forces soon began to mass in Eastern Europe. While Stalin's generals urged him to mobilize as quickly as possible, he was reluctant to do so, for fear of antagonizing Hitler. Stalin's order was that the Red Army was to offer 'No Provocation!'

Zhukov in particular was desperate to get their forces gathered in western Russia ready to counter any threat. He and Timoshenko started the process under the pretext they were going to conduct exercises in the western military districts. This was hampered by Stalin's dithering and continual refusal to believe that Hitler was preparing to attack. To compound matters, the Red Army was only just beginning to once again mass its armoured forces into large formations. After seeing the Germans triumph across Europe, Stalin had a change of heart and authorized the resurrection of the mechanized corps, the idea being that each would be able to mass about 1,000 tanks with 37,200 men.

By the summer of 1941 Stalin had an armoured force of well over 20,000 tanks, notably of varying quality, with which to protect the Soviet Union from the Nazi menace. The bulk of these were assigned to thirty newly-forming mechanized corps. Each was to comprise two tank divisions supported by a motorized infantry division, giving a total strength of sixty tank and thirty motorized divisions. The tank divisions were to comprise two tank, one motor-rifle and one artillery regiment. Authorized strength was 11,343 men, 413 tanks (of which 105 were to be KV-1s, 210 T-34s, 26 BT-7s, 18 T-26s and 54 flamethrower tanks), 91 armoured cars and 58 guns and mortars.

In early 1941, the organization of the tank regiments was revised, with a reduction of heavy tanks from fifty-two to thirty-one. This cut the number of tanks in a division to 375. This meant in theory each corps would have 750 tanks, which was much fewer than Stalin had envisaged. As already mentioned many of these mechanized corps were far from full strength and due to a lack of spares and supplies many of the tanks they did have were inoperable. Crucially, less than half the corps had been equipped by June 1941. Stalin's corps commanders faced an impossible task in the face of Hitler's impending attack.

Two of them are particularly noteworthy. The 9th was commanded by General Konstantin K. Rokossovsky, the future commander of the 1st Byelorussian Front. Rokossovsky was a survivor of Stalin's purges, who had been arrested, charged with treason and sent to the Gulag for three years. During his time there he was repeatedly tortured over trumped-up spying charges. Stalin, in need of senior officers, authorized his release in early 1940 and appointed him to take charge of a mechanized corps. Rokossovsky would rise rapidly through the ranks and command troops at all the major battles fought on the Eastern Front. In contrast the 4th Mechanized Corps was commanded by the infamous General Andrei Vlasov, who subsequently sided with Hitler and raised the ill-fated Russian Liberation Army.

Also of note was the 28th Tank Division, with 12th Corps, commanded by General Ivan D. Chernyakovsky, the future commander of the 3rd Byelorussian Front. He would be instrumental in organizing Stalin's much-needed replacement tank corps in 1942. For a time, he led the 18th Tank Corps, followed by the 60th Army, before assuming control of the Western Front reformed as the 3rd Byelorussian Front.

The first ten of Stalin's mechanized corps were formed in mid-1940 and early 1941, which meant that they were far from ready for combat. Most of them ended up being destroyed or disbanded in the wake of the German invasion. A few were later re-established as Guards mechanized corps. The 10th to 30th Mechanized Corps only came into being from March 1941 onwards and were even less prepared. At least five of these, the 23rd and 27th–30th, do not seem to have been allocated any divisions, so were essentially only paper formations. This rapid expansion of the tank corps required stripping the tank battalions from many of the rifle divisions. Only the cavalry divisions were allowed to retain their tank regiments.

Stalin's wholly inadequate and poorly-trained mechanized corps ended up stretched very thinly in defence of the western Soviet Union. The Northern (formed on 24 June 1941) and Northwestern Fronts had just two mechanized corps each, the 1st and 10th and the 3rd and 12th respectively. In the case of the Northern Front, although the 1st Mechanized Corps was held in reserve, it was weakened by having one of its tank divisions allocated to 14th Army. The Northwestern Front had no armoured reserves, as both its mechanized corps were assigned to its field armies.

Barring the road to Minsk and Moscow was Pavlov's Western Special Military District or Western Front. His command comprised just six of the mechanized corps, the 6th, 11th, 13th, 14th, 17th and 20th, with a total of twelve tank divisions and six supporting motorized divisions. The last two corps were held as Front assets, which in theory meant Pavlov had a mobile reserve that could conduct counter-attacks. Nonetheless, he was in the unenviable position of holding the Bialystok salient, trapped between East Prussia and German-occupied Poland. To add to the Red Army's difficulties, after moving into eastern Poland it had demolished most of the pre-1939 Soviet-Polish frontier defences. It was then necessary to build new defences in the western areas of the Western Special Military District. This left those Soviet forces in eastern Poland very vulnerable to attack. There was a suspicion that Stalin and Zhukov considered Pavlov's command a sacrificial lamb and that it was the Reserve Front's job to hold Hitler at the old frontier. Certainly by June 1941 the Western Front was far from up to strength.

In Stalin's mind, if Hitler should invade, he would undoubtedly go for the raw materials and abundant resources of Ukraine. As a result, many of his mechanized corps were with Colonel General M.P. Kirponos' Southwestern Front, covering the Kiev Special Military

District. This had a large number of armoured units including eight mechanized corps, comprising the 4th, 8th, 9th, 15th, 16th, 19th, 22nd and 24th. Two of these, the 19th, with the 40th and 43rd Tank Divisions and the 213th Motorized Division, and the 24th, with the 45th and 49th Tank Divisions and the 216th Motorized Division, were held as Front reserves.

Deployed at Lvov (Lemberg), in what had until recently been eastern Poland but was now part of Soviet Ukraine, was Vlasov's 4th Mechanized Corps. His command included the 32nd Tank Division equipped with 300 new KV-1 heavy tanks. When the time came elements of this division would offer effective if short-lived opposition to the panzers. His other unit was the 8th Tank Division.

Further east, protecting the Ukrainian capital Kiev, the key armoured formation was Rokossovsky's 9th Mechanized Corps, with the 20th and 35th Tank Divisions and the 131st Motorized Division. In reality it was mechanized in name only. Rokossovsky had only a third of his tanks and they were obsolete with worn-out engines; his motorized infantry lacked even horses and carts for transport. Soviet mechanics despaired at trying to maintain the vehicles in their charge. Once under attack Rokossovsky would work miracles and he proved to be exactly the type of general his country required in its hour of need. Rokossovsky's command formed part of 5th Army which included the 22nd Mechanized Corps.

To the south in the Odessa Military District were two more mechanized corps, the 2nd and 18th, while Stavka, the Soviet High Command, held five, the 5th, 7th, 21st, 25th and 26th, in reserve. The 23rd was deployed to protect the Orel Military District, the 28th the Transcaucasus Military District and the 17th the Central Asian Military District. Three days after the German invasion the Southern Front was formed, supported by the 2nd and 18th Mechanized Corps.

Understandably it was the infantry that constituted 75 per cent of the line divisions and the Soviets could muster four types, totalling 178 basic rifle divisions, 31 motorized rifle divisions (in theory deployed with the mechanized corps), 18 mountain rifle divisions and 2 independent rifle divisions. Despite being called motorized rifle divisions, the reality was that many riflemen ended up hitching a ride on the outside of tanks. Following the disastrous performance of the Red Army in Finland, the rifle division was reorganized, consisting of three infantry and two artillery regiments, plus anti-tank and anti-aircraft support. As all the armour went to the new mechanized corps, most rifle divisions were only left with sixteen light tanks. When Hitler struck most of their tank battalions were in the process of redeploying.

Hitler's Wehrmacht had perfected its 'lightning war' tactics in Western Europe, Scandinavia and the Balkans. In the face of the Nazis' tried and tested doctrine of combining armour with motorized infantry supported by overwhelming air and artillery strikes, the outcome for the partially-mobilized Red Army was perhaps inevitable. Hitler had at most 153 divisions, including reserves, available for operations on the Eastern Front by mid-1941; Stalin, though ill-prepared, had almost double that number. In total Hitler could muster about three million men, while Stalin had four and a half million at his disposal, with large reserves of manpower waiting in the wings.

Furthermore, for Hitler, geographically there was the problem of the Eastern Front funnelling out from 1,300 miles to 2,500 miles. The vast logistical problems were compounded by his lack of reserves; the Replacement Army had less than half a million men, sufficient only for the intended brief summer campaign. He only had three months' reserves of petrol and one month of diesel. He was gambling on a quick victory thanks to his panzers. Nor did Hitler seem inclined to consider the long-term value or reliability of his East European Axis allies in the shape of the Hungarian and Romanian armies. Equally worrying, the superiority of the panzers was not that marked. However, General Heinz Guderian, father of the Panzerwaffe, believed at the beginning of the campaign that the technical superiority of their tanks would cancel out the Soviets' massive numerical superiority.

Nonetheless, in the spring of 1941 a Soviet Commission's comments on viewing Hitler's panzers led German ordnance officials to conclude, 'It seems that the Russians must already possess better and heavier tanks than we do'. The German military really should have come to this conclusion after the Spanish Civil War. It was evident then that Soviet tank design was accelerating and the T-34 tank was about to make its appearance, which was equal to any existing German armour. This design and Soviet industrial might would be Hitler's ultimate undoing.

Hitler's titanic assault on Stalin was heralded at 0315 hours on Sunday, 22 June 1941 by air attacks on Soviet frontier airfields; the result was that the Red Air Force was swiftly taken out of the equation. Some 550 bombers and 480 fighters were involved in the massed raids. Hitler's strike force also included an additional 300 Stuka dive-bombers. A hail of fragmentation bombs fell on runways, taxiways and hangers. Soviet aircraft were either destroyed on the ground or shot out of the air as they rose to meet the Luftwaffe. They had lost 1,200 aircraft by noon. This left the Red Army struggling along open roads at the mercy of the marauding Luftwaffe. Soviet troop concentrations were bombed and strafed as they desperately sought to mass in order to conduct counter-attacks. German aircraft bombing Lvov airport also struck the barracks of Vlasov's 32nd Tank Division.

Hitler threw 3,200 panzers at Stalin's 20,000 tanks: in his favour only about 60 per cent of these were serviceable and most were obsolete, dating from the 1930s. Despite the Red Army having learned its lesson the hard way fighting the Japanese and Finns in 1939, the Germans were able to knock out huge numbers of Soviet tanks because they were poorly deployed and vulnerable, often cooking the crews.

Hitler's forces rolled very rapidly across eastern Poland, evicting the Red Army, and into Byelorussia. Army Group North thrust toward Leningrad, Army Group Centre struck toward Moscow and Army Group South cut into Ukraine. Further south combined German, Hungarian and Romanian forces drove toward the Crimea and the Caucasus, while to the far north the Finns thrust toward Murmansk and down the Karelian Isthmus as part of the 'Continuation War'. Soviet pre-1939 gains in both Poland and Finland were soon lost.

General Guderian's 2nd Panzer Group's key armoured formations comprised three panzer corps, which included five panzer divisions. General Hoth's 3rd Panzer Group included two further corps made up of four panzer divisions. In their path were Pavlov's 3rd, 10th and 4th Armies. His attempts at holding the Germans at bay proved futile as the 6th and 11th Mechanized and 6th Cavalry Corps' counter-attacks were crushed and Minsk encircled. Armoured units trapped in the Minsk Pocket included the 20th Mechanized Corps, the 4th and 7th Tank Divisions and the 8th Tank Brigade. In a state of panic Stalin and his generals became obsessed with launching rushed and ill-conceived counter-attacks and rapidly threw away their mechanized corps.

Within just three weeks Stalin lost two million men, 3,500 tanks and 6,000 aircraft to Hitler's unrelenting metal onslaught. Remarkably, within five months Hitler destroyed or captured 17,500 tanks (other estimates put the figure at 24,000), for the loss of 2,700 panzers, and reached the very gates of Moscow. By the beginning of December 1941 the Soviet field armies only had 1,984 tanks available, which were organized into separate battalions and brigades. Stalin's enormous losses were such that he could muster only 780 tanks for the Battle of Moscow. For a while the decimated Red Army suffered an acute shortage of tanks, guns and aircraft.

Chapter 4

Desperate Counter-Attacks

Most of Stalin's inexperienced tankers did not know what to expect when they came up against the battle-hardened panzer crews. Initially his new KV-1 and KV-2 heavy tanks proved a nasty shock to Hitler's Wehrmacht. Rokossovsky wrote with pride:

> The KV tanks literally stunned the enemy. They withstood the fire of every type of gun that the German panzers were armed with. But what a sight they were returning from combat. Their armour was pock-marked all over and sometimes even their barrels were pierced.

The Germans discovered the only way they could deal with the KV was by shooting off its tracks or wheels, thereby forcing the crew to abandon ship. The 1st Panzer Division, whilst invading Lithuania, hit a KV-2 more than seventy times using 50mm and 75mm guns, but failed to penetrate the thick armour. Its continued resistance was clearly testimony to the bravery of the crew. Whenever a KV tank was immobilized, artillery and satchel charges had to be used to finish it off. Most of the KV-2 losses were due to mechanical problems caused by its weight or by lack of fuel. For example, the 41st Tank Division had thirty-three KV-2s in its inventory, of which two-thirds were lost, but only five to enemy action. By July 1941 the Red Army had only 500 KV-1s and KV-2s remaining.

Likewise, the T-34 was an unwelcome surprise for the panzertruppen. One of the T-34's first combat operations took place with the 2nd Tank Division near Rassinye in Lithuania. It was under the control of the 3rd Mechanized Corps. About fifty tanks from the 3rd Tank Regiment sought to blunt the advance of the 1st and 6th Panzer Divisions on 24 and 25 June 1941. At first the Germans were alarmed to find that their 37mm anti-tank rounds bounced off the T-34's frontal armour, but their 88mm flak gun deployed in an anti-tank role rapidly brought the Soviet tanks to a halt.

South-east of Brest-Litovsk, in the opening stages of Operation Barbarossa, General Bogdanov's 30th Tank Division, equipped mainly with T-26 light tanks, was ordered to counter-attack the 18th Panzer Division on 22–23 June 1941. His unit formed part of the 14th Mechanized Corps assigned to the Western Front's 4th Army. He made no impression, suffering heavily at the hands of German anti-tank guns and dive-bombers. Poor crew training and lack of ammunition and fuel did not help matters.

Afterwards his tanks lay wrecked and abandoned. The crews quickly learned to loathe the T-26's petrol engine. Many of those photographed by the Germans were burnt out and surrounded by Soviet corpses. Often the crew, particularly the driver, burned with their tank or were gunned down trying to escape. Other tanks had their turrets blown off, either by direct hits or the ammunition 'cooking off'. Some received hits to the driver's hatch, killing the unfortunate driver instantly. Overall the T-26, despite its large numbers, did nothing to help save the Red Army.

On 22 June 1941 General Kirponos in the south tried to get his harassed 15th and 22nd Mechanized Corps to counter-attack the Germans' flanks. To his annoyance he found that his tankers were far from ready to go into battle. Only a weak element of 15th Corps' 10th Tank Division was committed, with little effect, and the panzers penetrated 24 miles to Berestechko. Likewise, the 22nd Corps' 19th Tank and 215th Motorized Divisions were unable to prevent the panzers reaching Lutsk. When finally mustered, the 15th Corps' 10th and 37th Tank Divisions, plus the 212th Motorized Division, were unable to stop the panzers pushing another 18 miles. The rapidity of the German advance was simply humiliating – nothing seemed capable of stopping them.

Similarly, Rokossovsky's 9th and General N.V. Feklenko's 19th Mechanized Corps were ordered to counter-attack north of Dubno, while to the south General I.I. Karpezo's 15th and D.I. Riabyshev's 8th Mechanized Corps were also to attack. Unfortunately, Zhukov and Kirponos' orders led to Vlasov's 4th Mechanized Corps being dispersed, which prevented it from supporting the 8th Corps. The counter-attack was launched on 26 June resulting in an enormous battle involving over 2,000 tanks.

The Red Army proved completely incapable of conducting coordinated mobile warfare on the same scale as the Germans. During the fighting the 8th Mechanized Corps was surrounded and the 15th made little headway. In the north the 19th Corps ran into two panzer divisions and was driven back to Rovno. Rokossovsky launched his attack on 27 June, only to suffer heavy losses, and was ordered back. While a failure, this Soviet counteroffensive delayed Hitler for a week and convinced him that he needed to secure Ukraine, which would have ramifications for Army Group Centre's decisive drive on Moscow.

In Byelorussia, Minsk fell to Army Group Centre on 28 June; with the liquidation of the Minsk Pocket the Germans claimed to have destroyed or captured 4,799 tanks and 9,427 guns and taken 341,000 prisoners. The subsequent seizure of Smolensk yielded similar results, as did the successful and massive encirclements at Vyazma and Bryansk. On 30 June Army Group Centre entered Lvov, the 32nd Tank Division having fled the city toward Kiev. Likewise, the rest of Vlasov's 4th Mechanized Corps were long gone.

Way to the south, the left flank of Kirponos' Southwestern Front was threatened when the Germans pierced Soviet defences in Moldova and their Romanian allies headed for the Black Sea port of Odessa. The Germans successfully captured Issay and reached the River Prut, driving off counter-attacks by Cherevichenko's 9th Army and Novosel'sky's 2nd Mechanized Corps.

Stavka's other counter-attacks launched the newly-arrived 5th and 7th Mechanized Corps against Hoth's 3rd Panzer Group in Byelorussia on 6 July. Their losses proved staggering. In five days of fighting near Senno and Lepel they lost 832 of their 2,000 tanks. This left the panzers free to press on toward the city of Smolensk. In a desperate move to restore the situation along the Dnieper, Zhukov instructed Timoshenko's Western Front to conduct counter-attacks along its full length.

Timoshenko threw the 6th and 17th Mechanized Corps, with a total of 700 tanks, at the flanks of the German 39th Panzer Corps north of Orsha. Lacking air cover, they headed for Senno and ran into the 17th and 18th Panzer Divisions, supported by the ever-present Luftwaffe. When the Germans occupied Berdichev this threatened to surround the Southwestern Front's left wing. In response Kirponos deployed the remains of Kaprezo's 15th Mechanized Corps and Sokolov's 16th Mechanized Corps into blocking positions south of Berdichev. A week later a German breakthrough heralded the encirclement of Smolensk and 300,000 Soviet troops were cut off between the city and Orsha.

During the first eighteen days of the war the Soviet Western Front, defending eastern Poland and western Byelorussia, lost more than 417,000 men killed, wounded, captured or missing, as well as 9,427 guns and mortars, plus 4,700 tanks and 1,797 aircraft. The Southwestern Front also suffered heavy losses: 241,594 men including 172,323 killed, captured or missing, 5,806 guns and mortars, 4,381 tanks and 1,218 aircraft. It seemed as if the Red Army had been completely crushed.

Crucially, at the end of July 1941 Hitler decided that Army Group Centre would go over to the defensive. The diversion of part of its forces to support Army Group South's capture of Kiev from the Soviet Southwestern Front fatally delayed the drive on Moscow. However, at Kiev two-thirds of a million Soviet troops were caught in a pocket the size of Belgium and for the first and last time the German Army outnumbered the Red Army. All eyes then turned back to Army Group Centre.

Following the successful evacuation of the Soviet tank-producing facilities east of the Urals during 1941, production of the T-34 was conducted at Chelyabinsk and Nizhny Tagil as well as a number of other subsidiary plants well out of the reach of the Luftwaffe. However, at the outbreak of war T-34 production was far from centralized, being spread over vast distances. The Kirov Factory manufactured the L-11 gun in Leningrad, while electrical components were made in Moscow at the Dynamo Factory. Initially the tanks themselves were built in 1940 in Kharkov at the No. 183 Factory, supplemented by production at the Stalingrad Tractor Factory in early 1941, then in the middle of the year the Krasnoye Sormovo Factory No. 112 in Gorky also began to manufacture T-34s.

Kharkov could not produce enough V-2 diesel engines for the tanks, which resulted in the Gorky T-34s having to be fitted with the BT tank's Mikulin M-17 gasoline aero engine and a substandard clutch and transmission. These tanks were to prove very troublesome when the fighting started. Likewise, radios were in short supply and were only installed in company commanders' tanks – the rest of the company had to rely on flags for communication. Production of the F-34 gun was undertaken firstly at Gorky and then Kharkov as well. Unsurprisingly, Hitler's attack on the Soviet Union swiftly focused Stalin's attention on the T-34 production lines.

After Hitler's invasion Stalin sought to safeguard his factories and established the People's Commissariat for Tank Production. Most of the Soviet defence plants, including their tank production facilities, only just escaped Hitler's grasp. Zhukov marvelled at what he called the 'Russian miracle', the swift dismantling and relocation of the Soviet Union's factories out of harm's way. About 1,300 major industrial enterprises were evacuated east. Before long these factories were churning out replacement T-34/76s and later the improved version known as the T-34/85, which had thicker frontal armour to withstand German anti-tank guns.

Hitler's remarkable victory in the summer of 1941 was due to his superior use of his panzers, speed, high morale and overall superior tactics and equipment. Nonetheless, the new T-34/76, once fine-tuned, was not found wanting, causing an acceleration in German tank design to try and counter it. The T-34 was well suited to the Russian weather; in particular its wide tracks and low ground pressure gave it good traction and speed. What the Red Army needed was replacement tanks and quickly before Hitler renewed his push on Moscow.

New tank plants sprang up east of the Ural Mountains, in particular at Uralvagonzavod in Nizhny Tagil and the Tractor Factory at Chelyabinsk that had to make good the appalling losses. The tank factory at Kharkov was evacuated to Nizhny Tagil to help create the Ural Tank Factory No. 183. Kharkov's diesel engine factory and Leningrad's Kirov Plant (Factory No. 100) and S.M. Kirov (No. 185) also moved to Chelyabinsk and combined with the Tractor Plant to became popularly known as 'Tankograd' or 'Tank City'. Leningrad's Voroshilov Plant (Factory No. 174) moved to Chkalov in 1941 and then to Omsk in 1942.

According to Zhukov the first batch of new T-34s were delivered from the Chelyabinsk production line a month after the relocation of the Leningrad factory. The Krasnoye Sormovo shipyards in Gorky on the Volga were also put to work producing T-34 tanks, and these were employed during the Battle of Moscow in the winter of 1941. Charged with defending the capital, Zhukov noted that they came just in time, though there were still not enough for his liking. He told Stalin he needed 200 additional tanks, but he did not get them.

On the road to Moscow the Germans had encountered the KV-1 and the T-34 and soon realized that their panzers were actually outgunned and under-armoured. The wake-up call came on 6 October 1941 when the 2nd Panzer Army under Heinz Guderian ran into a brigade of T-34s under Colonel Mikhail Katukov near Mtensk. They destroyed ten Panzer IIIs and IVs for the loss of only five of their own number. It was evident that the Germans' short 50mm and 75mm tank guns could only penetrate the T-34's sloping frontal armour at a death-defying 100m. In contrast the T-34 could kill the Panzer III and IV at 1,000m. On top of this, while the panzers were struggling with the ice and mud of the Russian winter the T-34 was able to plough ahead regardless thanks to its broad tracks. Only the German 88mm flak gun could stop the T-34 at any range.

Once it became clear that the 20,000 tanks of the Red Army had all but disappeared in the summer of 1941, all thoughts of the new T-34M design were shelved and the Model 1941 became the standard production version with another 1,886 built during the last six months of 1941 – although this was not enough as some 2,300 were lost trying to stave off the Nazis. Once the Kharkov production line had been shifted to Nizhny Tagil, work was undertaken to simplify the design with the Model 1942. This also saw the frontal armour increasing to 65mm, which added another two tons to the tank's weight. The shortcomings of the KV-1 meant that the T-34 was the only effective tank in production. With tank building cranked up, 12,553 rolled off the production line in 1942, but over 50 per cent were to become casualties of war.

The incredible rate of tank production was in part due to mechanical engineer Yevgeny Oskarovich Paton, who designed a portable fusion welder. Nikita Khrushchev recalled:

Thanks to the improvements he introduced in our tank production, tanks started coming off our assembly lines like pancakes off a griddle. He moved with our armour works to the Urals when we had to evacuate our industry from Kharkov early in the war.

Stalin refused to heed the hard-won lessons of the summer. He was impatient to forestall Hitler and instructed Zhukov on 14 November 1941 to conduct spoiling attacks south of Moscow and around Volokolamsk. Zhukov did not want to waste his precious tank reserves on an operation that was unlikely to end in victory. General Rokossovsky's 16th Army, which had been preparing in-depth defences, was instructed to abandon these and strike the enemy. He organized two mobile groups, one consisting of the 1st Guards and 17th Tank Brigades, the 89th Tank Battalion and the 40th Rifle Brigade, the other made up of the 145th Tank Brigade, 17th Rifle Brigade and the 44th Cavalry Division. Advancing just a mile, his men suffered heavy casualties. Rokossovsky held Zhukov personally responsible for his needless losses, but it was Stalin who was to blame.

Supported by an armoured brigade, a Soviet division newly arrived from the Far East attacked the German 112th Infantry Division protecting 4th Panzer's push on Venev on 18 November. The weakened 112th was overrun by T-34 tanks, having already suffered 50 per cent frostbite casualties. A week later German intelligence identified more fresh reserves thrown into the fighting, which had come from the Far East, including the 108th Tank Brigade as well as the 31st Cavalry and 299th Rifle Divisions.

By the end of the month Zhukov was pleased with the Red Army's efforts before Moscow, claiming:

In twenty days of the second phase of their offensive, the Germans lost 155,000 dead and wounded, 800 tanks, at least 300 guns and 1,500 planes. The heavy losses, the complete collapse of the plan for a blitzkrieg ending to the war, and the failure to achieve their strategic objectives depressed the spirit of the German forces and gave rise to the first doubts about a successful outcome of the war.

On 2 December 1941 von Kluge's German 4th Army was launched into the attack and elements of the 258th Infantry Division actually reached the suburbs of Moscow, but the brave Muscovites did not panic. Instead powerful Soviet counter-attacks persuaded von Kluge that he was not going to break through and that his advanced units should be withdrawn.

This proved to be prudent as Zhukov launched a hundred divisions into his general counteroffensive. However, he was very conscious of his shortage of both tanks and aircraft:

Late in the evening of 4 December the Chief [Stalin] telephoned me and asked, 'Is there anything else you need beyond what we gave you?'

I said I still needed air support from Supreme Headquarters reserve and the air defence forces and at least 200 tanks and crews. The front had too few tanks and needed more for the rapid development of the counteroffensive.

'We can't give you any tanks; we don't have any' Stalin said 'But you'll get your air support.'

Zhukov's available T-34s rolled round the Germans' positions, deliberately avoiding any centres of resistance in order to push as far as possible into the enemy's rear. Major-General von Mellenthin recalled:

In 1941 we had nothing comparable with the T-34, with its 50mm maximum armour, 76mm high velocity gun, and its relatively high speed with splendid cross-country performance. These tanks were not thrown into battle in large numbers until our spearheads were approaching Moscow; they then played a great part in saving the Russian capital.

By the time of Zhukov's counteroffensive, the German Army had suffered over 100,000 cases of frostbite. On 5 December 1941 Hitler's offensive was formally called off; two days earlier some local withdrawals had already been sanctioned. The net result was that Zhukov held Moscow in part thanks to the T-34.

Despite the Red Army's massive losses, it had 7,700 tanks by the beginning of 1942 and 20,600 by the following year. Soviet tank factories were churning out 2,000 a month, rising to almost 3,000 by the end of 1943. In the summer of 1942 the Soviets abandon their earlier piecemeal tactics and began to form entire tank armies, with armoured and mechanized corps.

Emboldened by their success before Moscow the Red Army attempted to recapture Kharkov in April 1942. Lack of experience was once again to play in the panzers' favour. A German counter-attack was to result in fourteen Soviet tank brigades, largely equipped with new T-34s, being scattered. It was a terrible waste of resources, but was symptomatic of Stalin's impatience to push back the Nazi invaders before the Red Army had fully recovered and rearmed.

Chapter 5

Tank City Falls

In 1941 Kharkov was one of the Soviet Union's most important strategic centres, due to its vital military factories and its railway and airport hub. It was not only a vital communications centre for the whole of Ukraine, but also connected the Crimea, the Caucasus, Dnieper and Donbas regions. The Caucasus held vital oilfields, while the Donets was rich in coal. All of which were obvious targets following Hitler's invasion of the Soviet Union in June 1941.

The city was host to one of the most important tank factories in the country and was where Mikhail Koshkin's brand-new T-34 tank was being built. Hitler was oblivious to the development of the T-34 and it was to be an intelligence blunder that was to cost him dearly. The failure to capture the T-34 factory at Kharkov before it escaped was to prove another strategic mistake. In addition to the vital Kharkov tractor and locomotive plants, the city was also host to the Kharkov Aircraft Plant and the Turbine Plant. These were churning out a plethora of military products including tanks, fighter aircraft, military tractors, mortars, small arms and ammunition.

Most notably Kharkov was home of the BT-5 and BT-7 fast tanks and the T-35 heavy tank which had gone into production there in the 1930s. It was also involved with the building of the T-26 light tank. Both the BT and T-26 formed the backbone of the Red Army's tank fleet in 1941. These though had already been proved to be obsolete during the Spanish Civil War and the Finnish Winter War. Koshkin was appointed head of the Kharkov design bureau in the mid-1930s to work on BT improvements; this led to the development of the T-34 that went into production in 1940.

As well as tanks Kharkov also manufactured tractors or tracked prime movers. Ukraine was the breadbasket of the Soviet Union so these tractors were invaluable to its agriculture. The first Soviet trucks and cars appeared in the 1920s coming out of Moscow's AMO and Spartak factories respectively. With the assistance of American Ford technicians, GAZ then set up a factory at Gorky in the early 1930s. Tractor and truck production also started in the early 1930s with civilian and military tracked tractors being built in Chelyabinsk, Kharkov, Kirov and Stalingrad. All of the Red Army's heavy artillery was hauled by tracked prime movers. Those produced at Kharkov's Komintern factory were used to tow the 152mm M1937 gun-howitzer. The Kharkov Aircraft Plant was home to Pavel Sukhoi's design bureau until its move in 1941 to Molotov. His Su-2 short-range bomber went into production in 1939 at Kharkov's Factory No. 135 and by September 1941 this was producing five aircraft a day. This factory was relocated in the face of the German advance and the aircraft was also constructed in Moscow and Taganrog.

While Hitler's main objectives before the winter of 1941 were the seizure of Leningrad, Moscow and the approaches to the Caucasian oilfields, Kharkov was clearly a key secondary objective. As well as protecting the flanks of their motorized columns, the German high command appreciated the value of Kharkov as a key rail hub and industrial centre that should be denied to the Soviets. Its capture would mean that the Red Army's Southwestern and Southern Fronts would have to rely on Voronezh and Stalingrad as their transport centres.

Despite his ignorance of the T-34, Hitler was well aware of Kharkov's military significance stating, 'The second in importance is south Russia, particularly the Donets Basin, ranging from the Kharkov region. There is the whole basis of [the] Russian economy; if the area is mastered then it would inevitably lead to the collapse of the entire Russian economy …' Hitler's assessment was right, but delays in securing Kharkov meant that its factories slipped from his grasp.

Following the German invasion, the T-34 was swiftly forced from its birthplace. Fortunately for the Red Army the Kharkov locomotive factory began to relocate to Nizhny Tagil in August 1941. Following the evacuation of the Soviet tank-producing facilities east of the Urals, production of the T-34 was successfully conducted at Chelyabinsk and Nizhny Tagil as well as a number of other subsidiary plants well out of the reach of the Luftwaffe.

While Kharkov is principally remembered as the birthplace of the famous T-34 tank, it is equally famous for the enormous Dzerzhinsky Square, which was photographed on numerous occasions during the war by both sides. This was bordered by massive and oppressive Stalinist tower blocks that were a fine example of totalitarian and utilitarian architecture. Perversely the square was named after Felix Dzerzhinsky the founder of the Cheka, the Bolshevik secret police and forerunner of the KGB. During the course of the fighting it was renamed by its conquerors as 'German Army Square' and then 'Leibstandarte SS Square'.

The evacuation of Kharkov's factories commenced before Hitler had a chance to attack. Three days before the German assault commenced on the city on 23 October seventy factories had been stripped and shipped east on 320 trains. The tank factory evacuated to Nizhny Tagil helped create the Ural Tank Factory No. 183. Likewise, Kharkov's diesel engine factory and Leningrad's Kirov Plant (Factory No. 100) and S.M. Kirov (No. 185) moved to Chelyabinsk and combined with the Tractor Plant to became popularly known as 'Tankograd' or 'Tank City'. In Molotov the Su-2 bomber was built from the component stock evacuated from Kharkov until late April 1942.

The Soviet 6th Army was reactivated in August 1939 in the Kiev Special Military District. It was involved in the invasion of eastern Poland in September 1939, then occupied defences along the Lvov axis as a premier military district 'covering army'. Under Lieutenant General I.N. Muzychenko, the 6th took the brunt of the main German attack in June 1941, falling back to Uman south of Kiev where it was trapped and destroyed with 12th Army. Muzychenko was captured and his command was deactivated on 10 August, only to be reactivated the following month around the nucleus of the 48th Rifle Corps and deployed in reserve in the Kharkov sector.

The 21st Army had only formed in the spring of 1941 at Kuibyshev in the Volga Military District. In July 1941, with the panzers approaching the Dnieper, it deployed to the Rogachev area where over three weeks it launched a series of desperate counter-attacks against Guderian's 2nd Panzer Group (the infamous 'Timoshenko counteroffensive'). During the fighting in September the 21st Army was destroyed in the Kiev Pocket.

Under Lieutenant General Dimitrii Riabyshev, the Soviet 38th Army had come into being in early August 1941 just after the loss of 6th and 12th Armies at Uman in western Ukraine. Based on survivors of 8th Mechanized Corps from the Uman Pocket and newly-raised Ukrainian divisions, it formed part of the Southwestern Front and was tasked with holding the Dnieper upriver from Kremenchug. After the surrender of those forces trapped at Uman on 1 August this task was given greater urgency.

At the end of the month Riabyshev was sent south to a new appointment and Major General Nikolai Feklenko assumed command of 38th Army. On 31 August it found itself resisting the German 17th Army's crossing of the Dnieper. This German bridgehead was to form the southern arm of a pincer designed to trap much of the Southwestern Front east of the river. The northern arm crossed the Desna 124 miles north-east of Kiev.

Although ordered to destroy the German Dnieper bridgehead, Feklenko was in no position to do so, especially once panzer divisions from the 1st Panzer Group crossed. The panzers broke through 38th Army's lines on 12 September and four days later linked up with the German armour moving south from Romny. As intended this trapped most of the Soviet Southwestern Front including much of 38th Army. Feklenko was replaced by Major General Vladimir Tsiganov. He was reinforced by reserve units from eastern Ukraine to try and stop the remnants of his army being driven back toward Poltava.

The Red Army's defeat at Kiev was even bigger than at Uman. When the Battle of Kiev came to a close on 26 September 1941, the German official news service claimed the pocket had given up 665,000 men killed or captured, 884 tanks and 3,718 field guns and mortars. Staggeringly five Soviet armies (the 5th, 21st, 26th, 37th and 38th), amounting to fifty field divisions, had been wiped off the Red Army's order of battle. Subsequently the Soviets contested these figures, claiming they lost no more than 175,000 men. The general feeling is that Moscow was trying to play down the situation, rather than the Germans over-inflating their victory. Despite the efforts of Military Commissar Nikita Khrushchev and General Semyon Mikhailovich Budenny to save them, Stalin remained content to leave these vast forces to their fate. When he did relent it was too late and thousands were killed trying to escape.

Thanks to the German victory at Kiev the Soviet Southwestern Front was smashed. The Soviet high command despatched reinforcements into the region between Kursk and Rostov in an attempt to stabilize the southern flank. Using the reformed 6th, 21st, 38th and 40th Armies, the front was reconstituted under Marshal Timoshenko. This though ended in failure in October when the Germans renewed their attacks. The 6th Army under Rodion Malinovsky and the 38th Army commanded by Victor Tsiganov were driven back after failing to coordinate their efforts. The situation at Vyazma and Bryansk meant that there were no reserves left forcing Timoshenko to retreat.

At the beginning of October, the 38th Army, comprising six rifle divisions and a tank division, was forced back toward Poltava. Tsiganov was saved by German armoured units being directed towards Moscow and Rostov and was able to avoid being encircled by the German 6th Army's plodding infantry divisions. The 21st Army's supporting 10th Tank Brigade fought alongside the 169th, 300th and 304th Rifle Divisions of 38th Army in the bitter fighting around Poltava and Kharkov in September and October 1941. It lost its twenty tanks in September and was refitted in early October.

The Ukrainian 169th Rifle Division was formed in the Ukranian Military District in the Kherson and Nikolaev region in the summer of 1939, taking part in the invasions of eastern Poland and Romanian Bessarabia. At the time of Hitler's attack on the Soviet Union the 169th was with the 55th Rifle Corps, which was acting as the Kiev Special Military District's reserve. It was with 18th Army during the fighting withdrawal across southern Ukraine. Then retreating eastward, it joined 6th Army's defence of the Dnieper river line and then 38th and 21st Armies defending the Kharkov sector. Major General S.M. Rogachevsky was appointed divisional commander on 3 October during the heavy fighting on the approaches to Kharkov.

Both the Ukrainian 300th and 304th Rifle Divisions were severely weakened by the ferocity of the autumn operations. By November their combined manpower was less than 2,680 men. Raised at Krasnograd south of Kharkov in July 1941, the 300th initially formed part of the Western Strategic Direction's reserve. The following month it was at Poltava and joined 38th Army's defence of the Dnieper line south of Kiev. Afterwards it fought with 38th Army in defence of Kharkov and during the winter battles that followed. Likewise, the 304th was raised near Kharkov at Solotnoscha in July 1941 using veterans and reservists from the disbanded 109th Motorized Division of the 5th Mechanized Corps that had been mauled in the battles at Lepel and around Smolensk.

The Soviet 38th Army was instructed to hold Kharkov while the city's vital military factories were dismantled and taken to safety. In reality the 38th was more concerned about conducting an orderly withdrawal, so it was really a case of buying time until the evacuation had been completed. This job fell to the 216th Rifle Division that had been reformed after its destruction at Kiev. Formed in May 1941 in the Kiev Special Military District at Staro Konstantinov as a motorized division with the 24th Mechanized Corps, the Ukrainian 216th Rifle Division was deployed south of Kiev at Proskurov when the war started. During July and August, it fought with 24th Corps in the Vinnitsa region and was trapped with 26th Army at Uman in late

August. The 216th was reformed around the division's survivors and served with 38th Army during the defensive battles on the approaches to Kharkov and Kupiansk.

Once Operation Barbarossa was underway, at the end of July 1941 Hitler issued Führer Directive 34 which reflected his intentions to secure the Leningrad area and the Caucasus before capturing Moscow. Army Group South was tasked with destroying those Red Army forces west of the Dnieper. Key amongst these was the 5th Red Army north-west of Kiev. Hitler despatched Army Group Centre's panzers to the flanks, moving them against Leningrad, a region that was simply not good for tank warfare, and into Ukraine. Kiev though was not Moscow, the epicentre of Stalin's power and the main traffic junction for western Russia through which passed nearly all of the Red Army's supplies. The loss of Moscow would have been a terrible blow and may have unseated Stalin in an ugly internal power struggle.

While Leningrad was enduring the first days of an artillery and air siege, events were moving quickly in Ukraine. After building up a superiority of 2:1 in men and artillery and 1.5:1 in aircraft on 30 July Hitler renewed the offensive along the Korosten-Berdichev-Letchev line. The first blow fell on the Kiev sector where the 5th and 25th Armies met. German troops reached the outskirts of Kiev by 7 August but were driven back by a determined counter-attack involving four rifle divisions of General A.A. Vlasov's 37th Army and two airborne corps fighting as infantry. Meanwhile General Paul von Kleist's 1st Panzer Group managed to pierce the Soviet defences and outflank the 6th Army from the north in the area of Belaya Tserkov. At the same time the German 17th Army broke though the junction of the Soviet 12th and 18th Armies and began a two-pronged advance, one to the north to link up with von Kleist and one south toward the Black Sea.

During the withdrawal the 6th and 12th Armies were transferred to General Tyulenev's Southern Front and were about to escape the German pincers when von Rundstedt switched von Kleist's panzers from the Kiev sector to the Southern Front. This greatly speeded up the arms of the northern pincer and on 2 August von Kleist severed the line of retreat of the 6th and 12th Armies east of Pervomaisk and linked up with 17th Army advancing from Uman. The Soviet 6th and 12th Armies resisted until 12 August when both army commanders were captured along with many thousands of officers and men. Part of the 18th Army was also trapped. After the encirclement of the 6th and 12th Armies, German mobile forces pressed southward and by 19 August had reached the Black Sea port of Nikolaev, threatening Odessa which was evacuated by mid-October.

A far more serious threat was hanging over the Southwestern Front. The 2nd Panzer Group began a new southward move on 8 August against the Central Front in the area of Gomel. The Germans planned to encircle Soviet troops in the Kiev area by advancing from Gomel across the Desna to the area of Konotop-Sevsk in northern Ukraine. There they hoped to link up with Army Group South fresh from its victory at Uman.

In mid-August Directive 34 was followed by a supplementary directive that called on Army Group South, 'To occupy the Donets area and the industrial area of Kharkov'. Despite the creation of the Bryansk Front under Ukrainian General Yeremenko (Yeryomenko), which counter-attacked south of Smolensk in the last week of August, the Soviet Central Front disintegrated and the main weight of defending Kiev from the north and north-east fell on the already overstrained Southwestern Front.

After the Battle of Kiev Army Group Centre was instructed to remain on the defensive before Moscow and the 2nd Panzer Group shifted northwards toward Bryansk and Kursk. Taking the panzer divisions' place were Walter von Reichenau's 6th Army and Carl-Heinrich von Stülpnagel's 17th Army. The strike formation of Army Group South, von Kleist's 1st Panzer Group, was sent south to advance toward Rostov-on-Don and the vital Caucasian oilfields. The 6th and 17th Armies spent three weeks regrouping and processing over half a million Red Army prisoners taken during the Battle of Kiev.

At the beginning of September, the German 17th Army was told to 'gain ground in the direction of Poltava and Kharkov'. After pushing the Red Army to the bend of the Dnieper, General von Kleist's panzers and the 17th Army returned to the area of Kremenchug, where they began to force a crossing of the river 150 miles south-east of Kiev. In the first week of September the newly-organized Soviet 40th Army, deployed to the right of 5th Army, fell back east of Kharkov. Part of 1st Panzer Group along with 17th Army had completed their crossing of the Dnieper at Kremenchug on 12 September and they drove back the Soviet 38th Army defending the river.

The 1st and 2nd Panzer Groups met near Romny three days later on 17 September and the forces of the Southwestern Front were trapped. The Soviet 5th, 21st, 37th, 38th and parts of the 40th and 26th Armies were encircled. Control of these forces collapsed, as two days earlier Marshal Budenny had been relieved of his command for recommending the evacuation of Kiev. The commander of the Southwestern Front, Colonel General M.P. Kirponos, and his chief of staff General V.I. Tupikov were killed by shellfire.

The commander of 5th Army, General M.I. Potapov, was captured, while the commander of the 24th Mechanized Corps, General V.I. Chistyakov along with Generals D.S. Pisarevski, A.I. Zelentsov and K.Ya. Kulikov were killed trying to escape the German trap. Estimates of the Red Army's losses vary but from a front of some 660,000 men about half were captured and less than 150,000 escaped east with their weapons.

At the end of September 1941 Marshal Timoshenko was appointed commander-in-chief of the battered Southwestern Strategic Sector. Nikita Khrushchev, who had previously served in Kiev under Budenny, was his chief political adviser, or commissar and political member of the military council, and Major General A.P. Pokrovski was his chief of staff. Gathering what troops he could from the Kiev disaster, Timoshenko withdrew slowly to the line of the Donets River from Belgorod to Kharkov while reserves were rushed to fill the gaps in his depleted order of battle.

At the end of July 1941 Guderian was convinced that the key threat to Army Group Centre was not the Soviet 5th Army, which lay behind him, but Red Army units gathering on his right flank north of the town of Roslavl. This in fact comprised the Soviet 28th Army, with little more than three divisions under Lieutenant General Vladimir Kachalov who had been tasked to relieve the Smolensk Pocket. Guderian proposed to Field Marshal Fedor von Bock diverting resources south with which to take Roslavl. His attack opened on 2 August and two days later the town had been captured along with 38,000 Soviet prisoners and 200 guns. The ease with which Guderian attained his victory should have warned him that this was not the main threat after all.

Eleven days had been wasted since the decision had been taken to destroy the Soviet 5th Army. Not even the destruction of the Soviet 16th Army and the 23rd Mechanized Corps on 5 August along with elements of the 19th and 20th Armies, resulting in 300,000 prisoners, 3,200 tanks and 3,100 guns taken, could compensate for this failure.

Budenny's request to withdraw his forces behind the Dnieper was approved by Stavka on 19 August. The Soviet 37th Army was ordered to remain in Kiev, but the withdrawn 5th Army and the new 40th Army (made up of remnants of other armies) were directed to form a line running south-east protecting Chernigov, Konotop and Kharkov. While this was a positive move, in reality Budenny's forces were already expended and he had no reserves left for his Southwestern Front. Everything hung on Yeremenko to defend Moscow.

Once the Battle of Moscow was underway, Hitler had to safeguard his flanks. On 6 October von Reichenau's 6th Army moved in the direction of Belgorod and Kharkov, driving through Sumy and Okhtyrka. At the same time Stülpnagel's 17th Army moved to protect the lengthening flank of 1st Panzer Army (formerly 1st Panzer Group). This was achieved by launching an offensive from Poltava towards Lozova and Izyum.

Chapter 6

The T-34 Escapes

Hitler had allocated units from the 17th Army to the 6th Army to assist with the capture of Kharkov. The result of this was to greatly weaken the 17th Army's attempts to screen 1st Panzer Army's flank and this contributed to the German defeat at the Battle of Rostov. The task of capturing Kharkov was assigned to General Erwin Vierow's 55th Corps, comprising General Josef Brauner von Haydringen's 101st Light Division and General Anton Dostler's 57th Infantry Division. The latter was supported by two batteries from Sturmgeschütz Battalion 197 commanded by Captain Kurt von Barisani.

General von Haydringen's men had fought their way to within four miles of the city by 21 October 1941. By now the Russian *Rasputitsa* or muddy season had begun to close in with the autumn and it was only by the middle of the month that the night frost had hardened up the roads. The gathering snow and the fall in temperatures hit the Germans hard as they had not been issued with winter clothing.

Haydringen's 228th Light Regiment acted as spearhead with the 1st and 3rd Battalions at the front with the 2nd Battalion in reserve. On 22 October the regiment was instructed to probe the Red Army's forward defences held by the 216th Rifle Division. This comprised a Soviet infantry battalion supported by tanks that launched an attack at noon that day.

The 3rd Battalion was strengthened by two guns from the 85th Artillery Regiment, a single 88mm anti-aircraft gun and a company of engineers. The 2nd Battalion was similarly reinforced but did not get an anti-aircraft gun. The 1st Battalion was assigned the role of regimental reserve. In addition, the 1st Battalion from the 229th Light Regiment was to act as flank guard while the 228th attacked along with the German 57th Infantry Regiment. The attack on Kharkov was set for noon, but the artillery was not ready so the attack had to be postponed until 1500 hours. There were also problems moving the anti-tank company forward as it fell afoul of the mud. When it did arrive it was instructed to allot a 37mm gun platoon to each of the front-line battalions.

As the evacuation of the city had already been completed, the Red Army was not obliged to conduct any major defensive operations. The escape of the city's factories, especially the T-34 plant, was to cost the Germans dearly in the coming years. Resistance by the Soviet 216th Division was sporadic and did little to hold up the Germans. By 24 October Kharkov was firmly in the hands of Dostler's 57th Infantry Division.

Administration of the city was given to 55th Corps with the 57th Division acting as the occupation force. The Red Army had left a nasty surprise for them. On 14 November a series of bombs on time fuses exploded in a number of buildings, killing General Georg Braun and his staff from the 68th Infantry Division. Reprisals were swift with the arrest of 200 civilians, many of them Jews, who were hanged from the balconies of the city's major buildings.

A month later the SS of Einsatzgruppe C herded 20,000 Jews into a hut settlement near the Kharkov Tractor Factor, where they were methodically exterminated. To add to the city's woes, the German garrison confiscated much of the available food, causing shortages for the civilian population. By January 1942 the population had been reduced to 300,000 and a third of them were facing starvation.

Meanwhile the defence of Moscow became a priority for the Red Army. Stavka's plan called for an offensive by all three fronts in the Moscow area: Konev's Kalinin Front to the north of the Sea of Moscow, Zhukov's Western Front either side of the capital and Timoshenko's Southwestern Front on Zhukov's left flank. Zhukov would provide the main effort, while on his right the fresh 1st Shock and 20th Armies were to open the attack supported by the 30th and 16th Armies on the flanks. They were to link up with Konev's 29th and 31st Armies. The intention was that opposite Moscow, Zhukov's front would tie down German forces, while the 10th and 50th Armies on the southern wing, along with Timoshenko's forces, attacked Guderian's Panzer Group.

Lelyushenko's 30th Army at Dmitrov, to the north of Moscow, made the deepest penetration into German lines on the first day. Its tanks advanced to the Moscow-Leningrad Highway, threatening the junction between the German 4th Army and 4th Panzer Group. Three days in, it had got to Klin and with the 1st Shock Army on the left flank seemed poised to achieve a successful encirclement. Rokossovsky's 16th Army and Vlasov's 20th Army made equally pleasing progress, taking Istra west of Moscow by 13 December 1941.

The Soviet 13th and 40th Armies belonging to Timoshenko's mauled Southwestern Front pierced the southern face of 3rd Panzer Group's salient, which it had created in November. By 9 December Timoshenko was threatening the Germans' main supply route, the Orel-Tula railway. In the meantime, the 50th and 10th Armies struck the northern edge of the salient driving a wedge between Guderian and Kluge. Once the Soviet 33rd and 43rd Armies had joined the offensive on 18 December the German 4th Army was increasingly pushed back westward.

To the north Konev's Kalinin Front drove the German 9th Army from Kalinin and thrust south-westward along the upper Volga towards Rzhev. In the far south von Rundstedt was ejected from Rostov-on-Don on 28 November having only occupied it five days previously. Hitler, incensed that his generals had not taken Moscow, sacked Field Marshal von Brauchitsch, CinC Army, von Bock, von Leeb and Guderian, while von Rundstedt was transferred west. Thirty-five corps or divisional commanders were also removed. The loss of Rostov was the first significant German withdrawal of the war.

As the 216th Rifle Division was conducting a holding action it was offered no support from any of 38th Army's other divisions or indeed from the higher command formations. The 216th moved to defend the western edge of the city, setting up machine-gun nests and mortar pits protected by minefields. It was evident that the first battle for Kharkov was going to be a very brief and one-sided affair. Forced to abandon the city, 38th Army later joined the Southwestern Front's January offensive toward Kharkov and in March 1942 seized the Staryi Saltov bridgehead just east of the city.

Lieutenant General Kirill Semenovich Moskalenko was appointed commander of 38th Army in March 1942, which by this stage consisted of six rifle divisions and three tank brigades. The 36th Tank Brigade, commanded by Colonel T.I. Tanaschisin, had been formed at Gorky in the Moscow Military District in November 1941 and joined the 38th Army shortly after its creation. The 13th and 133rd Tank Brigades had been formed in the summer of 1941 and already seen action with the armies of the Southwestern Front.

When the Germans had first invaded, Moskalenko, then a brigade commander, tangled with the 1st Panzer Group. After his force was destroyed he took charge of the 15th Rifle Corps, then the 6th Cavalry Corps and a cavalry mechanized group in fighting near Kiev, Chernigov and Elets. For his performance at Elets in late December 1941 he was promoted deputy commander of the 6th Army then attacking toward Kharkov. Moskalenko was vital in planning 6th Army's role in the January 1942 Barvenkovo–Lozovaya operation and as a reward was given 38th Army.

The Second Battle for Kharkov was to be a vastly larger and costlier affair than the first. By early 1942 the Soviet winter counteroffensive, which halted Hitler at the very gates of Moscow, had run out of steam and both sides paused to regroup. Stalin convinced himself that the German Army was now spent and could not cope with Mother Russia's bitter winter. He was confident that he could roll the Nazis back, but he was grossly overestimating the capabilities of the exhausted and much depleted Red Army

Encouraged by the Red Army's last-ditch efforts in stopping the Wehrmacht, Stalin was determined to launch another counteroffensive to capitalize on the situation. On 5 January 1942 he told his gathered generals:

The Germans are in disarray as a result of their defeat before Moscow. They've prepared badly for the winter. This is the most favourable moment to go over to a general offensive. The Germans hope to hold our offensive until the spring, so that they can resume active operations when they have built up their strength.

Our task is therefore to give the Germans no time to draw breath, drive them to the West, and force them to use up all their reserves before spring comes because by then we will have new reserves and the German reserves will have run out.

This was sound military thinking, but it did not take into account the resilience of the Wehrmacht or the true offensive capabilities of the Red Army. Stalin envisaged the main effort would be against Army Group Centre, with the aim of trapping it west of Vyazma; the Leningrad and Volkhov Fronts were to crush Army Group North and save Leningrad. It would be Timoshenko's job to deal with Army Group South, liberating Kharkov, the Donbas and Sevastopol in the Crimea. The attack toward Kharkov was to be two-pronged; from Volchansk to the north-east of the city and from Barvenkovo to the south.

On 5 April 1942 Hitler issued Directive 41 that struck an equally confident note, 'The winter battle in Russia is nearing its end. Thanks to the unequalled courage and self-sacrificing devotion on the Eastern Front, German arms have achieved a great defensive success.' He then laid out his plans for the coming summer, which gave the Wehrmacht the task of ejecting the Red Army from the Don region, the Donbas industrial region, the Caucasian oil fields and the Caucasus passes. He hoped that the latter operations would encourage neutral Turkey to finally side with the Axis.

Outlining his *General Plan* Hitler stated:

In pursuit of the original plan for the Eastern campaign, the armies of the Central sector [Army Group Centre] will stand fast, those in the *North* [Army Group North] will capture Leningrad and link up with the Finns, while those on the *southern flank* [Army Group South] will break through into the Caucasus.

In view of the conditions prevailing at the end of winter, the availability of troops and resources, and transport problems, these aims can be achieved only one at a time.

First, therefore, all available forces will be concentrated on the *main operations in the southern sector*, with the aim of destroying the enemy before the Don, in order to secure the Caucasian oil fields, and the passes through the Caucasus mountains themselves.

In early 1942 the Germans began to conduct their deception plan codenamed Kremlin, designed to convince Stalin that the German summer offensive would be directed toward finally capturing Moscow. Leaks were made to the foreign press and Army Group Centre conducted poorly-concealed preparations that indicted that Hitler would again attack the Soviet capital in force.

Meanwhile, during the spring the Germans began preparing for their real massive southern summer offensive, known as Operation Blue. Their first moves were to secure their flanks. Way to the south this meant driving the Red Army completely from the Crimea and capturing Sevastopol. This would protect the right flank of Field Marshal Fedor von Bock's Army Group South and enable General Erich von Manstein's 11th Army to cross the Straits of Kerch in support of 1st Panzer Army and 17th Army's offensive along the eastern coast of the Black Sea once they were across the lower Don and Donets.

Von Manstein moved to eliminate the Red Army from the Kerch Peninsula on 8 May 1942 in Operation Bustard Hunt, diverting all his forces except for 54th Corps which remained before Sevastopol. In total six German and three Romanian divisions were thrown at the Soviet 44th, 47th and 51st Armies. With Luftwaffe support, the Germans sliced through the thin Soviet defences. By the evening von Manstein's 30th Corps had pierced the Soviet 44th Army's front and eleven Soviet divisions were driven into the Sea of Azov on 11 May. The rest of his forces reached Kerch five days later. The Soviets could not hold on in the Crimea and evacuated. In the chaos that followed they lost 170,000 prisoners, 260 tanks, 1,140 guns and 300 aircraft. Von Manstein's forces suffered 7,500 casualties. He could now devote all his attention to reducing the last remaining Soviet stronghold in the Crimea – Sevastopol. This was defended by about 100,000 men of Lieutenant General I.E. Petrov's Independent Coastal Command.

In Ukraine, while Timoshenko and his Southwestern Front were preparing to liberate Kharkov, von Bock's Army Group South was planning to destroy the Barvenkovo-Lozovaya bridgehead that stretched west from Izyum beyond the Donets south of Kharkov. General Friedrich Paulus deployed his forces between Belgorod and Balakleya north and south of Kharkov respectively, while von Kleist further to the south was at Pavlograd west of the Soviet bridgehead. Their intention was to cut off and destroy the Soviet salient, straighten the German line along the Donets and then launch their main offensive. Ironically Timoshenko obliged von Bock by putting more troops into the noose.

This salient had been created by a Soviet offensive launched on 18 January against Army Group South. They had planned that the Soviet 6th, 57th and 9th Armies of the Southwestern Front as well as the Southern Front would drive west over the Donets between Balakleya in the north and Artemovsk in the south before swinging south to the Sea of Azov at Melitopol, trapping German forces in the area. The tanks of the Southern Front never got beyond their start point and the Southwestern Front ground to a halt on 31 January having created a considerable salient containing two armies.

Nikita Khrushchev, head of the communist party in Ukraine and Stalin's regional enforcer (his official title was Military Commissar of the Southwestern Direction), recalled:

Perhaps my most perilous hour was during the disastrous counteroffensive toward Kharkov in 1942. We had broken through the enemy's front line of defence easily – too easily. We realized that there were no forces massed against us. We seemed to have a clear road ahead, deep into enemy territory. This was unsettling. It meant we had stumbled into a trap.

Disastrously, two-thirds of the Soviet armour along with General Kharitonov's 9th Army and General Gorodnyanski's 6th Army moved into the salient ready to liberate Krasnograd south-west of Kharkov. This was to be followed by a push on Kharkov and Poltava way to the west. Their attack was to be supported by the Soviet 28th and 38th Armies north-east of Kharkov in the Volchansk bridgehead.

If von Bock had struck first he would have had to contend with nearly 600 Soviet tanks, but instead Timoshenko beat him to the post by attacking a week earlier on 12 May. Those forces launched from Volchansk made little impression against Paulus' fourteen divisions. In the south Romanian forces could not prevent the fall of Krasnograd and Kharkov seemed within Timoshenko's grasp. The Soviet 9th Army rolled on to Karlovka west of Kharkov. Worryingly though, the Red Army's tanks were unable to widen the breach south of Izyum and Barvenkov, which meant the pocket got bigger but not the breach.

If both the Soviet 6th and 9th Armies had struck toward Merefa just south of Kharkov things might have gone differently, but with Kharitonov heading west on the 17th warning signs began to appear. This was the Soviets' first attempt at an armoured offensive on such a scale and it had clearly not brought the Germans main combat strength to battle, which was now identified as laying on their southern flank. It was imperative they shifted to a defensive posture and move their armour, anti-tank guns and artillery to protect their exposed left flank. Realizing the danger, Timoshenko and Khrushchev called a halt with a view to helping 9th Army, only to be overridden by Stalin. Despite Khrushchev's efforts to get Stalin to stop the offensive, his orders were to press on.

On the 18th the Germans counter-attacked. Eleven divisions from von Kleist's Army Group struck against the 9th and 57th Armies from

Slavyansk-Kramatorsk and within two days had broken through on the left wing of the Southwestern Front in the Petrovsky region. Von Kleist was assaulting the left flank of the salient northwards toward Izyum in an attempt to cut off the 57th and 9th Armies as well as the 6th Army and Group Bobrin (the last two had been halted in the preceding days trying push westward towards Krasnograd on the key railway line south-west of Kharkov). Izyum fell on the 18th and the Soviets fell back in a state of chaos and the Germans sped on to reach the Oskol River.

Khrushchev wrote:

Catastrophe struck a few days later, exactly as we expected. There was nothing we could do to avert it. Many generals, colonels, junior officers, and troops perished. The staff of the 57th Army was wiped out completely. Almost nobody managed to escape. The army had advanced deep into enemy territory, and when our men were encircled, they didn't even have enough fuel to escape. It was too far to return on foot. Many were killed, but most taken prisoner. General Gurov somehow managed to escape in a tank.

With the noose tightening around the Soviets' forces, Timoshenko despatched his deputy General Kostenko to try and save the 6th and 9th Armies. When General Friedrich Paulus' panzers arrived at Balakleya on 23 May, linking up with those of von Kleist, the trap was snapped shut. By the 26th the survivors were squeezed into an area about six square miles. The main pockets of resistance were quickly broken up into a series of ever-shrinking pockets that were swiftly overwhelmed. Less than a quarter of the two Soviet armies got away, and all their heavy equipment was left littering the west bank of the Donets.

Officially the Soviets acknowledged 5,000 killed (including General Kuzma Podlas, commander of 57th Army), 70,000 missing and 300 tanks lost. The Germans claimed to have captured 240,000 men, something which Khrushchev confirmed to Stalin when he reported to Moscow shortly afterwards. This implied the bulk of the Soviet troops surrendered and the Germans also claimed to have taken or destroyed 1,200 tanks. Timoshenko only had 845 tanks in total, but the German figure may include all armoured fighting vehicles. It is doubtful that any Soviet armour escaped the southern pocket, though the 28th Army may have saved a few tanks in the north.

In the face of such an unmitigated disaster Timoshenko sought to gather his remaining troops by appealing to their stomachs. When Khrushchev returned from a tense meeting with Stalin in Moscow he observed:

> Marshal Timoshenko told me that the army had been so utterly routed by the enemy that the only way to rally the troops was to set up mobile kitchens and hope the soldiers would return when they got hungry. He was drawing on his Civil War experience here. We set up field kitchens and slowly but surely reorganized our defences.

The cost of the failed Kharkov offensive for the Red Army was considerable, and while the tank ratio during 1942 had stood at 5:1 in their favour, it was now 10:1 against them, which did not bode well in light of the coming German summer offensive. Operation Fridericus II, to clear the Kupyansk area and secure a bridgehead over the Oskol, was conducted on 22–26 June. Moving from south-east of Kharkov the Soviets were again driven back, losing 40,000 more prisoners and sealing the destruction of the Southwestern Front.

Inevitably someone had to take the blame for the failed Kharkov offensive and initially Khrushchev feared he was going to face a firing squad when he flew to Moscow. Certainly Stalin accused Khrushchev of acting independently of Timoshenko when halting the offensive and going over to the defensive, but Khrushchev denied this, saying he had Timoshenko's agreement. Both men knew it was the only logical course of action.

To be fair, despite the wrangling with Stalin, the Red Army was not given time to react, because the danger was not appreciated until the Germans had launched their counteroffensive and their deadly encirclement was rapidly underway. Rather unfairly Timoshenko was demoted from Deputy People's Commissar of Defence and Commander-in-Chief Southwestern Strategic Sector as a consequence of the Kharkov disaster. In contrast, Zhukov took over as Deputy Supreme Commander under Stalin.

Chapter 7

The Stalingrad Flank

Hitler's continuation of Operation Barbarossa, Case Blue, was conducted between 28 June and 24 November 1942. In preparation his Army Group South (one of three operating on the Eastern Front) was divided into two – A and B. The former was instructed to fight its way south-east through the Caucasus Mountains to reach the major oil fields at Baku on the Caspian Sea. The latter was to attack eastward toward the Volga and the major industrial city of Stalingrad. The Caucasus was not good tank country.

Army Group A was placed under Field Marshal List with the task of advancing into the Caucasus. At this point it seems that Hitler and the Army's Chief of Staff, General Halder, misunderstood each other's intentions. Hitler resolved to capture Stalingrad not only because it was Stalin's namesake city but also as a way of safeguarding the northern flank to cover his swing to the south-east into the Caucasus, but Halder was working on the opposite proposition, assuming that Stalingrad was the primary goal while operations to the south were more diversionary.

Von Kleist, who was given command of the armoured thrust into the Caucasus, received personal instructions from Hitler. He clarified:

> The capture of Stalingrad was subsidiary to the main aim. It was only of importance as a convenient place, in the bottleneck between the Don and the Volga, where we could block an attack on our flank by Russian forces coming from the East. At the start Stalingrad was no more than a name on a map to us.

Hitler had summoned von Kleist in early April and the Field Marshal expressed severe doubts about the wisdom of what was being proposed:

Hitler said we must capture the oilfields by the autumn because Germany could not continue the war without them. When I pointed out the risks of leaving such a long flank exposed, he said he was going to draw on Romania, Hungary and Italy for troops to cover it. I warned him, and so did others, that it was rash to rely on such troops, but he would not listen.

Von Kleist was told that once he had taken Maikop, his next objective would be to secure Tbilisi, the capital of the Soviet Republic of Georgia. After that he was to take Baku on the Caspian Sea, the capital of the Soviet Republic of Azerbaijan. The latter's oilfields had been producing crude oil since at least the seventeenth century.

The local geography favoured the Red Army and local militias before reaching the mountains. There were numerous stop lines that presented ideal defensive positions. First the Germans would have to get over the Terek river, then beyond that the land was steep and densely wooded. Inevitably the advance was also at risk from what might happen on the left flank between Stalingrad and the Caspian.

Although the Caucasus was far away and lacked public interest in Britain compared to Stalingrad, the British media still reported on the fighting there. In particular the pundit Major-General Sir Charles Gwyn was a regular commentator on that part of the world. He astutely noted that Marshal Timoshenko's failed counteroffensive at Kharkov in May 1942 had greatly disrupted German plans for an early offensive towards the Caucasian oilfields. Gwyn wrote:

The drive towards Caucasia will probably be restaged, for it is even more important for the Germans to deprive Russia of oil than it is to obtain new sources of oil supply for themselves. But Timoshenko has secured a position from which he can threaten the flank of a southern offensive and check a cooperative attempt from Kharkov.

Moscow's Ministry of Information took delight in issuing a photo of German officers and men captured near Kharkov. However, what Gwyn did not know was just how badly Timoshenko had been mauled.

Operation Blue consisted of three different components that were conducted from late June through July. The first part saw von Bock's Army Group South advance east of Kursk to the line of the river Don between Livny and Rossosh capturing the city of Voronezh. This offensive conducted by 2nd Army and 4th Panzer Army formed the left flank protection for the 'Donets Corridor' along which 6th Army would push toward Stalingrad.

The second part of Operation Blue saw General Paulus' 6th Army attacking toward Stalingrad. It reached its first objective on the Don's eastward bend at Kachalinskaya by 22 July. The third part was undertaken Field Marshal List's Army Group A. This employed the 1st Panzer Army and 17th Army between Izyum on the Donets and Taranrog on the Sea of Azov, with the aim of securing the right flank of 6th Army. Their goal was to take the region as far south as the Don between Tsimlyansky and Rostov. Its success ensured that Hitler would be able to eventually thrust into the Caucasus.

The attack towards the Volga and Stalingrad was dubbed Operation Heron and involved General Friedrich Paulus' 6th Army (with eighteen divisions divided into five corps) as well as part of Hoth's 4th Panzer Army. The error in this strategy was immediately obvious. Whereas the task had originally been allocated to von Weichs' Army Group B to create a defensive front along the Don as a subsidiary to Army Group A's southward thrust, Stalingrad now became a strategic offensive in its own right. Paulus was left with insufficient forces, especially when Stalin made it clear he would not give up the city by creating the Stalingrad Front under Marshal Timoshenko on 12 July.

Hitler's offensive achieved huge success because the Red Army had not recovered from its massive losses of men and equipment in 1941. The newly-formed armies were still in the process of gathering their strength. Hitler's left wing made good progress from Kursk to Voronezh. This was helped by Stalin directing what reserves he had to hand to the Moscow area. Also other Red Army forces launched an offensive towards Kharkov.

Hitler issued his orders for the subjugation of the Crimea on 11 July 1942. In his mind it was vital that his forces were over the Kerch Straits by early August. 'The aim of this operation', he explained 'will be to thrust forward on either side of the western foothills of the Caucasus in a south-easterly and easterly direction.' Hitler added that the codename for the operation would be Blücher and that the crossing would be dubbed 'B1-day'. The German 11th Army would then advance to occupy the ports of Anapa and Novorossiysk, thereby denying the Soviet Black Sea Fleet its key bases. Marshal Antonescu of Romania was to be Hitler's partner in crime in the invasion of the Caucasus. He committed half a dozen divisions including mountain units to fight alongside the Germans.

Hitler had no intention of stopping:

> After that, the operation will continue to the north of the Caucasus, its main thrust in a general easterly direction. In this connexion it is especially important that the Maikop area be quickly occupied. The decision whether small forces should also be landed on the coast along the Black Sea in the Tuapse area can only later be taken.

The 11th Army was directed to carry out deception operations with bogus movements that would convince the Red Army it was moving to the north of the Sea of Azov and not to the south-east. Hitler also proposed special forces operations, with paratroops dropping on the Maikop area to protect the oil installations in 'Undertaking Schamil', sabotage against the bridges in the Kuban and attacks on Soviet ports and coastal installations.

Amongst those German units committed to the invasion of the Caucasus was General Hubert Lanz's 1st Mountain Division, appropriately known as the 'Edelweiss' because its divisional badge was the white Alpine flower. It had fought in Poland, France and Yugoslavia. On the Eastern Front, Lanz and his men were further battle-hardened at Lvov and Kharkov. General Karl Eglseer's 4th

Mountain Division was also involved and they were likewise combat veterans of the invasion of Yugoslavia. This unit wore the regulation Edelweiss insignia, but in addition had a Gentian flower in blue on a shield as it emblem.

German intelligence officer Colonel Reinhard Gehlen optimistically assessed:

> Even if the coming operation was insufficient to destroy the Red Army or to bring about an early collapse, the physical occupation of the vital Caucasus region, and the blocking of the Volga as a Soviet waterway, would cause untold harm to the enemy's economy.

He then added a note of caution:

> Between us and the military goals of the coming year, there lay, however, yet another Russian winter, in which the enemy could rely on his superiority in winter combat, as he had the year before, to inflict such a drain of manpower and equipment on us that we would have to dismiss all thought of renewing the German offensive in 1943, particularly in view of our obligations in other theatres.

It was a prophetic warning that would come true in the summer of 1943 and thwart the Germans at Kursk. Zhukov suspected that Hitler was going after the Caucasus in part to sever one of the routes used to deliver Lend-Lease military equipment. He said 'A specific aim of the capture of the Caucasus and the Volga was to cut the Soviet Union's means of communication with its allies in the anti-Hitler coalition'.

On 29 July 1942 the Germans cut the last direct rail link between central Russia and the Caucasus. Von Kleist's 1st Panzer Army headed for Maikop in the western Caucasus foothills. He needed to act quickly to prevent the Soviets blowing up the vital oil wells. Hitler's special operations Brandenburg Regiment was called on to secure the city's key facilities ahead of Von Kleist's advance.

Zhukov was alarmed at the progress Hitler's forces seemed to be making in the Caucasus:

In mid-August the enemy occupied Mozdok and broke through the River Terek. By 9 September the Soviet 46th Army had been dislodged and enemy forces were in possession of nearly all the mountain passes. The city of Sukhumi was seriously threatened.

In these testing days the peoples of the Caucasus did not waver or lose faith in the strength and viability of the Soviet multinational state.

However, von Kleist was having major problems in terms of manpower and supplies. In just six weeks the Germans had seized the more westerly oilfields, but they never took the main ones that lay beyond the mountains. Von Kleist's initial problem was acute fuel shortages, rather than Soviet tanks. Fuel supplies could not come via the Black Sea because that route was not safe. Some oil was delivered by air, but it was simply not enough. This left his forces reliant on supplies shipped by rail from Rostov.

General Sir Alan Brooke, visiting with part of a senior British delegation, was not impressed by what he had seen of the region's defences. He had flown to Moscow from Tehran via Baku on 12 August 1942 over one of the main lines of attack from Russia into Iran. His aircraft flew below 200ft to keep out of the way of German fighters, ensuring he got a good view of the surrounding countryside. He was dismayed by what he witnessed:

I did not expect very much.... I had, however, expected to find more than I saw, which consisted of only one half-completed anti-tank ditch, badly revetted and without any covering defences. The work was unfinished.... Beyond that nothing to be seen, not a man, gun, lorry, tank or defence of any kind. In fact this back door seemed wide open for the Germans to walk through for an attack on the Russian southern supply route, and more importantly still, the vital Middle East oil supplies of Persia and Iraq.

In Moscow, where Churchill was holding difficult talks with Stalin, Marshal Voroshilov claimed that the Red Army had twenty-five divisions defending the Caucasus. Brooke did not believe him and pressed the marshal about the seemingly poor defences in the Caucasus:

> I then turned to the main approach route between the Caucasus and the Caspian. Here I drew him on and extracted out of him details of their strong lines of defence with anti-tank ditches and concrete pill-boxes for anti-tank guns and machine guns – a complete pack of lies from what I had been able to see for myself.

Despite Brooke's misgivings, Stalin remained confident, at least publicly. Churchill had flown up the eastern coast of the Caspian so had not taken the same route as Brooke. Whilst having drinks with the Soviet leader in the Kremlin, Churchill also raised the issue of holding the Caucasus passes. Stalin had responded by spreading out a map and saying with calm confidence 'We shall stop them; they will not cross the mountains'. Before they parted Stalin told his guest that they were planning a counteroffensive before the winter.

It is unclear if Stalin was stung into action by the rate of German gains or the vocal Allied concerns. Belatedly he did all he could to prepare the defences of Grozny and Baku. During August and September around 90,000 civilians were 'mobilized' to work day and night constructing fortifications and anti-tank ditches at Grozny, Makhach-Kala and the 'Debrent Gate' on the Caspian. In total ten defence lines were built around Baku. General Tyulenev wrote:

> Within a few weeks the entire Caucasian theatre of war became a network of defences. People worked till they nearly collapsed, with bloody rags around their blistered hands. Sometimes they

had little or nothing to eat for days, but they still went on with the work even at night, and despite enemy air raids … By the beginning of the autumn about 100,000 defence works were built, including 70,000 pillboxes and other firing-points. Over 500 miles of anti-tank ditches were dug, 200 miles of anti-infantry obstacles were built, as well as 1,000 miles of trenches; 9,150,000 working days were expended on this work.

It is possible that none of this work had commenced when General Brooke flew north. An alternative scenario is that the Soviet pilot had deliberately taken a route that would reveal little to the prying eyes of the British delegation. However, it is still strange that Brooke saw no signs of activity, suggesting that the construction of defences in the Caucasus did not really get underway until mid-August.

The Germans took Khulkhuta, halfway between Elista and Astrakhan, on 13 September 1942. It was not until the end of October that German and Romanian troops took Nalchik, the capital of Kabardino-Balkaria in the north Caucasus, but they were stopped once again west of Grozny at Ordzhonikidze. Von Kleist's troops struggled in the face of fresh Soviet reinforcements brought from the southern Caucasus and Siberia. He recalled 'This flank concentration of theirs was helped by the railway that the Russians built across the Steppes, from Astrakhan southward'. The city at the mouth of the Volga was not only instrumental in supporting the Red Army in the Caucasus, but also helped throw a valuable lifeline to Stalingrad to the north. The Germans tried destroying sections of the rails but as soon as they did they were swiftly repaired.

'My patrols reached the shores of the Caspian', said von Kleist 'but that advance carried us nowhere, for my forces in this quarter were striking against an intangible foe. As time passed and the Russian strength grew in that area the flanking menace became increasingly serious.' Doggedly von Kleist continued his efforts until the onset of winter. He attempted attacking at different points, but his troops struggled to unhinge Soviet defences. Initially he had attempted a direct approach by attacking toward Grozny from Mozdok, but this failed. He then tried from Nalchik on his western flank and reached Ordzhonikidze. When the weather began to turn bad his enemies struck back. 'In this counter-attack, a Romanian division, which I reckoned as a good one, suffered a sudden collapse and threw my plan out of joint. After that, a stalemate set in.' This unit was the Romanian 3rd Mountain Division which was almost destroyed by a Soviet counter-attack on 25–26 September.

In late September 1942 General Gwyn was reporting that Hitler's Caucasus campaign was evidently not going according to plan:

In the Caucasus the weight of the German attack had obviously been reduced by the necessity of using all reserves on the Volga front. The drive eastwards along the Baku railway towards the Grozny oilfields and the Caspian coast was maintained; but after a precarious foothold had been secured across the Terek river it was brought to a standstill.

There had been no slackening, however, in the attack on Novorossiysk and, five days after a premature claim by the Germans to have effected its capture, the Russians were forced to evacuate the port. It remains to be seen whether this loss will fatally affect the activities of the Black Sea fleet. If it is unable to prevent the Germans making use of the port for the supply of their southern armies the consequences will be serious.

During October the Germans intensified their attacks in the Mozdok region and renewed their attempts to reach Tuapse by road over the mountains as well as the coast road from Novorossiysk. The vital oil pipeline from Grozny to Rostov passed through Mozdok. The Soviet defenders in the Mozdok area and in the Western Caucasus continued to defy the Germans, who were hampered by the deterioration in the weather.

Closely monitoring the progress of the fighting, General Gwyn readily admitted that it was difficult to piece together exactly what was happening:

> The operations in the Mozdok region are not easy to follow, but apparently the Germans are engaged in a two-prong attack. One prong is directed up the Terek valley towards Ordzhonikidze, where the military road across the mountains to Tbilisi starts. The other is attempting to advance by the Baku railway towards the Grozny oilfields. The object may be to develop a pincer movement on Grozny, but the capture of Ordzhonikidze would also provide flank protection for the communications of a major advance on Baku, preventing Russian forces which might threaten them from using the military highways as a line of supply.

German patrols got as far as the railway between Kizlyar, north-east of Grozny and Astrakhan, but this marked the furthest point of their advance toward the Caspian Sea. Von Kleist was hampered by the region's formidable terrain and fuel supplies remained a major problem. On occasions his tanks were left hanging around for weeks waiting for petrol. In the end the Germans had to use camels to bring supplies forward. Von Kleist also lacked specialist units. Most of the mountain troops had been deployed with 17th Army to support its push along the Black Sea coast. To make matters worse, when the latter was stopped at Tuapse between Novorossiysk and Sochi he had to send them reinforcements. This inevitably weakened his operations against Grozny's oilfields.

General Günther Blumentritt, chief of staff of 4th Army, remembered the arguments, observing 'But the clamour for the reinforcement of the Tuapse operations prevailed, with the consequent splitting of our efforts in the Caucasus, until it was too late'. However, the Germans still managed to launch a new offensive from a point south-west of Mozdok against the weakly defended Soviet left flank at Nalchik. This seems to have caught the Red Army by surprise and succeeded in taking the town and placed them firmly on the road to Ordzhinikidze.

It was the 13th Panzer Division, with the Romanian 2nd Mountain Division, that captured Nalchik at the end of October along with 10,000 prisoners. This relatively small number showed that the Red Army was withdrawing in good order and not allowing itself to become trapped as it had in the summer of 1941. Nalchik had a Jewish population, known as the Mountain Jews who originated from Iran, who soon found themselves being persecuted by the invaders.

Chapter 8

Save the Oil

In the Kremlin, Stalin was once more panicked by the prospect of Grozny falling to Hitler. Should he lose the oil supplies of the Caucasus, his tanks and aircraft would grind to a halt. The Germans were stopped west of the city at Ordzhonikidze. Although they took Alagir in early November, the Alagir-Beslan-Malgobek line became the furthest south they got. On 4 November 1942, Stalin held a council of war with a dozen of his most senior generals and it was clear that aside from Stalingrad that the Caucasus was in the forefront of his mind. Stalin did not want the Germans getting their hands on anything of value. They agreed that 'it is vital to salvage industrial and public-utility installations in good time by evacuation, ... orders [were] issued for the dispersal of refineries and machine-tool factories from Grozny and Makhachkala to New Baku, Orsk and Tashkent ...'

Interestingly, Stalin also showed signs of being less callous with his troops and equipment than was usual. His orders stated that operations should be conducted cautiously to avoid heavy casualties and that the loss of ground was unimportant. He had finally recognized that mobility was key to avoiding large pockets of soldiers becoming trapped and forced to surrender. The meeting also agreed that 'all planned attack-operations are to be executed before 15 November if possible, insofar as weather permits. These are primarily from Grozny towards Mozdok ...' The weather on the Mozdok front brought the Red Army some relief from German attacks. To the west German progress towards Tuapse was slowed, though it was clear they were in a better situation to stabilize the front in the Caucasus than at Stalingrad.

General Gwyn seemed baffled by Hitler's intentions:

It is inconceivable that the Germans intended at this season to attempt to cross the mountains by this road which leads to Tbilisi or by the other road leading to Batumi on which they gained a footing, for both passes reach an altitude of 9,000ft, and are already snowbound. On the other hand, the occupation of the upper Terek valley would deprive the Russians of a valuable base of operations and source of supplies; and it would provide the Germans with winter shelter.

Moscow announced on 19 November 1942 that the Red Army had inflicted a heavy defeat on the Germans at Ordzhonikidze. According to Soviet figures the Germans lost 5,000 killed and an even greater number wounded. Winter in the Caucasus finally took the pressure off the Soviet forces fighting for possession of the Georgian Highway as their opponents hunkered down.

Reporting on the battle, General Gwyn noted:

The drive made in formidable force pressed back the Russians, who fought stubborn rearguard actions, until the arrival of reinforcements enabled them to bring it to a standstill. The critical situation now seems to have passed, since, although the Germans in the Mozdok area renewed their attacks, they made no progress.

In the face of Soviet counter-attacks the 3rd Panzer Division suffered heavy losses at Mozdok.

In late 1942 Gwyn accurately concluded:

On the Caucasus front German reports speak of Russian counter-attacks developing into a major offensive, but the Russians make no such claim. Any pressure that they are exercising certainly complicates the German problem; and should a collapse occur at Stalingrad the German position in the Mozdok region in particular would become precarious.

By now the yawning gap between Hitler's Army Groups A and B was a tempting opportunity for a Red Army counter-attack. A single unit, the 16th Motorized Infantry Division, was all that was protecting the left flank of 1st Panzer Army and the roads towards Astrakhan. The Germans had little choice but go over to the defensive in the Caucasus while the battle for Stalingrad played itself out.

Due to the rapidly deteriorating situation on the southern Eastern Front, in early 1943 the Germans steadily withdrew from the Caucasus toward Rostov and the Kuban in the Taman Peninsula. That January witnessed the Red Army liberating Mozdok, Stavropol, Armavir and Maikop. The following month Soviet forces landed near Novorossiysk, though the port was not freed until mid-September 1943 and Krasnodar was retaken. By mid-February 1943 the Soviet flag was once more fluttering over Mount Elbrus.

Toward the end of January, it was obvious that German resistance at Stalingrad was coming to an end. Von Manstein assessed that the Soviet tanks tied up at Stalingrad would be 'about our ears within two or three weeks'. When these units redeployed they were expected to put pressure on the gap between Army Group B and his Army Group Don.

Von Kleist and von Manstein would have preferred to evacuate the whole of the Caucasus via Rostov, but on 23 January 1943 Hitler reverted to type and instructed they maintain their bridgehead in the Taman to deny Novorossiysk to the enemy. This peninsula divided the Sea of Azov from the Black Sea and lay directly east of the Kerch Straits. It meant dividing their forces in the region just as 1st Panzer Army had reached a point where it was expected to pass through Rostov to help hold the advancing Soviets on the Donets.

Once again Hitler's generals were exasperated by his ever-changing priorities. Initially he had agreed that part of 1st Panzer Army would not withdraw into the Kuban bridgehead. He then changed his mind and decided the whole of 1st Panzer Army should be withdrawn through Rostov. The problem with this was that its southern flank was still at Armavir, which meant tying down 4th Panzer Army south of the Don even longer to keep the Rostov gap open.

Von Manstein wanted 1st Panzer Army reassigned to Army Group Don, but was vexed that Army Group A's slow withdrawal in his view needlessly delayed the panzers. He was then displeased to discover that the 13th Panzer Division and 50th Infantry Division were being sent to the Kuban. 'Thus both these divisions were withheld from the crucial battle ground', he grumbled, 'while some 400,000 men lay virtually paralysed in the Kuban.'

Part of the delay was caused by the need to stock up the Kuban with supplies and ammunition. The Germans had to safeguard the Rostov-Tikhorets railway to the north of Armavir to permit almost ninety supply trains to reach the Kuban. This meant that the Red Army needed to be held on the Manych River to the north-east for as long as possible. As a result, by 23 January the left wing of Army Group A was still at Belaya Glina, 30 miles east of Tikhorets, and could not reach the latter until early February. The diversion of all available trains to the Kuban caused a petrol shortage. In turn this hampered launching local panzer counter-attacks on the lower Manych.

Once his forces had recovered the initiative, Hitler optimistically saw the bridgehead as a jumping-off point for a renewed effort against the Caucasian oilfields later in the year. The Kuban river flows through the Taman Peninsula and the German 17th Army, supported by some Romanian units, was ordered to hold defensive positions on both banks. These were dubbed the 'Goth's Head Position'. In total some fourteen German and seven Romanian divisions were to remain needlessly tied up in this bridgehead.

The German naval presence in the Black Sea was fairly limited and its main task was to keep the Red Navy bottled up and to intercept convoys. It therefore fell to the Luftwaffe to maintain the Kuban bridgehead. Just three days before the fall of Stalingrad the Luftwaffe's 8th Air Corps established *Lufttransporteinsatz Krim* or 'Transport Mission Crimea'. General Martin Fiebig's pilots were given two tasks. Firstly, to airlift troops and wounded men from east of the Kerch Straits to the Crimea. Secondly they had to ship supplies and fuel from the Crimea and from the airfields north of the Sea of Azov into the bridgehead.

The final airlift to the Kuban was conducted on 30 March 1943. The very next day the 8th Air Corps was transferred to Luftflotte 4's northern flank. It was replaced by the 1st Air Corps which was given responsibility for supporting the men in Kuban. It was commanded from General Günther Korten's HQ at Simferopol in the Crimea and through an advanced command post at Kerch.

As well as the airlift from the Kuban, troops were withdrawn across the Kerch Straits, the narrow stretch of water separating the Taman from the Crimea. One ferry in particular made 2,000 trips carrying troops and their equipment as they withdrew from their last foothold in the Caucasus. In total the operation successfully evacuated over a quarter of a million personnel with all their equipment across the Straits into the Crimea. There on Hitler's orders they made a pointless last stand the following year and were overwhelmed.

Up to this point the Luftwaffe had been able to conduct its operations largely unimpeded by the Red Air Force. Now while the 17th Army was preparing its defensive positions in the Kuban the Red Air Force began to attack German airfields and ports. The strengthened 9th Flak Division under General Wolfgang Pickert (who was later to serve in Normandy as a flak corps commander) was in charge of the air defences in 17th Army's area of responsibility. They were able to call on two weak fighter and one dive-bomber gruppen as well.

Alexander Novikov was promoted to Marshal of Aviation, the first appointment of its kind in the Red Air Force, on 17 March 1943. He instructed General K.A. Vershinin, the North Caucasus Front air force commander, to centralize control of the 4th and 5th Air Armies. By the beginning of April, the former under General N.F. Naumenko had 250 aircraft while the latter under General S.K. Goryunov had 200. They were supported by another 120 aircraft from the Black Sea Fleet and the local air defence forces.

On 20 April Vershinin received reinforcements which gave him a total of 900 aircraft, including 370 fighters, 170 ground-attack aircraft, 165 day bombers and 195 night bombers. This did not bode well for the defenders of the Kuban bridgehead. In addition, the Red Air Force received numerous British and American aircraft thanks to Lend-Lease. Many of these planes were flown into the Caucasus from Tehran. The Red Air Force relied on Lend-Lease fighters throughout the Kuban air campaign.

The most popular with Soviet pilots was the US-supplied Bell P-39 Airacobra which they flew with great skill during the battle. For example, the 16th Guards Fighter Air Regiment was equipped with Airacobras at Baku. In the spring of 1943 it was then deployed to Krasnodar where it served with the North Caucasus Front and the 9th Guards Fighter Regiment.

Also in the skies above the Kuban were British-supplied Spitfire Mk VBs. Stalin had first made a specific request for Spitfires (the British fighter contribution consisted largely of Hurricanes) in October 1942. A total of just 143 Spitfires were delivered by March 1943. Further deliveries of Spitfires did not arrive until the following year.

To oppose the Red Air Force by mid-April 1943 Luftflotte 4 deployed some 820 aircraft in the Taman and Crimea, while another 200 aircraft were on call from airfields in southern Ukraine. These forces included the 51st and 54th Fighter Groups equipped with a mix of the latest versions of the Bf 109 and the Fw 190. A massive air battle for the Kuban was looming. As far as the Luftwaffe was concerned this was a wholly unnecessary diversion of valuable resources and pilots that were needed elsewhere.

By the end of June, the Luftwaffe had been defeated. On 7 July 1943 Vershinin reported that 'control of the air passed to our hands'. During the campaign the Red Air Force claimed perhaps somewhat excessively to have flown about 35,000 sorties and destroyed 1,100 German aircraft, most of which were as a result of air-to-air combat.

The 13th Panzer Division remained in the Taman Peninsula until July when it crossed the Kerch Straits into the Crimea. It was not until early September that Hitler finally decided to abandon the 'Goth's Head' and withdraw 17th Army's remaining units. This effort mirrored the German evacuation from Sicily a few weeks earlier across the Strait of Messina.

Once back on the Dnieper von Kleist launched a counteroffensive that finally halted the Red Army's triumphant march from Stalingrad. So successful was this that it enabled the Germans to recapture newly-liberated Kharkov and resulted in a lull until the summer. Hitler's fate then rested on the outcome of the battle for Kursk. The Soviets announced on 9 October 1943 that the Kuban had been cleared.

General Blumentritt aptly summoned up the irony of Hitler's ill-fated and fruitless Caucasus campaign. 'Although it was not possible to contradict economic experts who asserted that it was essential to obtain oil, if we were to continue the war, events disproved their contention. For we managed to carry on the war until 1945 without ever securing the Caucasus oil.'

Chapter 9

New Tank Armies

Through 1941 and early 1942, Stalin and his commanders learned a salutary lesson – their pre-war mechanized corps were completely unwieldy and inflexible. Similarly, the Barvenkovo operation also taught them that their light mobile forces, consisting of tank brigades and cavalry corps, were simply not effective enough against powerful German mechanized units, or indeed once behind enemy lines against hastily-assembled battle groups. They simply lacked firepower. The net result was that in the spring of 1942 the Red Army was ordered to create new mechanized and then tank corps, that would be able to tackle the panzers on equal terms. The latter consisted of three tank and one motorized brigade, the former of three mechanized and one tank brigade.

Having learned the hard way about not dispersing their tank forces, the Red Army also began to form the first of six tank armies. Employing the 55th Army as the basis, this came into being in May 1942 and was designated the 3rd Tank Army. Under the command of General Rybalko, it comprised the 12th and 15th Tank Corps, which later in the year were reinforced by the 3rd Tank Corps. Infantry support was provided by three rifle divisions, one of which was motorized. All these forces took time to gather and train, however.

The Soviet 1st Tank Army, under General Moskalenko, was formed in July 1942 using the 38th Army. Its forces included the 13th and 28th Tank Corps, the 158th Tank Brigade and the 131st and 399th Rifle Divisions. The 4th Tank Army, commanded by General Kryuchenkin, also came into being that summer with the 22nd and 23rd Tank Corps and a single tank brigade, as did the 5th Tank Army comprising the 2nd and 11th Tank Corps, one tank brigade and a rifle division. It was led by General Romanenko and would play a key part in crushing the Germans and their allies at Stalingrad at the end of the year. The 2nd Tank Army was not created until early 1943 using the 3rd Reserve Army. It consisted of the 11th and 16th Tank Corps, plus three rifle divisions. The 6th Tank Army was formed in early 1944 with the 5th Guards Tank Corps and the 5th Guards Mechanized Corps.

These new tank armies and corps were to be blooded at Kharkov, on the Bryansk Front, the Voronezh Front and on the approaches to Stalingrad. To start with their deployment was largely a case of trial and error, more often than not resulting in heavy losses as they fell foul to the panzers' superior tactics. Eventually though a growing confidence paid off, with notable results at Stalingrad.

In the summer of 1942, von Bock launched the general German offensive with Operation Blue. This was to push east of Kursk against the Soviet Southwestern Front to a line on the river Don between Livny and Rossosh, capturing Voronezh. Conducted by General von Weichs' 2nd Army and Hoth's 4th Panzer Army, it was to create left flank protection for the 'Donets Corridor' along which Paulus' 6th Army could advance to Stalingrad.

On 28 June the Germans struck from the Kursk area in the direction of Voronezh, attacking the Bryansk Front's 13th and 40th Armies. From the start the Soviets were outgunned and outnumbered. In the face of Hoth's panzers the Soviet 40th Army disintegrated within 48 hours and the 13th Army was obliged to withdraw northwards. On the 30th the German 6th Army attacked Ostrogozhsk, penetrating the defences of the 21st and 28th Armies (the latter having been mauled at Volchansk in May), and both were caught in the open by German firepower. Two days later the Germans struck south of Kharkov, with von Kleist leading 1st Panzer Army over the Donets. Once again Stalin's armoured forces were in disarray.

The newly-created Stalingrad Front absorbed the battered Southwestern Front, which was reinforced with the newly formed 1st and 4th Tank Armies. By 22 July the Stalingrad Front numbered thirty-eight divisions; sixteen divisions were deployed in the main defensive zone. It was their job to fend off the eighteen divisions of the German 6th Army.

The Germans attacked Stalingrad's first defensive line on 17 August, with General Gustav von Wietersheim's 14th Panzer Corps breaking through five days later to reach the Volga north of the city. His corps split the Stalingrad defence near Vertyachi and the Soviet 62nd Army was cut off from the Stalingrad Front and was transferred to Yeremenko. German bombers pounded Stalingrad to rubble and the following day the corps attacked toward the Tractor Works but was cut off for several days by a Soviet counter-attack. To the south of the city the Southeastern Front was forced to withdraw on the outer and then the inner defences.

The 4th Panzer Army's two corps reached the second line of defence by the end of the month and the third by mid-September. The battle then turned into bitter urban warfare that dragged on until 18 November, by which time the Germans had reached the limit of their offensive. From that point on they were on the defensive

According to Soviet intelligence, by early November 1942 Hitler's strength on the Eastern Front totalled about 6.2 million men organized into 266 divisions equipped with 5,080 tanks and assault guns. Soviet industrial muscle had ensured that by this stage their massive losses of 1941 had been made good. Manpower stood at about 6.6 million men, equipped with 7,350 tanks. On top of this the Soviet high command had considerable reserves. It was time for them to strike back again.

The main attack for Stalin's Operation Uranus was to be launched over 100 miles north-west of Stalingrad and would drive south-east. At 0630 hours on 19 November 1942 Russian guns opened up on the Romanian 3rd Army's positions. These were smashed as the barrage ranged in and pounded their defences relentlessly. Then came the dreaded T-34s clanking across the snow-draped landscape followed by supporting riflemen. Most of the Romanian defenders took fright and fled as they lacked adequate weapons with which to stop the enemy tanks. The Soviets almost immediately broke through in two places. This was achieved by Romanenko's 5th Tank Army launching itself from the bridgehead south-west of Serafimovich and General I.M. Chistyakov's 21st Army attacking from the Kletskaya bridgehead. The Romanian 1st Tank Division and 7th Cavalry Division were called on to halt the 5th Tank Army. It was an impossible task and both divisions were easily brushed aside.

The Soviet 26th Tank Corps' advance guard seized a bridge over the Don on 26 November. The Germans mistook the attack for an exercise using captured Russian tanks and the enemy armour rumbled over the bridge unhindered. Kalach lay just 1.25 miles away, but the German defences were not overwhelmed until Soviet reinforcements arrived. Far to the south-east the Romanian 4th Army suffered a similar fate, just 24 hours after the Southwestern and Don Fronts had opened the offensive.

In an attempt to stem the armoured advance on Kalach, the 16th and 24th Panzer Divisions unsuccessfully counter-attacked. By 1600 hours on 23 November Soviet tanks were in the vicinity of Sovetsky east of Kalach. It was only a matter of time before a link-up was achieved, trapping the Germans deployed between the Don and the Volga. The next stage was to destroy the Axis forces trapped in the *Kessel* or 'Cauldron', as the Stalingrad Pocket became known.

Stalin also launched Operation Mars on 25 November 1942, designed to crush the German forces in the Rzhev salient. This involved the Kalinin Front supported by the 1st and 3rd Mechanized Corps, as well as the Western Front supported by the 5th, 6th and 8th Tank Corps and the 2nd Guards Cavalry Corps. Unlike Uranus, this offensive was not destined to be a resounding success. The intended victims were not ill-prepared and ill-equipped Romanians, but tough German divisions well dug in. Furthermore, help was at hand. At Rzhev the German 9th Army had the 1st and 9th Panzer and Grossdeutschland and 14th Panzergrenadier Divisions in reserve, while the 19th and 20th Panzer Divisions were also within reach; Western Front was faced by the 5th Panzer Division.

On the 25th the two mechanized corps broke through the German defences north and south of Beyli, and only bad weather and determined German resistance finally brought them to a halt. To the north 39th Army hit the Germans north-east of Rzhev, while to the west it struggled to cut the Rzhev-Olenio railway. During December German reserves succeeded in destroying the 1st Mechanized Corps and the 6th Rifle Corps. The 3rd Mechanized Corps was driven back and contained. The Western Front alone lost 42,000 dead and 1,655 tanks by 14 December.

Von Manstein's highly capable and experienced 11th Army HQ was formed into a new Army Group Don to coordinate Operation Winter Storm – the relief of 6th Army trapped at Stalingrad. This mission was assigned to the rump of 4th Panzer Army remaining outside Stalingrad, now grandly named Armeegruppe Hoth under General Hoth. It was intended that Hoth would make a single concerted thrust using General Friedrich Kirchner's 57th Panzer Corps comprising the 6th and 23rd Panzer Divisions, later bolstered by 17th Panzer. Looking at the map both von Manstein and Hoth realized that the shortest route to Stalingrad was from Nizhne Chirskaya, but this was not the best path for success. In the region lay the 5th Tank and 5th Shock Armies of Lieutenant N.F. Vatutin's Southwestern Front, the key players in the success of Operation Uranus.

With 230 tanks of 6th and 23rd Panzer, plus air support from the Luftwaffe, the operation commenced on 12 December. Initially it made some headway, but waiting in reserve were the Soviets' 4th and 13th Mechanized Corps. Quickly realizing what was going on, the Soviets not only committed the 4th Cavalry Corps, but also the 7th Tank Corps and the 2nd Guards Army belonging to the Southwestern Front. In the face of such resistance the panzers could get no further. Having smashed the Romanians so effectively, Stalin set about crushing the other Axis armies. Following the encirclement of Stalingrad, Operation Saturn smashed the Italian 8th Army to create another pocket of trapped Axis forces. On 16 December Soviet tanks crashed into the Italian army and two days later it was surrounded.

By early 1943 one of Stalin's priorities was to again to attempt liberating Ukraine's second city. A general Soviet offensive on

12 January 1943 began with the intention of pushing Field Marshal Maximilian Freiherr von Weichs' Army Group A and von Manstein's Army Group Don away from the Don and into Ukraine. This opened between Orel in the north and Rostov in the south employing Lieutenant General M.A. Reiter's Bryansk Front, Colonel General F.I. Golikov's Voronezh Front, General N.F. Vatutin's Southwestern Front and General A.I. Eremenko's Southern Front. It was resisted from north to south by the German 2nd, the Hungarian 2nd, the Italian 8th and the Romanian 3rd Armies and the German 4th Panzer Army. By the end of January Army Group A's 17th Army was isolated in the Kuban. The battered Army Group B was placed in reserve and its formations given to Army Groups Centre and South. Fortunately for the Germans the Red Army began to lose momentum.

The Red Army's tanks pressed forward to the Oskol, Donets and Don Rivers. As well as thrusting on south-west to Kharkov, the Soviets also opted to punch west toward Kursk in order to exploit the 200-mile gap torn between Field Marshal von Kluge's Army Group Centre and von Manstein's Army Group Don (shortly renamed South). On 1 February 1943 Stalin launched Operation Star with the 13th and 38th Armies of the Vorenezh Front attacking toward Kursk and the 60th, 40th and 3rd Tank Armies striking for Kharkov. In the meantime, the Southwestern Front's 6th Army and 1st Guards Army swung south-west to take Mariupol on the Sea of Azov, cutting Army Group Don's communications with Army Group A still in the Caucasus.

Chapter 10

Other People's Tanks

Stalin's 1st and 4th Tank Armies were involved in the counter-attack north of Kalach on the River Don on 19 December 1942. The fighting was such that they were both disbanded, with the first remerging as the 1st Guards Army the following year and the 4th became 65th Army, but was later re-established. It was Romanenko's 5th Tank Army, spearheaded by Butkov's 1st Tank Corps and Rodin's 26th Tank Corps, that was instrumental in breaking through the Romanian forces on the Don and reaching Kalach.

It is not generally appreciated that a Romanian armoured division fought alongside the Germans in the winter of 1942 at Stalingrad, in a vain effort to stem the Soviet counter-attack that trapped the German 6th Army. At the outbreak of the Second World War in 1939 Romania created its very first tank regiment; this was combined with a motorized rifle regiment two years later to form an armoured brigade. The 1st and 2nd Armoured Regiments were combined in April 1941 and were mainly equipped with Czech LT-35 and some CKD light tanks. The Romanian Army also had six cavalry brigades (the 1st, 5th, 6th, 7th, 8th and 9th), some of which were issued with light tanks.

Bad blood between the Romanians and the Hungarians forced them into Hitler's evil embrace. In 1940 Romania lost Bessarabia and Bukovina to the Soviet Union, followed by half of Transylvania to Hungary and the southern Dobrudja to Bulgaria. That same year the Romanian king abdicated in favour of his son, but the pro-Nazi Marshal Ion Antonescu became the power behind the throne. In October 1940 the German 13th Motorized Infantry Division crossed Hungary into Romania, followed by the 16th Panzer Division two months later, to ensure Romanian 'security'.

Six months before Operation Barbarossa, Hitler secretly allocated Romania a key role. He directed, 'It will be the task of Romania to support the attack of the German southern flank, at least at the outset, with its best troops; to hold down the enemy where German forces are not engaged; and to provide auxiliary services in the rear areas'. 'Of course I'll be there from the start', exclaimed Antonescu when told of Hitler's invasion of the Soviet Union, just ten days before it was due to commence. 'When it's a question of action against the Slavs, you can always count on Romania', he added, little realizing the bloody consequences. Antonescu willingly provided the largest number of troops of any of the Axis satellites and his finest troops, including his fledgling armour units. General von Rundstedt's Army Group South included the equivalent of fourteen Romanian divisions.

The Romanians had almost 300 tanks in June 1941, comprising 35 Czech CKD/Praga R-1 light tanks, 126 Czech LT-35s (known as the R-2 in Romanian service), 73 French R-35s and 60 French FT-17s, but few of these were suitable for front-line service. While the LT-35 was capable of taking on the various Russian light tanks such as the T-26, T-37, T-40 and T-60, up against anything heavier it was in trouble. Although reasonably armoured at the front to a thickness of 35mm, the LT-35's 37mm anti-tank gun was simply not capable of taking on the Russian T-34/76 armed with a 76.2mm or the similarly-armed KV-1.

The 1st Armoured Regiment with the LT-35s was the first Romanian unit to take part in the invasion of the Soviet Union, though the 2nd Armoured Regiment was held back because of the condition of its R-35s. Many of these French tanks had been appropriated from the fleeing Polish Army, in particular the 21st Armoured Battalion, but a lack of spares meant that they were not committed to the invasion of Russia. Similarly, the wholly inadequate R-1s were held back with the Royal Cavalry.

In 1941 Romania fielded its 3rd Army, consisting of the Mountain Corps and Cavalry Corps totalling six brigades, as well as the 4th Army consisting of four divisions. Altogether these forces totalled about 150,000 men, but later with reinforcements were to swell to over 300,000. Under pressure to supply more manpower Romania also drafted 2,000 rapists, looters and murders – never the best basis for an army. Romanian troops wore khaki uniforms with very distinctive Dutch-style helmets, so were clearly distinguishable from their German allies.

On 22 June 1941 the Romanians pushed into southern Russia. The 3rd Army's Mountain Corps fought with the German 11th Army in the Crimea and the Cavalry Corps with 1st Panzer Army. With a 5:1 numerical superiority, the 4th Army attempted to capture Odessa on 10 August, but made little headway against determined Red Army resistance. The attack petered out five days later, but was resumed on the 20th and for a month the Romanians struggled to get within nine miles of the city. Headway was finally made when the Germans swung down into the Crimea. After suffering an appalling 98,000 casualties, the exhausted 4th Army was withdrawn in October 1941 to refit.

As in the case of Hungary and Bulgaria, Hitler's tank deliveries to Romania were modest, totalling less than 350 throughout the war. During 1942 Romania received twenty-six replacement LT-35s, eleven Panzer IIIs and eleven Panzers IVs. To address their need for a mobile anti-tank weapon the Brasov factory was instructed to convert some LT-35s into self-propelled guns by installing captured Soviet 76mm guns; a number of Soviet T-60 light tanks were also supplied by the Germans fitted with a 76mm and these were designated TACM (*Tun autopropulsat cu afet mobile*) R-2 or T-60 respectively. The cavalry brigades also became divisions in 1942.

During the summer of 1942 Romanian forces were involved in the attack on Sevastopol and fought across the Kerch Straits, while others were in the Caucasus with the 3rd Panzer Army. Crucially, by the autumn the fate of Hitler's stalled ambitions for conquering the Soviet Union rested firmly on the shoulders of two ill-equipped Romanian armies bereft of tanks and anti-tank guns. Fatefully the Romanian 3rd Army, consisting of nine divisions under Colonel General Dumitrescu, came back into the line in October 1942 to the north-west of Stalingrad. To their left was the Italian 8th Army, which served as a buffer between them and the Hungarians, such was the national enmity between the two. Another Romanian corps, part of 4th Army, moved into place on the southern flank followed by a second in November, providing six divisions to the German 4th Panzer Army. Perhaps as window dressing Hitler suggested that General Constaninescu's 4th Army should take charge of the 4th Panzer Army, despite the fact the Romanians were incapable of commanding such forces. He also proposed that the 3rd and 4th Romanian Armies along with the German 6th Army should form Army Group Don under Marshal Antonescu. The forthcoming Soviet offensive prevented such plans being implemented.

The Romanian generals called on their tanks to try and save the day. The 1st Tank Division and 7th Cavalry Division were thrown into the fight to halt the 5th Tank Army. However, the Romanians' inadequate Czech tanks were easily brushed aside and the 5th Romanian Corps' HQ overrun. While some of the Romanian troops fled, most simply threw down their weapons and surrendered.

Following the Romanian Army's mauling at Stalingrad, the remnants of the Romanian 1st Tank Division and Cavalry Divisions were regrouped for refitting. To make good Antonescu's losses Hitler sent fifty Panzer 38(t)s, thirty-one Panzer IVs and just four StuG III assault guns. First to arrive were the 38(t)s, which were delivered in March 1943 and used to re-equip the 1st Tank Regiment. The 1st Tank Division spent 1943–4 re-equipping and training. Only in 1944 did Hitler despatch any significant numbers of tanks to the Romanians, consisting of 100 Panzer IVs and 114 StuG assault guns. The 1st Tank Division was re-established along the lines of a German panzer division in April 1944 and given the title *Romania Mare* (Great Romania). Equipped with German tanks it returned to the Eastern Front and continued to resist the Red Army until Romania defected in August 1944. Panzer IVs of the 2nd Armoured Regiment then fought alongside the Red Army in Hungary and ended up in Czechoslovakia the following year, where Romanian R-35s were deployed armed with Russian 45mm anti-tank guns.

Similarly, the 1st, 5th, 7th and 8th Cavalry Divisions all suffered heavy losses during the fighting around Stalingrad. The 7th was beyond repair and disbanded, while the others were reformed during 1943. In particular, the 5th was supposed to become a motorized division but its tanks and other vehicles were never supplied. It had also been intended that the 8th Cavalry Division become a motorized division in late 1942, but these plans were halted by Stalingrad. In July 1944 it was decided to use it to create Romania's 2nd Armoured Division, but this was not completed before the Romanians defected to the Soviet camp. The German instructors manning the 4th Armoured Regiment seized the panzers supplied by Hitler and used them to help cover the German withdrawal from Romania.

Hungary was the only Eastern European country with an indigenous tank-building capability. Hungarian ruler Admiral Horthy's total contribution to Hitler's armoured forces were modest, amounting to about 1,500 tanks, assault guns and armoured cars (including German-supplied vehicles) between 1941 and 1944. These were used to equip two armoured divisions and eight assault artillery battalions. The leading Hungarian manufacturers were Ganz and Manfred Weiss at Csepel and MAVAG and MVG at Raba.

Hungary's armoured vehicle production was painfully slow and amounted to just under 900 vehicles for the whole of the war. One hundred and twenty indigenous 38M Toldi light tanks, some 500 40M Turán medium tanks (a version of the Czech LT-35), 60 43M Zrinyi assault howitzers, an unknown number of 40M Nimród self-propelled guns and 171 39M Csaba armoured cars were constructed between 1939 and 1944. The Hungarian Army was also equipped with a few hundred German-supplied LT-35/38s, Panzer IVs and StuG III as the Hungarian Turán was very late going into production. Horthy provided two motorized brigades and a cavalry brigade equipped with about 150 Toldi light tanks, Italian-supplied L.35 tankettes and Csaba armoured cars for Hitler's invasion of Yugoslavia in April 1941. However, Horthy's armoured forces proved an embarrassment. His troops reached Novi Sad on the Danube, but one armoured unit ran out of petrol after driving only 30 miles south of the border.

By June 1941 the Hungarians had just 189 tankettes, light tanks and armoured cars. Nonetheless Horthy committed large numbers of troops to Hitler's Operation Barbarossa including the Carpathian Group of two brigades and the Mobile Corps of three brigades. The latter had to seize civilian transport to supplement their obsolete Toldis, Csabas and L.3s. Forming part of the German 17th Army, the Mobile Corps fought well in the Ukraine, but after reaching the Donets was withdrawn home in November 1941.

In the summer of 1942, with Hitler desperate for reinforcements, Horthy despatched the 2nd Army, consisting of the 3rd, 4th and 7th Corps, bringing his contribution up to 200,000 men. This was supported by a single Hungarian armoured division equipped with Panzer 38(t)s, Panzer IIIs and IVs, Toldi light tanks, Csaba armoured cars and Nimród self-propelled guns. In June the 2nd Army under General Jany reached the front at Kursk and moved to hold the line along the Don south of Voronezh. In the face of the Russian winter and T-34 tanks Hungarian morale soon fell.

After smashing the Romanian and Italian armies around Stalingrad, the Russians moved to destroy the 2nd Hungarian Army on 15 January 1943. The Hungarian 1st Armoured Division, under German tactical control, was held back and not permitted to counter-attack in time to help restore the situation. The Hungarians lost 30,000 casualties, 50,000 prisoners and all their tanks and heavy equipment. It was the worst military disaster ever experienced by the Hungarian Army, who were quick to blame the Germans for abandoning them to their fate. Horthy ordered the remains of 2nd Army home in March, leaving behind two weak corps for security duties.

In mid-1943 the Hungarians reconstituted their battered 1st Armoured Division and created a second. Both were organized along German lines, but equipped with a mixture of Hungarian Turán and Turán II medium tanks. In addition, eight assault artillery battalions were created, which were to have been equipped with the Hungarian

Zrinyi assault gun. However, there were only enough of these to arm two battalions so the others used German-supplied StuG IIIs. The Hungarians also raised the 1st Cavalry Division, which was later renamed the 1st Hussar Division. Between 1942 and 1944 Hitler was obliged to supply Hungary with almost 400 German-built panzers to try and prop up their army.

Chapter 11

Triumph at Kursk

The turning point on the Eastern Front came in 1943. By the middle of the year General Vannikov's tank factories were outproducing the Germans by nearly 3:1. A total of 15,812 T-34/76 tanks were built in 1943, with monthly production at around 1,300. Such output is hard to credit. The T-34's immediate foes, the Panther and Tiger, only made up about 41 per cent of German panzer production in 1943, with the Panzer IV remaining the backbone of the Panzerwaffe. During 1943 the Red Army lost over 14,000 T-34/76s, including some 6,000 expended in the battle with Army Group South during July to December 1943. Crucially though, Soviet production was able to keep pace with the Red Army's quite staggering tank losses.

The tank designer Alexander Morozov came up with the Model 1943 in mid-1942 that incorporated a hexagonal turret with two hatches instead of the heavier single one on the earlier models. This turret also had thicker armour at 70mm but the commander's visibility problems were not solved until a cupola was fitted in mid-1943. The Model 1943 T-34 comprised the bulk of the T-34s deployed in Ukraine in the summer of 1943. This need to keep on pouring out high volumes of tanks showed that Soviet tank design had all but stagnated – the T-34 was still armed with the 76.2mm gun and was increasingly vulnerable to improved German anti-tank guns. The T-34/76 had been intended to withstand anti-tank guns in the 37mm–50mm calibre range, but things changed when the Panzer IV F2 appeared in May 1942 armed with the 75mm KwK 40 L43 gun. This could take on the T-34 at 1,000m, which now gave the panzers a much-needed stand-off capability that could help cope with superior Soviet numbers.

By 1943 the T-34's F-34 tank gun was out of date. Its standard armour-piercing round could penetrate the Panther's side armour at 1,000m, but could only tackle the glacis armour at some 300m and could not get through the frontal armour of the turret. This meant that the Red Army fighting in Ukraine was supported by a tank that no longer enjoyed any real technical advantage over the panzers. One saving grace was that by 1943 Soviet tank units enjoyed a 70–90 per cent reliability rate with the T-34 – in contrast German units equipped with the Panther could only manage half this.

Further compounding the T-34 crews' woes, their armour had only been increased from 45mm to 75mm – when they need 90mm to offer protection against the KwK 40. Because of the low nickel content, Soviet armour plate had a nasty habit of spalling when hit, sending steel splinters flying around the inside of the tank causing appalling injuries to the crew.

Hitler pinned his hopes on the upgunned Panzer IV and Panther, armed with a high-velocity 75mm gun, and the Tiger, armed with an 88mm gun, killing vast numbers of T-34s at Kursk. While Stalin sought to win the war using a simple and well-rounded tank design, Hitler opted for producing a series of different tanks as well as numerous armoured fighting vehicles that had specialized roles as self-propelled guns, assault guns and tank destroyers. While the latter found a use for the chassis of the more obsolete of the panzers, it meant that production was never solely dedicated to the Panzer IV, the Tiger and the Panther. The Germans desperately sought a technical solution to their predicament on the Eastern Front but this simply slowed up production, especially in the case of the Tiger, which was time-consuming to manufacture. The Soviets on the other hand realized that the T-34 was as good as they were going to get in the interim and opted to delay a modernization programme in favour of replacing their shattered tank fleet as swiftly as possible. The upgunned T-34/85 was not ready until 1944, by which time the Red Army already had the upper hand.

These contrasting approaches to armoured warfare went head to head in Ukraine in the summer of 1943 as this offered by far the best open tank country. Here the combination of tanks, anti-tank mines and anti-tank guns came together in a deadly killing ground. The German generals understood that if they could contain the Red Army in Ukraine and fight it to a standstill then there was some chance of victory – or, as was more likely, some sort of much-needed ceasefire. At the same time the Soviet generals knew that the outcome of the Second World War hung on Ukraine. If they could defeat Hitler's panzer armies there, then this would open the road to Eastern Europe and Nazi Germany.

Stalin's operations left him in possession of the vast salient around Kursk, flanked by enemy forces centred in the south on Kharkov and in the north on Orel. Belatedly Hitler's intention was to snip the salient off employing all available means. Capitalizing on his spring victory on the German right, Field Marshal von Manstein's Army Group South, spearheaded by Hoth's 4th Panzer Army and General Werner Kempf's Armeegruppe Kempf, was to attack northward from Belgorod and Kharkov.

For the Battle of Kursk Hitler gathered the greatest force ever assembled on such a small front. Operation Barbarossa had flung 3,200 panzers at the Soviet Union along a 930-mile front: for Operation Citadel, Hitler squeezed 2,700 tanks along just 60 miles. Some 63 per cent of all battleworthy German armour on the Eastern Front was assigned to von Kluge and von Manstein. While this sounded impressive, with 1,850 front-line panzers, 200 obsolete panzers and 533 assault guns divided amongst 16 panzer and panzergrenadier divisions and three assault gun brigades, the units were under-strength. By 1943 a panzer division had a theoretical strength of up to 200 panzers and 15,600 men. In reality the average strength was just seventy-three tanks. However, the 2nd SS Panzer Corps' divisions averaged 166 panzers and assault guns.

Hitler's generals though were hoping his newly-deployed armour would help counter the Red Army's growing strength. These offered the opportunity to destroy Soviet tanks at arm's length and stop them closing, which would prevent the panzers from being overwhelmed by superior numbers. Indeed, for the first time since Barbarossa Hitler was fielding tanks and self-propelled guns that had a distinctive qualitative edge. He placed great faith in his menagerie of tanks and fighting vehicles named after wild beasts, notably the Tiger, Panther, Elefant (Ferdinand), Rhinoceros, Bison and Grizzly Bear. It was anticipated that these would tear great holes in the ranks of the Soviet tank corps

Crucially though, none of these vehicles were available in decisive numbers. There were less than 90 Ferdinands, about 200 Panthers and about 100 Tigers; over 1,000 older Panzer IIIs and IVs remained the backbone of the panzer forces. Also making their debut was the Hummel, the Nashorn or Hornisse and the Marder III or Wespe self-propelled guns. Again numbers available were a problem: all three had only gone into production in early 1943, with about 100 of each type ready for the summer. To help smash Soviet fortifications were sixty-six newly-built Grizzlys or Brummbär comprising a short 150mm howitzer mounted on a Panzer IV chassis.

Stalin was not only well prepared for Hitler's massed panzers but ready to switch over to his own offensive once they had been stopped. Soviet defences around Kursk were formidable: by June 300,000 civilians had dug a series of eight in-depth defensive lines stretching back almost 110 miles. Just to be on the safe side the reserve Steppe Front had dug its own defences to protect the eastern bank of the Don.

The fields of wheat and corn ripening in the summer sun concealed another deadly secret that would tear machines and men apart with ease. Soviet sappers toiled to sow over 40,000 mines across the length and breadth of the salient. In the killing grounds between the strongpoints they meticulously concealed about 2,400 anti-tank and a further 2,700 anti-personnel mines per mile. Initially as the panzers and supporting infantry blundered through these they would be deluged by fire from howitzers and heavy mortars supported by anti-aircraft guns.

Once through the minefields the panzers would encounter 'pakfronts' consisting of groups of anti-tank guns supported by anti-tank rifles, machine guns and mortars. The plan was that along expected axis of attack the panzers would meet clusters of guns whose job it was to funnel them into yet more minefields. There was little doubting the quite extraordinary volume of fire that the Central and Voronezh Fronts could call upon – at their disposal were 6,000 anti-tank guns, 20,000 guns and mortars and 920 Katyusha rocket launchers.

Operation Citadel commenced on 4 July 1943, making little headway before being checked. General Hausser's 2nd SS Panzer Corps struck toward Bykovka with 365 tanks and 195 assault guns. The SS took the town, while other units cut the Oboyan-Belgorod road only to be obstructed by the Soviet 96th Tank Brigade. Similarly, a penetration was made on the right flank but the panzers could get no further. The strength of the Soviet defensive positions stopped the Germans breaking through north of Belgorod, which was to cause Hoth problems.

Model got just six miles before being halted in front of Olkhovatka and Ponyri, losing 25,000 men, 200 panzers and 200 aircraft in the process. Von Manstein's forces managed 25 miles, losing 10,000 men and 350 panzers. Stavka was not slow to react and during the night of 8/9 July they hastened to get General Pavel Rotmistrov's 5th Tank Army with 630 tanks and self-propelled guns and 5th Guards Army to the Prokhorovka region.

It was at Prokhorovka that the T-34 bested the Tiger and Panther. This was achieved by the tanks of 5th Tank Army engaging the panzers at very close range in order to fire on their side and rear armour. The German 4th Panzer Army lost 300 panzers, including 70 Tigers, at Prokhorovka. The Red Army lost about 400 tanks, but Soviet industry quickly replaced them. It was also left in possession of the battlefield, which meant that many of the more lightly-damaged T-34s could be salvaged. As a result, the German panzers in Ukraine were severely outnumbered by the Red Army's tank fleet at the close of 1943.

Within six days Citadel had run out of steam and decisively it was the first occasion a German panzer offensive had been stopped before achieving a breakthrough. By 13 July von Manstein claimed those forces facing him had lost 24,000 men captured as well as 1,800 tanks. Also that day von Manstein and Kluge were summoned to East Prussia, where Hitler informed them that Citadel must be called off as the Allies had landed in Sicily, thereby threatening Italy. Once the Germans had been fought to a standstill at Kursk, Zhukov unleashed his massive counteroffensive sweeping back the panzers' hard-won gains and pushing them out of their Orel and Kharkov salients to the north and south of the Kursk bulge.

Hitler gambled on the Panther being a successful counter to the T-34 but it had been rushed into production and then into combat and paid the inevitable price. The Panther had offered some tactical success for the German Army, but did little to change the overall strategic situation. During the fighting in the Ukraine from July to December 1943 the Panthers claimed around 500 T-34s, which equated to about 10 per cent of the Soviet tanks lost there. The T-34 only claimed about a dozen Panthers, but the T-34s had kept the Panther under pressure and on the move, which played havoc with its mechanical reliability. Any advantages the Panther's gun may have offered were increasingly overshadowed by the Soviet 85mm and 122mm anti-tank guns by mid-1944. This was especially the case with the appearance of the T-34/85.

Chapter 12

Battles for Kharkov

Spearheading Operation Star in the Ukraine was General Rybalko's 3rd Tank Army on the Voronezh Front's southern flank. By 5 February 1943, just three days after the last pocket in Stalingrad surrendered, his tanks had reached the Donets east of Kharkov. The Voronezh Front liberated Volchansk, Belgorod, Oboyan and Kursk and by 11 February had successfully reached the outskirts of Kharkov. Meanwhile the Southwestern Front was soon deep in the rear of Army Group Don. The Soviets had every prospect of trapping the 1st Panzer Army, the 4th Panzer Army and Army Group Hollidt against the Sea of Azov. Only after the personal intervention of von Kluge and von Manstein did Hitler agree to a withdrawal to the River Mius.

At Kharkov the newly-arrived SS Panzer Corps stood in the Soviets' way but was pushed back. Its commander General Paul Hausser, fearing Kharkov could become another Stalingrad, disobeyed Hitler's orders to stand firm and withdrew from the city on 15 February. Von Manstein was concerned that Army Detachment Lanz was expected to hold Kharkov and strike toward Losovaya to relieve the pressure on Army Group South's left flank. It was only in a position to conduct one of the two tasks and von Manstein wanted to avoid being trapped at all costs. His proposal was to abandon Kharkov, strike south, defeat the Red Army and then reoccupy the city, but Hitler did not want to give up the Soviet Union's fourth-largest city. The SS Panzer Corps, outside the authority of German Army's high command, took matters into its own hands to avoid being surrounded. Fortunately for von Manstein this permitted the Army units to withdraw as well.

To compound von Manstein's problems Hitler flew into the factory town of Zaporozhye south-west of Kharkov to be briefed on the situation. Alarmingly the Field Marshal was unable to guarantee Hitler's safety as the town was only garrisoned by a defence company and a few anti-aircraft units. When they met on 17 February Hitler refused both to discuss von Manstein's plans and to admit the Red Army was posing a very dangerous threat to the junction of 1st Panzer Army and Army Detachment Lanz. Von Manstein assumed this was because Hitler was keen to see the SS Panzer Corps roll back into Kharkov, but the reality was the threat to the Dnieper crossings had to be dealt with first. Also it was now a race against time because the impending thaw would soon put a halt to operations between the Dnieper and Donets rivers.

The mud actually came to von Manstein's rescue because the 3rd SS Panzer Division was bogged down between Kiev and Poltava. If the 1st and 2nd SS Panzer Divisions were not comfortable holding the city on their own, they were unlikely to retake it without the assistance of their sister division. In the light of this Hitler acquiesced to von Manstein's plans, but refused to countenance shortening the 470-mile front held by Army Group South's thirty battered divisions. Despite von Manstein's intelligence Hitler refused to acknowledge the Red Army's gathering strength in manpower and tanks. Von Manstein observed diplomatically 'We lived, it seemed, in two entirely different worlds'. Perhaps more importantly he noted, 'I had the impression that Hitler's visit to my headquarters had helped to bring home to him the danger of encirclement which immediately threatened the southern wing of the Eastern Front'.

In the meantime, the main Soviet threat was a salient thrusting toward Dnieperopetrovsk containing the 1st Guards and 6th Armies as well as Group Popov. While the Germans held the Red Army west of Kharkov, von Manstein orchestrated a counter-attack on 19 February using the SS Panzer Corps striking south from Krasnograd south-west of Kharkov towards Pavlograd. Three days later Hoth's 4th Panzer Army linked up with the SS at Pavlograd.

On the southern side of the salient 1st Panzer Army's 40th Panzer Corps joined the attack, defeating Group Popov near Krasnoarmeysk.

Stalin interpreted these operations as a means of covering 1st Panzer Army and Army Group Hollidt's withdrawal from the Mius to the Dnieper. In response the Southwestern Front was instructed to hold the Germans on the Mius. However, von Manstein's success at Pavlograd enabled his forces to push forward 150 miles, thereby threatening recently-liberated Kharkov. Indeed, von Manstein had unhinged the junction of the Soviet Southwestern and Voronezh Fronts. In the fighting the Soviet advances were stopped, having lost 23,000 dead, 9,000 prisoners, 615 tanks and 354 artillery pieces.

Having once gained victory between the Donets and the Dnieper, the Germans were ready to tackle those Red Army units in the vicinity of Kharkov. Von Manstein was very clear on what was to happen, 'Our object was not the possession of Kharkov but the defeat – and if possible the destruction – of the enemy units located there.' This principally meant crushing the Soviet 3rd Tank Army using the 4th Panzer Army and the SS Panzer Corps. General Rybalko's 3rd Tank Army swung south to take on the SS Panzer Corps on 24 February. The SS withdrew to lure the Soviets into a trap, which resulted in the Red Army losing another 9,000 dead, 61 tanks, 60 motor vehicles and 225 guns. Rybalko's defeat left newly-liberated Kharkov open to the Germans once more. His 3rd Tank Army had to fight its way out of the Kharkov area and Stalin agreed to a withdrawal to the Donets 40 miles away. 'In the end it was possible to bring the SS Panzer Corps round to the east. The city fell without difficulty, and we succeeded in cutting of the retreat of considerable numbers of the enemy across the Donets', recorded von Manstein in his usual no-nonsense manner.

Following the Soviet victory at Stalingrad, in early 1943 Stavka planed an offensive to capitalize on the successes of the Bryansk and Voronezh Fronts along the Voronezh-Kursk axis and support the Southwestern Front's push through the Donbas to the Dnieper and the Sea of Azov. This was scheduled to begin on 12 February when the Western Front's 16th Army and the Bryansk Front's 13th and 48th Armies were to surround the Germans' Orel salient. The two fronts, supported by the Central Front, were to clear the Bryansk region and gain bridgeheads over the Desna between the 17th and 25th. Afterwards the Kalinin and Western Fronts were to take Smolensk and help destroy Army Group Centre in the Rezhev-Viazma salient.

Rokossovsky's Don Front (formerly the Stalingrad Front) attempted a left hook behind the Orel salient, launched from the Soviet salient around Kursk; this offensive was halted by the German 2nd Army at Sevsk. In the Donbas von Manstein threw back the Southwestern Front and the Western Front failed in the Zhizdra area. Also Rokossovksy's offensive was delayed to 25 February. His Don Front (renamed the Central Front) was to spearheaded by the 2nd Tank Army and the 70th Army from the Stavka reserve with the 65th and 21st Armies redeployed from Stalingrad. Within two weeks the 2nd Tank Army had gained Sevsk, while a Cavalry-Rifle Group from the 2nd Guards Cavalry Corps reached Trubchevsk and Novgorod-Severskii. However, south of Orel the progress of 65th and 70th Armies was slow and on the left flank the 38th and 60th Armies were tied up trying to turn the German 2nd Army's left flank.

Rokossovsky was denied victory by the delayed arrival of 21st Army from Stalingrad (which was subsequently diverted to Oboyan to counter von Manstein's move on Belgorod), bad weather and by von Manstein's counterstroke that smashed the Voronezh Front south of Kharkov. The fighting continued until 23 March, but Rokossovsky's troops gave up Sevsk to take up positions that significantly would become the northern and central face of the Kursk salient.

Von Manstein was then able to launch the second phase of his powerful counteroffensive on 6 March and by the 14th was back in control of Kharkov. The Germans claimed to have killed another 50,000 Soviets and captured 19,594, as well as destroying 1,140 tanks and 3,000 guns. In just over two months the SS Panzer Corps sustained over 11,000 casualties, the 1st SS Panzer Division losing 4,500 of these during the recapture of Kharkov.

Alarmed by the situation in the south, Stalin summoned Zhukov, his deputy supreme commander, to Moscow on 14 March. Zhukov found himself sent to the Voronezh Front, where his prognosis was dire, 'All available forces from the Stavka's reserves must be deployed here; otherwise, the Germans will capture Belgorod and continue their offensive on the Kursk sector.' Stalin had already decided to despatch the 1st Tank, 21st and 64th Armies to the Belgorod area, but they could not be in place quickly enough to save the city which fell to von Manstein on the 18th. Nonetheless, the Soviet 21st and 64th Armies were able to move into blocking positions north-east of Belgorod and this thwarted von Manstein's attempt on Kursk.

Once the three Soviet divisions (52nd Guards Rifle, 67th Guards Rifle and 375th Rifle) from 21st Army had taken up defensive positions the Germans were unable to dislodge them. The 1st Tank Army deployed south of Oboyan and the 64th Army along the Seversky Donets. Zhukov managed to stabilize things by 26 March and the spring thaw brought the mobile warfare to a halt. The Germans in turn dug in.

In a stroke of genius von Manstein had defeated Stalin's Operation Star. He had saved Army Group South and put the Germans back on the Mius/Donets line. While impressive, such a victory could not offset the disaster at Stalingrad. Although checked by the SS Panzer Corps, the Red Army threatened the whole region from Kharkov via Belgorod to Kursk. The latter would ultimately be Hitler's undoing on the Eastern Front.

Just after Hitler's calamitous defeat at Kursk, a fourth and final battle was fought for Kharkov during 12–23 August 1943. The panzers did all they could to halt the Soviet attack and inflicted huge losses, but the lack of manpower and critical shortages of ammunition meant there could be only one outcome. Following Hitler's failed attempt to cut off the Kursk salient, Zhukov unleashed his massive counteroffensive, sweeping back the Germans' hard-won gains and pushing them out of their Orel and Kharkov salients to the north and south of the Kursk bulge. The first Operation Kutuzov, the Orel Strategic Counteroffensive, ran from 12 July to 18 August 1942, designed to destroy the German Army's positions at Orel.

This capitalized on the Wehrmacht's shortcomings and further emphasized that the strategic and operational initiative had passed over to the Red Army and the Red Air Force. The Soviets intended not only to liberate the salient, but also ensnare as much of General Walther Model's 2nd Panzer Army (its previous commander Rudolf Schmidt had been sacked on 11 July) and 9th Army also commanded by Model, both of which formed part of von Kluge's Army Group Centre.

Stalin launched his attack with the relatively fresh forces of General V.D. Sokolovsky's West Front and General M.M. Popov's Bryansk Front, neither of which had been directly involved in the Kursk fighting. It was intended that the West Front's 3rd and 63rd Armies would push west from the Novosil area over the Susha River cutting through the junction of 2nd Panzer Army and 9th Army to liberate Orel. This would pin the Germans down while 3rd Guards Tank Army pushed its armour through to exploit the situation further west. Meanwhile, the West Front's 11th Guards Army was to attack south from the Belev area to smash the left shoulder of the German salient, which would allow the 4th Tank Army to press on and cut off 2nd Panzer Army, ensuring the destruction of its armoured forces.

Model and von Kluge were not ignorant of Soviet intentions, photoreconnaissance and radio intercepts having provided a clear picture of what the Red Army was intending. Model simply did not have sufficient manpower to conduct any spoiling attacks, but this intelligence did enable his men to prepare in-depth defences. This was especially important for General Dr Rendulic's 35th Corps that would bear the brunt of the 63rd Army's attack. In the event the latter was only able to make slow progress toward Orel. To the north the 11th Guards Army pushed the Germans back 16 miles in two days in the face of bitter resistance.

Operation Kutuzov overlapped with Operation Polkovodets Rumyantsev, the Belgorod-Kharkov Strategic Offensive, from 3 to 23 August 1943. This was the Red Army's counteroffensive against the southern sector of the Kursk bulge following Hitler's Operation

In 1941 Soviet dictator Joseph Stalin had the largest tank fleet in the world, but he and his generals did not know how to deploy it effectively. (All images sourced by author)

Georgi Zhukov, future Hero of the Soviet Union, gained valuable experience in tank combat fighting the Japanese in 1939 and ended up Stalin's deputy commander.

Konstantin Rokossovsky started the war as a mechanized corps commander and went on to take part in all the major battles on the Eastern Front, including Moscow, Stalingrad, Kursk and Operation Bagration.

The T-34/76 medium tank first came off the Kharkov factory production line in January 1940. The Model 1940 (T-34/76A) is identifiable by the low-slung barrel of the 76.2mm L-11 anti-tank gun, below a distinctive bulge in the mantlet housing the recoil mechanism.

Similarly, the KV-1 heavy tank had first gone into production in February 1940 at Leningrad's Kirov works and was available only in limited numbers.

The first production version of the KV-1 was designated the Model 1939. It is easily recognizable by the rounded recuperator above the 76.2mm L-11 tank gun barrel. The Model 1940 T-34 had a similar arrangement.

Model 1940 KV-1 uparmoured with 35mm plates which were bolted on. The Germans dubbed this version the KV-1E.

Abandoned KV-1 with added turret applique armour.

German soldiers examine the remains of a KV-1. It has the uparmoured turret which has done nothing to save the tank from destruction.

It is not clear if this KV-2 was in a hull-down position to guard an airfield, or whether it simply sank under its own weight.

The KV-2 with its enormous turret housing the 152mm M1938/40 howitzer. This could not be traversed unless the tank was on level ground, which severely restricted its ability to fight off-road.

Horse-drawn German baggage wagons pass a KV-2 left on the roadside.

Two KV-2s left derelict on the road by their unit. The nearest has 'I Kompanie' scrawled on the side of the turret, the victors having already laid claim to it.

This side view shows an impact hole between the first and second return rollers. It was this that severed the track. The gun suffered damage as it has been holed.

This KV-2 put up a fight before succumbing. Three impact marks can be seen just to the right of the hull machine gun and on the right-hand side of the main gun mantlet.

The bulk of the Soviet fast tanks consisted of the BT-5's uparmoured successor the BT-7, seen here with the newer conical turret, which went into production in 1935.

Overturned BT-7 Model 1935 with the rounded hull nose and early cylindrical T-26-style turret.

One of hundreds, if not thousands, of BT drivers who died with their machines.

German troops examine captured BT-7s caught in an ambush.

BT-7 fast tanks abandoned at the roadside. Up to 5,000 of these were built at the Kharkov Locomotive Factory along with the T-34 medium tank.

The single-turret T-26B light tank appeared in 1933 (the earlier T-26 had twin turrets) and was armed with a 45mm or 37mm gun. Its low speed and poor mobility compared to the BT-5 resulted in production being abandoned in the mid-1930s.

The T-26 was obsolete even in 1940; while its 45mm gun could destroy all German armoured vehicles except the Panzer IV, it suffered from common problems amongst Russian tanks – mechanical unreliability and thin armour.

A disabled Soviet T-26 tank with the sloped turret. The one in the background is fitted with the earlier cylindrical version.

The crew of this T-26 Model 1933 never managed to escape.

Knocked-out Soviet T-26.

A decapitated T-26.
Around 2,000
Model 1938/39s
were built.

T-26s destroyed
defending the
road to Moscow.

Another disabled
T-26 with one of its
crew.

The cumbersome-looking T-28 went in production by 1932, fitted with three turrets, one mounting a 76.2mm gun and two with machine guns. It was one of the world's very first medium tanks.

Abandoned T-28B Model 1938 medium tank bearing the skull and crossbones.

The massive T-35 heavy tank weighing 45 tons, which appeared a year after the T-28, was a similar beast but only about sixty were ever built.

A slightly later T-35A Model 1938 fitted with the horseshoe radio antenna. Although an impressive-looking monster with a maximum armour thickness of 30mm and a minimum of 10mm, it could be pierced by most anti-tank guns.

A German cyclist passes a T-35 left on the road.

From the mud splattered up the side of this T-35 it managed to travel some distance before breaking down.

The T-20 Komsomolets armoured artillery tractor was designed in 1936 at the Ordzhonikidze Moscow Plant No. 37.

The T-20 was unsuitable as a weapons or troop carrier. Nonetheless, it was used offensively with predictably fatal results.

German officers and NCOs take a good look at an abandoned T-34/76B or Model 1941.

This BT-7 came off worst during an engagement defending Moscow and is being looted for souvenirs or warm clothing.

This T-34 has been blown over onto its turret.

T-34 Model 1943s being mass produced. These are readily identifiable by the hexagonal and flat fronted turret with twin hatches.

This T-34 deployed on the Leningrad Front did not fare well against the Finns.

This German is standing by the remains of a battered T-34/76 Model 1940. The gun barrel has been bent out of shape and there is damage to the mantlet.

Germans examining a new T-34/76B Model 1941 with the rolled plate turret and one-piece hatch.

This T-34/76B or Model 1941 has a welded turret with the single large turret hatch.

Model 1941 abandoned on the road. Early in the war the T-34 was prone to mechanical problems leading to breakdowns.

This was an only too familiar sight in the early days of the fighting on the Eastern Front – a tank in a crater.

T-34/76 stuck fast in the mud. One of the exhaust pipes and its armoured covering is missing.

Soviet 'tank riders'. Due to the Red Army's lack of transport, infantry had to hitch a ride on the tanks where they were dangerously exposed to enemy fire.

A column of T-34/85s waiting to go into action. During the spring of 1944 Soviet Guards armoured brigades were issued with this new tank for the first time.

The enlarged turret of the T-34/85 allowed for an 85mm main gun and provided space for three crewmen, freeing up the commander who had previously acted as commander/main gunner.

This shows the very crude finish on the T-34/85 turrets – the casting and welding was much better on the earlier T-34/76.

Another shot clearly showing the casting seams on the front of the T-34/85 turret.

T-34/85s and their tank riders on manoeuvres.

T-34 tanks and supporting infantry in the Ukraine.

T-34s and tank riders clearing enemy defences.

T-34 tank crew celebrate
their arrival in Romania.

After defeating the
Germans in the Ploesti
area, T-34/85 tanks
of the Red Army's 4th
Guards Corps rolled
into Bucharest on 31
August 1944.

SU-76 self-
propelled guns
moving up for
the Red Army's
summer offensive
in 1944.

Nothing could withstand the ISU–152 armed with the powerful 152mm ML–20S gun-howitzer. This was capable of destroying German Panther and Tiger tanks.

IS–1 heavy tank armed with a massive 122mm gun.

The crew of an IS-2 pose for the camera.

A column of IS-2s.

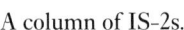

IS tanks in the woods outside Berlin.

IS tanks on the streets of Berlin heralding the final defeat of Nazi Germany.

The T-34 proved to be a real war-winner despite suffering heavy losses.

A preserved T-34/85 tank acts as a permanent memorial to the Battle of Debrecen that heralded the Battle for Budapest.

Citadel. The Soviet Steppe Front committed four armies, comprising the 7th Guards, 57th, 69th and 5th Tank, supported by 800 tanks. This force was to push back von Manstein's Army Group South with the aim of liberating both Belgorod and Kharkov.

On the night of 5/6 August General Erhard Raus' 11th Corps (little more than an ad hoc battle group drawn from five different infantry divisions) evacuated Belgorod and took up positions between the Donets and Lopan Rivers north of Kharkov. These though were compromised by Soviet forces up to 20 miles behind them and 11th Corps was forced to withdraw toward Kharkov, which it reached on the 12th having successfully conducted a rearguard action to the Donets.

Once Soviet tanks cut the Poltava–Kharkov rail link, General Raus' position at Kharkov was seriously jeopardized. Despite the presence of large numbers of administrative and logistical personnel in the city, 11th Corps could only muster 4,000 infantrymen. In addition, ammunition was precariously low. Thanks to the Battle of Kursk, the intense fighting had consumed half of what had been set aside for the end of August and early September. As a result, the supply depot in Kharkov had five trainloads of spare panzer tracks but not much else.

When General Werner Kempf, commanding Army Detachment Kempf, requested permission to abandon the city on 12 August von Manstein agreed. In response Hitler insisted it be held and von Manstein replaced Kempf with General Otto Wöhler and his former command became the German 8th Army. Hitler was worried that the loss of Kharkov would damage his prestige with Turkey, which while neutral was pro-Nazi. In the spring the Turkish commander-in-chief had inspected Kempf's defences, pronouncing them 'impregnable'. Kharkov was in a long line of towns and cities that Hitler decreed should be held to the last – thereby shackling the Wehrmacht to innumerable costly defensive battles and depriving them of the initiative.

The mood in General Raus' headquarters cannot have been a happy one, but to be fair German generals had found themselves in this type of situation on innumerable occasions and had still turned the tables on the enemy. Raus was actually Austrian, but was an experienced pair of hands having commanded the 6th Panzer Division during the early part of the war.

Examining his maps, Raus anticipated that the Red Army would attempt to cut off Kharkov by breaking through the defensive arc to the west of the city. He therefore rushed every anti-tank gun and 88mm flak gun to the high ground on the northern edge of the precarious bottleneck, which would have to be kept open to facilitate the escape of withdrawing units. Despite the efforts of the Red Air Force these defences were was reinforced by the welcome and timely arrival of panzers from the 2nd SS Panzer Division, giving Raus ninety-six Panthers, thirty-five Tigers and twenty-five Sturmgeschütz III assault guns, all of which were capable of giving Soviet tanks a very bloody nose.

The Red Army began to mass for its attack on 20 August and were promptly set upon by the Luftwaffe's Stuka dive-bombers. Raus recalled:

Dark fountains of earth erupted skyward and were followed by heavy thunderclaps and shocks that resembled an earthquake. These were the heaviest, two-ton bombs, designed for use against battleships, which were all that Luftflotte 4 had left to counter the Russian attack. Soon all the villages occupied by Soviet tanks lay in flames.

Soviet tanks advanced through the broad cornfields, emerging on the east-west highway several hundred metres from Raus' main defences. Initially the Panthers held the T-34s at bay, but weight of numbers got them to the Germans' forward positions. Raus recalled:

Here a net of anti-tank and flak guns, Hornet 88mm tank destroyers, and Wasp self-propelled 105mm field howitzers trapped the T-34s, split them into small groups, and put large numbers out of action. The final waves were still attempting to force a breakthrough in concentrated masses when Tigers and

StuG III self-propelled assault guns, which represented our mobile reserves behind the front, attacked the Russian armour and repulsed it with heavy losses.

The 5th Guards Tank Army lost 184 T-34s that day. In total the Red Army lost 450 tanks during the Belgorod-Kharkov offensive.

Although the Luftwaffe and panzers had done all they could to stop the Soviets, with their ammunition and strength spent there was little more they could achieve. To insist that the garrison remain at their posts was simply a waste of valuable manpower. On 21 August 1943 von Manstein abandoned battered Kharkov for a second time and two days later the Red Army was in the city centre once more. The retreating Germans blew up their remaining ammunition and fuel dumps and set fire to parts of the city to slow down the advancing enemy. To the south of Kharkov, the German rearguard fought desperately to hold open the escape corridor as troop convoys sped to safety. Despite repeated Soviet attacks and attempts to cut them off, Raus and his 11th Corps fought their way back to the Dnieper.

Elements of the Soviet 183rd Rifle Division triumphantly reached Dzerzhinsky Square at 0200 hours on the 23rd, where they met with soldiers from the 89th Rifle Division. They proceeded to hoist the Red Flag over the ruins. The city was completely liberated by 1100 hours and the fourth and final battle for Kharkov was over. The success of this operation meant that German forces in Ukraine were forced to withdraw beyond the Dnieper, paving the way for the liberation of Kiev in early November.

At the end of July events in Italy now took a hand as Mussolini was ousted following the Western Allies' landing in Sicily. Field Marshal von Kluge was ordered to evacuate the Orel salient. Despite the committal of the Soviet Central Front on the southern shoulder of the salient the Germans were able to withdraw to the half-completed Hagen Line in front of Bryansk. There was to be little respite, for on 23 August Zhukov launched an offensive to push the Germans back from Nevel south to the Black Sea defended by Army Groups Centre, South and A.

The Soviet victory at Kursk came at a terrible price. Casualties for the three Soviet Fronts totalled 177,847 men, and 1,614 tanks and self-propelled guns, three times those of the Wehrmacht. German losses were just short of 50,000 (Army Group South 29,102 and 9th Army 20,720), although while 1,612 panzers were damaged only 323 were irreparable losses. On top of this was the subsequent loss of Belgorod and Kharkov. From this point on Hitler, like it or not, was on the strategic defensive on the Eastern Front.

Fearful of being outflanked, the bulk of the German forces in the Soviet Union fell back on the Dnieper River. West of Moscow, from early August to the beginning of October the Red Army struggled in a series of operations to push back the Wehrmacht and liberate Smolensk. These were conducted by the Kalinin and Western Fronts against Army Group Centre. Smolensk was liberated in late September at the cost of 450,000 casualties; German losses were assessed at around a quarter of a million. This finally removed the strategic threat to Moscow.

The heavy losses suffered by the Wehrmacht in July and August 1943 crippled both Army Groups Centre and South. Notably the Polkovodets Rumyantsev and the concurrent Kutuzov operations were the first time that the Germans were unable to defeat a major Soviet summer offensive. Von Manstein was unable to launch another Kharkov comeback and the Red Army's momentum of 1943 was to continue unabated in 1944, with catastrophic consequences for Hitler.

Chapter 13

Victory in the Crimea

In early 1944 the 19th Tank Corps was to play a leading role in the liberation of the Crimea. This unit, along with the 20th Tank Corps, had been formed in December 1942 and was to fight until the very end of the war. The 2nd Guards Mechanized Corps was also to be involved, despite the Crimea, like the Caucasus, being poor tank country. This unit had been created in October 1942, but was not based on the original 2nd Mechanized Corps, as this had been converted into the 7th Guards Mechanized Corps the previous year.

With the Red Army's tanks thrusting into western Ukraine, General Erwin Jaenecke's 17th Army, cut off in the Crimea by the 4th Ukrainian Front and the North Caucasian Front, faced annihilation. The fate of his command was almost a repeat of 6th Army's at Stalingrad. Despite the strength of their formidable defences, the prospects for the German and supporting Romanian forces, totalling around 195,000 men, equipped with 215 assault guns and self-propelled guns, 3,600 guns and mortars and 148 aircraft, were extremely bleak.

After clearing the Black Sea coast to the mouth of the Dniester River, the Red Army was well placed to liberate the Crimea. Common sense would have dictated it was a good time to evacuate Jaenecke's command before the inevitable blow fell. Instead Hitler was adamant that holding the Crimea was necessary to safeguard Romanian oil and to keep Turkey neutral. General Jaenecke was in an unenviable position. Hitler wanted Sevastopol held as a fortress, but the city's inner defences had remained in ruins since the 1941–2 campaign. Jaenecke, who had been at Stalingrad, understood perfectly well what happened when a surrounded and unsupported army was ordered to hold its ground to the last.

Jaenecke was not idle and his troops had done all they could to reinforce their outer defences. He had confidence in the fortifications behind which his eleven divisions held Perekop, Kerch, the Ak–Monai positions and Sevastopol itself. The lagoons of the Sivash Sea had not frozen and they seemed to present the Red Army with a considerable obstacle. The Romanians left only a covering force to screen the salt flats and marshes and dug in on the nearby high ground.

The German 49th Mountain Corps, commanded by General Rudolf Konrad, defended the northern Crimea, with the German 50th Infantry Division blocking the Perekop Isthmus and the German 336th Infantry Division and the Romanian 10th and 19th Infantry Divisions south of the Sivash Sea. In reserve supporting these units were the German 111th Infantry Division and Mountain Regiment Krym. The German 5th Corps, commanded by General Karl Allmendinger, was deployed at Kerch to the east consisting of the German 73rd and 98th Infantry Divisions and the Romanian 3rd Mountain and 6th Cavalry Divisions. The Romanian 1st Mountain Corps was on coastal defence and anti-partisan duties.

The Red Army planned a two-pronged assault in the spring of 1944. Tolbukhin's 4th Ukrainian Front, attacking from the north, and Yeremenko's Separate Maritime Army, striking from the eastern end of the Kerch Peninsula, could field 470,000 men, 559 tanks and self-propelled guns, and almost 6,000 field guns and mortars. General K.A. Vershinin's 4th Air Army assigned to Yeremenko and General T.T. Khryukin's 8th Air Army assigned to Tolbukhin with a total of some 2,255 aircraft backed the ground assault. The Germans claimed 604 Soviet aircraft downed over the Crimea in the six months leading up to their evacuation, with one Luftwaffe pilot remarkably claiming 247 of the kills!

Tolbukhin planned to strike across the Perekop Isthmus and the Sivash lagoons employing G.F. Zakharov's 2nd Guards Army, which included the 2nd Guards Mechanized Corps, and Y. Kreizer's 51st Army, supported by the 19th Tank Corps, respectively. His intention was that the main attack would come through the lagoons bringing his forces into the rear of the German units in the Perekop, followed by a drive on Simferopol and Sevastopol. The Sivash operations required engineers and pontoons in order to traverse water so salty that horses would not enter it. At the other end of the Crimea, General Yeremenko's Coastal Army would drive into the interior from its bridgehead. It would liberate Kerch, destroying the Axis defences, block the escape route through Ak-Monai and pin down the Germans to stop them interfering with Tolbukhin's attack.

The push into northern Crimea started on 8 April just as Odessa was being liberated. The 4th Ukrainian Front launched the assault across the Perekop Isthmus followed by the Kerch attack the following day. At 0800 hours Soviet artillery in support of the 2nd Guards opened fire on the German 50th Infantry Division's positions. Two hours later the 51st Army's guns opened up on the German 336th Infantry Division and the Romanian 10th Infantry Division in the Sivash sector.

Under covering smoke Zakharov's guardsmen forced their way into Armyansk while Kreizer's infantry ferried their artillery and light tanks on pontoons across the salt lagoons. Once across the Sivash, the goal was to come ashore at the southern end of the ruined Chongar Bridge. After the rafted artillery and vehicles were clear of the water they were to strike out into the rear of the Axis Perekop defences. The right flank of the German 49th Mountain Corps quickly crumbled once the 10th Romanian Infantry Division collapsed.

Intensive night bombing attacks over Kerch were a prelude to the 4th Air Army's mass strikes in support of the Separate Coastal Army's invasion. A special forward command post was set up from where the Deputy Air Army Commander, General Slyusarev, directed fighter cover over the beachhead. The Soviet Coastal Army reached Kerch on 11 April. The following day it secured the Ak-Monai position which constituted the last fortified German line of defence on the Kerch Peninsula. On 13 April the Coastal Army liberated the city of Feodosiya, followed by Sudak to the south-west two days later.

On 12 April Axis forces hastily withdrew on Sevastopol, seeking the protection of its fortifications. As they went the Soviet 19th Tank Corps and other mobile units continually attacked them. Mountain Regiment Krym, part of the 49th Mountain Corps, made a stand at Dzhankoy to cover the escape south. The Soviet 4th and 8th Air Armies constantly pounded the Crimean ports and hit ships at sea. In the Black Sea Soviet submarines and torpedo boats attacked enemy convoys. Partisans also caused upheaval with attacks behind Axis lines. By 16 April the German 17th Army was in full retreat toward Sevastopol.

Once 17th Army was squeezed into the south-western corner of the Crimea there was little the Luftwaffe could do to help. On 13 April, Simferopol, the Crimean capital, was liberated by Kreizer's 51st Army with 19th Tank Corps taking the honours. This meant that German and Romanian aircraft were confined to the few airstrips in the Sevastopol area. The Red Army reached the outskirts of Sevastopol toward the end of the month. Jaenecke flew to Berchtesgaden to meet Hitler to persuade him not to sacrifice the remaining 65,000 men of 17th Army and authorize rescuing the Sevastopol garrison. Hitler was unmoved and General Allmendinger, the German 5th Corps commander, replaced Jaenecke, but the Romanian-led evacuation continued.

The Germans desperately needed to keep the Soviet guns out of range of Sevastopol's docks and wharves, as equipment and men were now being shipped out in ever-growing numbers. This meant that the northern defences were vital and most of the mobile German artillery was deployed there. A smaller force of two divisions was deployed to the east and south-east to hold the formidable Zapun Heights.

In late April, Zakharov's 2nd Guards began to attack from the north across the Mackenzie Heights, but Tolbukhin then shifted his main attack to his left flank against the Zapun with the 19th Tanks Corps sweeping from the south into the German rear. Its task completed, the headquarters of the 4th Air Army was transferred to the 2nd

Belorussian Front and Vershinin's air regiments, now absorbed into the 8th Air Army, remained to take part in the capture of Sevastopol.

The Guards opened the attack from the north on the morning of 5 May. They fought their way up the Mackenzie Heights and through an extensive German minefield. Two days later Tolbukhin unleashed his main attack from the east. Kreizer's 51st Army crossed the Bakchisarai Mountains during the night and deployed before the northern slopes of the Zapun Heights. The Soviet 77th Rifle Division under Colonel Rodionov was poised to strike once Colonel Pavlov's 12th Assault Engineer Brigade had cleared a route. The Coastal Army to the south had seized Balaklava and was also poised to assault the southern end of the Zapun Heights. The 11th Guards Rifle Corps was to act as spearhead for the final push in the southern sector.

By mid-morning Kreizer had gained a foothold on the ridge and the Red Flag was hoisted by a sapper from the 12th Assault Brigade. During the afternoon the 51st and Coastal Armies barged their way up the western slopes and forced their way into the Inkerman valley. By this point the way to Sevastopol was open. In the northern sector German soldiers, after offering fierce resistance, were soon falling back towards the Inkerman Bridge or the ferries. The 51st Army's spearhead, formed by the 10th Rifle Corps, was soon involved in heavy street fighting. From the Zapun Heights Soviet troops fought their way into the outskirts of Sevastopol, reaching the main station. By the evening of 9 May the city had been liberated.

After the fall of Sevastopol, the remaining Axis forces withdrew into the Khersones Peninsula for a last stand while as many men were evacuated by sea as possible. Stalin instructed Tolbukhin on 10 May 1944 that the Crimea should be completely liberated within the next 24 hours. The Soviet Separate Coastal Army was tasked with clearing resistance on the Khersones. The aim was to affect a junction with the Soviet 19th Tank Corps. Soviet fighter-bombers, dive-bombers and artillery pounded those enemy troops escaping from Sevastopol by boat. They also targeted the last remaining airstrip still controlled by the Germans in Khersones.

The remnants of the 17th Army tried beating off the Soviet Coastal Army using their remaining anti-aircraft guns firing over open sights. The situation was chaotic as Soviet artillery ranged freely over the remaining spit of land still held by the Axis. General Erich Gruner, commanding the German 111th Infantry Division, and Colonel Paul Betz, acting commander of the 50th Infantry Division, were killed and the 336th Infantry Division's commander General Wolf Hagemann was wounded. Gruner was caught by Soviet tank fire.

During their fighting retreat to Sevastopol, the Germans lost 12,221 men and the Romanians 17,652 along with most of their armour. Whilst the 17th Army held out in Sevastopol until 9 May, the desperate Axis resistance in the Khersones bridgehead did not cease for another three days when the last 3,000 defenders were overwhelmed, Soviet artillery having prevented their evacuation by sea. Some 25,000 German troops surrendered at noon on the 12th. Many of them were gathered on the Khersones auxiliary airfield at the northern end of the peninsula, which under German occupation had been used as a Luftwaffe repair facility.

While about half of the 17th Army escaped across the Black Sea, approximately 117,000 men were killed, wounded or captured. The Germans lost 65,100 causalities (31,700 dead and missing in action and 33,400 wounded). Their Romanian allies lost 31,600 (25,800 dead and missing and 5,800 wounded); some 20,000 local Soviet 'volunteers' suffered an unknown fate. Soviet casualties during the offensive amounted to some 83,000 men, 171 tanks, 521 artillery pieces and 179 aircraft. The 4th Ukrainian Front suffered the highest losses with 13,000 killed and 50,000 wounded and the Coastal Army 4,000 killed and 16,000 wounded.

The Soviet authorities claimed that during their offensive west of the Dnieper in Ukraine and in the Crimea, the Red Army destroyed ten divisions and forced the Germans to dissolve another eight, while a total of sixty-eight German divisions lost 50 to 60 per cent of their manpower. It seemed impossible to conceive that the Wehrmacht could weather such bloodletting. In the aftermath Army Group A was re-designated Army Group South Ukraine and Army Group South became Army Group North Ukraine.

At the end of April 1944 Zhukov noted:

> Even though throughout the winter and spring campaign, the actions of our forces had resulted in signal victories I felt the German troops were still strong enough to put up a stiff defence on the Soviet-German front. As far as the strategic proficiency of their High Command and the local army group commands were concerned, after the disaster in the Stalingrad area and particularly after the Kursk battle it had drastically declined.

His comments on the Red Army's victory in the Crimea were perfunctory. 'An offensive by the 4th Ukrainian Front, the Independent Maritime Army and the Black Sea Fleet culminated in the complete rout of the Crimea group of enemy forces. On 9 May the Hero City of Sevastopol was freed, and on 12 May the operation to liberate the Crimea was completed.'

'Hitler's decision to hold the Crimea was one of his most insane inspirations', wrote American war correspondent Alexander Werth. He saw the liberation of the Crimea as a clear indication that German morale was faltering and concluded:

> It will remain one of the great puzzles of the war why, in 1941-42, despite overwhelming German and Romanian superiority in tanks and aircraft, and a substantial superiority in men, Sevastopol succeeded in holding out for 250 days and why in 1944, the Russians captured it within four days. ... Was there not something lacking in German morale by April 1944?

Chapter 14

Stalin's Armoured Steamroller

Through late 1943, Stalin fought to liberate the Ukraine west of the Dnieper, thereby undermining Hitler's exposed flank in Byelorussia to the north. The 1st Ukrainian Front included two tank armies, and these forces were soon in Kiev driving back the 4th Panzer Army. Then in the New Year, 370 tanks moved to successfully trap those German units in the Korsun-Shevchenovsky salient. This victory crushed the last of Hitler's offensive strength in Ukraine. By the beginning of 1944, despite massive losses sustained at Kursk and in Ukraine, thanks to Soviet industry the Red Army was still able to field 5,357 tanks and self-propelled guns.

Stalin's six tank armies had nearly forty armoured corps. The tank corps each numbered around 200 tanks and 60 self-propelled guns, whilst the mechanized corps fielded fewer tanks but the same number of self-propelled guns. For the Byelorussia offensive in June that year, Stalin committed the bulk of his armoured forces, including five tank armies. The 6th Tank Army, formed in January 1944 with the 5th Guards Tank Corps and 5th Guards Mechanized Corps, fielded about 600 tanks and self-propelled guns, 500 guns and mortars and 30,000 men. Stalin also employed independent infantry brigades, self-propelled artillery and heavy tank regiments to reinforce them.

During the spring of 1944, the Red Army's Guards tank brigades were issued with the very first new T-34/85s. Once production was in full swing it became the standard medium tank in all armoured units, although the T-34/76 remained in widespread service. While many units were re-equipped for the coming Operation Bagration offensive, they did not all get the T-34/85, instead having to make do with the earlier 76.2mm-armed Model 1942/43 as battle replacements.

The Red Army also introduced a series of new heavy tanks. Very limited numbers of the KV-85, essentially a remodelled KV armed with an 85mm gun, and the IS-1, also armed with the same gun, appeared in late 1943. These were quickly abandoned in favour of the IS-2 armed with a 122mm gun. A combination of this weapon and thicker armour meant it was able to give a good account of itself against the German Tiger I and Tiger II. This provided the Red Army with a tank that could provide powerful long-range support. However, the IS-2 struggled to penetrate the sloped armour of the Panther at ranges over 600m. Luckily for Soviet tankers, a growing German shortage of manganese resulted in them subsequently using high-carbon steel, alloyed with nickel, for the Panther's armour. This made it brittle, especially on the welds. Also in 1944 the Red Army began to receive the SU-85 and then the SU-100 tank destroyers, armed with 85mm and 100mm guns respectively, based on the proven T-34 chassis.

From January to March 1944 the Red Army lifted the siege of Leningrad in the north. Then in late March, more German troops were caught in the Kamenets-Podolsk Pocket as Soviet armour sought to crush the 1st and 4th Panzer Armies. The following month the Germans and Romanians were swiftly ejected from the Crimea. It was during this time that the panzers started to come up against growing numbers of the Red Army's next generation of heavy tanks. The 1st Guards Heavy Breakthrough Regiment, equipped with the IS-1, fighting at Staro-Konstantinov in early March 1944, found the tank could stand up to the Tiger I. However, like the KV-85, its gun was not powerful enough against the Tiger's armour.

In contrast, in April 1944, the 72nd Independent Guards Heavy Tank Regiment with the IS-2 allegedly accounted for forty-one Tiger Is and Elefant tank destroyers over a period of 20 days. One of the latter scored five direct hits at 1,500–2,000m, but the IS-2 survived until being destroyed from 700m. Ironically the regiment lost more tanks to mechanical failure than to the enemy. This engagement confirmed that the IS-2's hull could withstand the German 88mm armour-piercing round at over 1,000m. Its 122mm gun could penetrate 160mm of armour at the same range, thereby posing a severe threat to the Tiger. No other tank could outshoot the IS-2; the Germans did develop the massive Jagdtiger armed with a 128mm gun, but less than 100 were ever built.

Throughout May and June 1944 Hitler was misled by fake build-ups in the 3rd Ukrainian Front and 3rd Baltic Front areas, convincing him that Stalin's major attacks would take place in Ukraine or the Baltic States rather than Byelorussia. However, many of Hitler's commanders remained very uneasy about maintaining the 'Byelorussian Balcony', as the highly-exposed bulge in Army Group Centre's line was nicknamed. Field Marshal von Busch, commanding Army Group Centre, pleaded with Hitler to pull out of Byelorussia, or at least to shorten the line, but to no avail.

Although originally intended to coincide with D-Day on 6 June 1944, Operation Bagration commenced at 0500 hours on 23 June with a barrage that lasted for over two hours and to a depth of nearly four miles. For fifteen minutes Red Army gunners furiously poured hot metal onto the Germans' positions to a depth of two miles, followed 90 minutes of fire directed at observed targets, artillery positions and weapons pits. There was also 20 minutes of general bombardment dropped onto the Germans' main line of resistance and their rear areas. For the troops of Hitler's Army Group Centre, the density of this was truly shocking. Stalin's forces brought to bear 24,000 guns and mortars along the 430-mile line. Up to 90 per cent of the artillery was deployed on the breakthrough sectors, which only represented up to 20 per cent of the overall width of the front under attack.

This was to be no amphibious assault as in Normandy, but a massive armoured charge led by the T-34 across the length and breadth of the Soviet republic of Byelorussia. Opposite Hitler's Army Group Centre were four Soviet Fronts, meaning that over 40 per cent of the entire Red Army was committed to Bagration. Stalin gathered a staggering 118 rifle divisions, eight tank and mechanized corps, six cavalry divisions, thirteen artillery divisions and fourteen air defence divisions. These forces, including support troops, numbered 1.7 million men, more than double the strength of Army Group Centre. Most notably, for the opening stages of the offensive Stalin's generals had massed 2,715 tanks and 1,355 assault guns, about six times the number deployed by Army Group Centre. The vast majority of them were T-34/76s, T-34/85s and SU-85s/100s. Nothing could withstand such brute force.

To make matters worse for Hitler the loss of armoured units to northern Ukraine and France meant that the Army Group Centre was largely an infantry force. Critically it only had 553 of the 4,740 tanks and assault guns on the Eastern Front and most of these were in fact assault guns. The bulk of the armour, 40 panzers (including 29 Tiger Is) and 246 StuG IIIs, were deployed with General von Tippelskirch's 4th Army defending the city of Orsha. On top of this Army Group Centre had no real reserves except for a weak panzer division, the remains of a panzergrenadier division and an infantry division. Overall, the balance sheet favoured Stalin who had a 3:1 superiority in manpower, 10:1 in tanks and self-propelled artillery and 8:1 in guns and mortars. The correlation of forces was such that Hitler's troops would be overwhelmed if they did not conduct a swift fighting withdrawal.

General Reinhardt's 3rd Panzer Army held the northern wing. Despite its name, this formation had no panzer or panzergrenadier divisions. On the right of 3rd Panzer lay 4th Army south of Mogilev, running northward between Mogilev and Orsha. It could muster just two panzergrenadier divisions. General Jordan's 9th Army, holding the Bobruisk area running roughly south to north, had a single panzer division at Bobruisk

Following the massive artillery and rocket barrage and air attacks, Stalin's armoured steamroller, spearheaded by the T-34, struck on 23 June 1944. The deluge of hot metal pouring onto their positions stunned the defenders and whole units were simply swept away. By mid-afternoon Army Group Centre had informed the German high command that in the face of Stalin's pincer movement the situation around Vitebsk looked precarious. Furthermore, Reinhardt's 3rd Panzer Army did not have the resources to restore the situation.

The T-34-based PT-34 mine roller played a leading role in Stalin's offensive. One notable unit equipped with specialized armoured fighting vehicles was the 116th Separate Engineering Tank Regiment. They were used to clear the way to the strategic Minsk-Moscow highway from Smolensk to Orsha. This area was heavily fortified and held by the powerful German 78th Sturm (Assault) Division. To counter it, the 11th Guards Army's attack toward Orsha was supported by special engineer and tank units tasked with breaching the thick defensive belts.

The attacking rifle divisions were preceded by armoured assault forces each led by a company of ten PT-34s followed by heavy tanks and assault engineer battalions. At least five regiments of OT-34 flamethrowers were also deployed during Bagration: the 148th and 253rd with the 3rd Byelorussian Front, the 40th with the 3rd Shock Army and the 119th and 166th with the 1st Byelorussian Front. The PT-34s did not only have to contend with German minefields, barbed wire, anti-tank ditches, trenches and bunkers: 78th Sturm Division, although an infantry unit, was equipped like a panzergrenadier division and bolstered by StuG III assault guns. In addition, German anti-tank gunners, once they realized what the mine rollers were doing, made them priority targets.

Unfortunately for the Red Army, the resulting smoke and early morning fog on 23 June greatly hampered the supporting air attacks by the Red Air Force. Only General Chernyakovsky's 3rd Byelorussian Front enjoyed clear weather allowing bombers to carry out 160 sorties. The ground-attack Shturmoviks had to wait until the artillery and rocket launchers had finished their work. Afterwards the Soviet infantry surged forward to seize tactical ground that could be exploited as a springboard for the impending breakthrough by the T-34s.

To the north the collapse of Army Group Centre's forward defences at Vitebsk was very rapid. German corps commander General Gollwitzer signalled at 1312 hours on 25 June, 'Situation has changed.

Completely encircled by constantly reinforcing enemy. 4th Luftwaffe Field Division exists no longer! 246th Infantry Division and 6th Luftwaffe Field Division in heavy combat on several fronts. Various penetrations into the city of Vitebsk ...' Ominously at 1500 hours his HQ added, 'Situation at its climax'.

By early afternoon General Butkov's 1st Tank Corps had reached the Dvina and taken a damaged bridge. In Chernyakovsky's sector Lyudnikov's 39th Army was also pushing on the river and, supported by some elements of the 43rd Army, was assigned the task of destroying those German units trapped at Vitebsk. The Germans tried to break through the Soviet cordon, launching twenty-five counter-attacks on the 25th and a similar number the following day without success.

Traut's men were used to and expecting heavy Soviet bombardment, but the ferocity of the shelling on 23 June stunned even them. Carefully-prepared minefields and barbed wire were obliterated, sandbags were torn apart and scattered, weapon pits and trenches became gaping craters. Heavy weapons caught on the surface were soon useless twisted pieces of steel. They then found themselves under attack by the PT-34s as they ploughed a furrow through what remained of the minefields. The mine rollers did not have it all their own way as they came up against the assault guns assigned to Traut's division as well as his well dug-in anti-tank guns.

The plan was that General K.N. Galitskiy's 11th Guards would overwhelm the German defences along the Moscow-Minsk highway, which would permit Marshal Pavel Rotmistrov's 5th Guards Tank Army to deploy and exploit the breakthrough. Although the 11th Guards struggled against the determined resistance from Traut, the 1st Guards Rifle Division forced its way between him and the 256th Infantry Division to the north. Galitskiy then pushed General Burdenyniy's 2nd Guards Tanks Corps through this gap along a railway line.

Soviet tanks swiftly overwhelmed Tippleskirch's 39th Panzer Corps and 9th Army fell apart. General Jordan received permission to commit 20th Panzer to try and stem the onslaught of T-34s. The division could muster just seventy-one Panzer IVs. At that moment the 65th Army broke through on the southern approaches to Bobruisk and the 1st Guards Tank Corps moved to exploit this breach. Perhaps panicking, Jordan ordered 20th Panzer to retrace its tracks and head south, where it bumped into the Soviets near Slobodka south of Bobruisk.

Now not only was Bobruisk under threat but also those German divisions still east of the Berezina River. By 26 June the armour of 20th Panzer had been driven back to the city with the Soviet 9th Tank Corps bearing down on them from the east and the 1st Guards Tank Corps from the south, which cut the roads from Bobruisk to the north and north-west on the night of 26/27 June.

Two German pockets were created in the Bobruisk area, trapping nearly 40,000 men. Attempts by von Lützow's 35th Corps to break out to the north, spearheaded by 150 panzers and self-propelled guns, were smashed on the evening of 27 June. The 20th Panzer Division led the break-out north-west along the western bank of the Berezina, with the rearguard instructed to hold until 0200 hours on 29 June. The panzers and panzergrenadiers soon found themselves under attack by marauding T-34s and fighter-bombers.

Between Vitebsk and Bobruisk a sense of panic began to overwhelm those Germans defending Orsha, and some units began to fall back but it was too late. Burdenyniy's tanks swept north of the city toward the end of the 26th and his T-34s rolling to the west caught a German train full of wounded being evacuated from Orsha and blew it off the rails. That night the 11th Guards and 31st Armies overran the city.

South of Orsha, General Zakharov's offensive opened with Grishin's attack north of Mogilev, supported by General K.A. Vershinin's 4th Air Army, his men beginning to cross the Dnieper on 26 June. To the south General I.V. Boldin's 50th Army also thrust toward Mogilev. East of the city the tanks of the 33rd and 49th Armies hit the German 337th Infantry Division and broke through on the Ryassna-Mogilev road. Once the first and second German trench lines were breached,

T-34s poured into the rear area of General Weidling's 39th Panzer Corps.

By the morning of 27 June General B.S. Bakarov's 9th Tank Corps had secured the Berezina crossings. Sensing the time was right, General Rokossovsky committed the 1st Guards Tank Corps and 1st Mechanized Corps from Batov's 65th Army, sending them toward Baranovichi south-west of Minsk. The 1st Guards had been formed in December 1942. Although 1st Mechanized Corps had been disbanded in the summer of 1941, it was reconstituted the following summer. Rokossovsky's 1st Byelorussian Front trapped a sizeable number of German troops east of Bobruisk. Any withdrawal or break-out attempt was too late.

Effectively the fall of the defensive line Vitebsk–Orsha–Mogilev–Bobruisk meant that it was all over for Army Group Centre. The entire German defensive system collapsed in one fell swoop. By 30 June the first phase of the battle of Byelorussia was over. According to the Soviets they killed 132,000 Germans and took another 66,000 prisoner as well as capturing or destroying 940 tanks, over 5,000 guns and about 30,000 motor vehicles.

General M.F. Panov's 1st Guards Tank Corps, from the 1st Byelorussian Front, followed the T-34s of the 3rd Byelorussian Front to Minsk from the south-east. The city was liberated by the evening of 3 July and the people danced in the streets and rode on the tanks. In France the Allies would not liberate Paris until late August. The near-total annihilation of Army Group Centre in just under two weeks cost Hitler 300,000 dead, 250,000 wounded, and about 120,000 captured. Stalin's losses included 2,957 tanks, 2,447 artillery pieces and 822 aircraft, but his factories would enable him to shrug these losses off.

For Hitler Bagration was a vastly more serious blow than the catastrophes at Stalingrad or in Normandy. The destruction of Army Group Centre was a much bigger and swifter disaster than the loss of Army Group B's 7th Army and 5th Panzer Army in mid-August 1944 at Falaise. Although overall total German losses in France were comparable to those in Byelorussia, the former occurred over a two and a half month period, not a matter of weeks. Stalin's D-Day was a formidable achievement thanks in part to the T-34/76 and T-34/85 paving the way in German dead.

Nikolai Zheleznov, serving with the 63rd Tank Brigade, 10th Guards Tank Corps, 4th Guards Tank Army, observed:

> The next operation in which I participated was the Lvov-Sandomierz offensive. I fought in a T-34/85 there. There were still only a few of them at that time – my platoon had just one. Our corps was sent to exploit the breakthrough. We marched towards Lvov, not encountering any resistance.

The work of Stalin's Bagration steamroller was complete; his armour now looked to liberate the rest of Ukraine and strike into southern Poland. Between 20–29 August the Red Army thrust into eastern Romania, with the Jassy-Kishinev offensive. The denuded Army Group South Ukraine only had three armoured units and was quickly overwhelmed.

Chapter 15

Punishing Traitors

Following the utter destruction of Hitler's Army Group Centre in June 1944, Stalin instructed Zhukov to coordinate his next massive counteroffensive to be conducted by Marshal I.S. Konev's 1st Ukrainian Front on 13 July. Konev's forces included the 1st, 3rd and 4th Guards Tank Armies, which would have to take on the 900 panzers and assault guns of Hitler's Army Group North Ukraine. He was not too worried about this, because 1st Ukrainian Front had been considerably reinforced and could muster 10 tank and mechanized corps, as well as almost 80 cavalry and rifle divisions – in total they had up to 2,200 tanks and assault guns.

Nonetheless, sitting in Konev's path ready to counter-attack were some 20,000 crack Ukrainian SS troops, who had thrown their lot in with Hitler. Many Ukrainians hoped they would gain independence from Moscow by helping the Germans. The Ukrainian Liberation Army (*Ukrainske Vyzvolne Viysko* – UVV) was little more than a Nazi propaganda tool and two Ukrainian divisions numbering 40,000 men designated the Ukrainian National Army (UNA) in 1945 were never really effective as such.

Significantly Ukrainians proved eager recruits for a Waffen-SS division. These were largely Galician Ukrainians as Reichsführer-SS Heinrich Himmler stipulated they must come from western Ukraine (formerly Polish Galicia) and be Greek Catholic rather than Russian Orthodox, thereby excluding Soviet Ukrainians. The idea was that anti-communist volunteers would be drawn from the area of Poland that had once been part of the Austro-Hungarian Empire and therefore loyal servants of the Habsburg Emperor.

When recruitment commenced in April 1943 there were a staggering 100,000 applicants for 30,000 places (typically a Waffen-SS division numbered about 15,000 fighting men and 5,000 support troops). Many of the others were not turned away and were recruited to form five Galician police regiments. Himmler placed an Austrian major-general, the elderly and professorial-looking Fritz Freitag, in charge. About 350 Galician volunteer officers and 2,000 NCOs were despatched to Germany. After their training was completed in May 1944 the 14th Waffen-SS Grenadier Division *Galizien* was shipped to the Eastern Front just in time to face Konev's Lvov-Sandomierz offensive.

North of Lvov the 3rd Guards and 13th Armies, 1st Guards Tank Army and General V.K. Baranów's mechanized cavalry corps were to strike in the direction of Rava-Russkaya and 4th Panzer Army. In the south the 60th and 38th Armies, plus the 3rd and 4th Guards Tank Armies and General S.V. Sokolov's mechanized cavalry group, were to push on Lvov, cutting their way through 1st Panzer Army. Even further south the 1st Guards and 18th Armies, with the 5th Guards Army following up were to attack the weak Hungarian 1st Army guarding the approaches to Stanislav.

Resistance by 1st and 4th Panzer Armies was much stronger than that conducted by Army Group Centre's shattered divisions. Konev threw his tanks in a two-pronged attack. The right forced its way across the Bug and headed north for Rokossovsky's planned push on Lublin and the Vistula; but panzer and SS divisions initially held up his left as it fought its way south toward Lvov. The northern attack ran into the prepared positions of the weak 291st and 340th Infantry Divisions, but these were easily penetrated. To the north-west into the gap either side of Radekhov, Konev poured Cavalry-Mechanized Group Baranów and the 1st Guards Tank Army. It took 13th Army two days of tough fighting to surround Brody.

With his defences east of Lvov just about holding, General Harpe decided to commit his tactical reserves, the 1st and 8th Panzer Divisions, in an attempt to stifle the Soviet offensive on 14 and 15

July. Although Konev had been ordered by Stalin to hold back the 3rd and 4th Guards Tank Armies until a deep penetration had been made, he knew he must act quickly to exploit the situation.

Konev had trouble bringing his tank armies to bear in the Lvov attack because the 15th Infantry Corps from 60th Army had only managed to hack a two and a half to four-mile wide corridor to a depth of 11 miles. General P.S. Rybalko, commander of the 3rd Guards Tank Army, took the decision to shove his men down this corridor on the 16th and was followed up by General D.D. Lelyushenko's 4th Guards Tank Army. This was the only time during the war that two entire tank armies were committed to combat on such a narrow front and while the flanks were being counter-attacked. With German artillery bombarding this 'Koltiv Corridor' the 1st and 8th Panzer Divisions prepared to counter-attack supported by Freitag's Ukrainian 14th SS.

Once Rybalko's men were in the corridor, General Arthur Hauffe's German 13th Corps knew it must withdraw and fell back to the *Prinz Eugen Stellung* defensive position. By 17 July the Soviets had captured parts of this strongpoint, which Freitag's Galician Ukrainians attempted to recapture, until the appearance of powerful Soviet IS-2 tanks. On the evening of 18 July the 1st Ukrainian Front cut through Harpe's defences to a width of 125 miles, advanced 30 to 50 miles and surrounded 45,000 men near Brody. Despite pleas to General Hauffe by his subordinates, there was little he could to help the four divisions in the Brody salient escape.

The 48th and 24th Panzer Corps attempted to reach 13th Corps but to no avail. On the 18th General von Mellenthin, taking command of 8th Panzer Division, tried to cut his way through to the trapped men of 13th Corps at Brody. The Soviets were waiting for him with minefields and concentrated artillery and tank fire. Mellenthin wrote:

Two days later the bulk of 13th Corps, led by Generals Lasch and Lange, succeeded in fighting their way through to our lines. Thousands of men formed up in the night in a solid mass and to the accompaniment of thunderous 'hurrahs' threw themselves at the enemy. The impact of a great block of desperate men, determined to do or die, smashed through the Russian line, and thus a great many of the troops were saved. But all guns and heavy weapons had to be abandoned, and a huge gap was opened in the front. Marshal Konev's tanks poured through and the whole German position in southern Galicia became untenable.

Those forces remaining in the Brody Pocket resisted for four miserable days until it was cut in half and they were finally wiped out on the 22nd. The Germans suffered 30,000 killed and 15,000 captured as well as losing 68 panzers, 500 guns and 3,500 lorries. Unable to resist the Soviet tanks, 14,000 men of Freitag's 14th SS Division were caught in the Brody area and just 2,000–3,000 managed to escape. Those caught could expect little mercy from their captors. Despite the severe mauling of his untested division, there was no doubting Freitag's courage and he was decorated with the Knight's Cross. His exhausted survivors were sent to Slovakia to refit and the division was rebuilt using Soviet Ukrainians, which was reflected in its re-designation as 14th SS Grenadier Division (*ukrainische Nr.1*). They were not redeployed until 1945 and then fought in Czechoslovakia and Yugoslavia.

The 29th Tank Corps, assigned to the Guards 4th Tank Army, reached Lvov on 23 July and several days later was reinforced by the 10th Guards Tank Corps (formerly the 30th Urals Volunteer Tank Corps). Both these units had been formed the previous year. The city was liberated on 27 July and only half of the 40,000-strong German garrison escaped. The 1st, 3rd and 4th Guards Tank Armies then pushed west toward Sandomierz on the Vistula with the aim of securing a bridgehead. During this advance the 6th Guards Mechanized Corps and 10th Guard Tank Corps, both with the 4th Guards Tank Army, suffered considerable casualties. One battalion from the 63rd Tank Brigade, belonging to the 10th Guards, crossed the river with just five of its T-34s remaining. One of those had a damaged gunsight and proved incapable of hitting anything.

The Germans counter-attacked, but on 12 August a solitary T-34/85, from the 53rd Guards Tank Brigade, successfully ambushed three Tiger IIs. The following day eleven IS-2s, from the 71st Independent Heavy Tank Regiment, halted another attack by fourteen Tiger IIs. At a range of 600m the IS-2s bested their enemies and destroyed four and damaged seven. The 71st Regiment lost three of its tanks and seven were damaged. This was not the IS-2's first time in combat, as it had seen action earlier in the year. Embarrassingly for the Germans it was the Tiger II's debut on the Eastern Front and it was clearly inauspicious. Sandomierz was taken shortly after and the Germans were unable to eliminate the Red Army's bridgehead. Konev's offensive claimed to have destroyed 1,900 tanks and assault guns and killed or captured 140,000 German troops.

The Soviet summer 1944 offensive saw the Red Army cut through Ukraine and into Poland to the very gates of Warsaw. This spelled the end of Bulgaria, Finland, Hungary, Romania and Slovakia's alliance with Hitler. Once they had become front-line states they were swift to swap sides, but by this stage most of their tank forces had been destroyed. Disastrously, Romania's defection in mid-1944 exposed Hungary's southern frontier. Desperately trying to stem the Soviet and Romanian forces pushing from the east, the Hungarian 7th Assault Artillery Battalion succeeded in briefly giving Soviet tanks a bloody nose at Arad on the River Lipova. However, Horthy's government began to wobble and by the end of 1944 the Hungarian 1st Army had withdrawn into Slovakia and the 2nd Army had been disbanded. Units were transferred to the battered Hungarian 3rd Army south of Lake Balaton or to the German 6th and 8th Armies in northern Hungary. Budapest, the Hungarian capital, came under the protection of General Otto Wohler's Army Group South.

By October 1944 it was apparent that Horthy was intent on joining Romania and Bulgaria in defecting to the Soviet camp. The Germans temporarily stabilized the situation by installing a puppet government with Operation Panzerfaust, but the Soviets were soon hammering at the gates of Budapest. The mixed German-Hungarian garrison included the Hungarian 1st Armoured, 10th Mixed and 12th Reserve Divisions as well as a number of armoured car and assault artillery battalions.

Having stretched its supply lines to the very limit, the Red Army was unable to penetrate the German positions so switched their attentions east of Budapest. The 6th Guards Tank Army attacked from the north-east and the 46th Army from the south encircling the city. Efforts to relieve the Hungarian capital in January 1945 got to within 12 miles of the city. On 11 February the garrison desperately attempted to break out, but this ended in bloody disaster and Budapest capitulated the following day. Elements of the Hungarian Army continued to fight alongside the Germans, but their armour was long gone.

Chapter 16

Stopped Before Warsaw

The 2nd Tank Army and 3rd, 8th and 16th Tank Corps were committed to the battle for Warsaw. Stalin knew that to safeguard the Soviet Union in the future he would need to carve out a massive security buffer in Eastern Europe. To do this, as a minimum, he needed to establish communist governments in Poland, Hungary, Romania and Bulgaria. Poland presented a potential problem because unlike the others it was not a German ally. He also understood that if the Red Army took Berlin before the Allies, then eastern Germany would become communist as well.

A communist Polish army was formed in the Soviet Union as the military wing of the so-called Union of Polish Patriots, which came into being with Stalin's approval in 1943. General Zygmunt Berling's Soviet-raised Polish 1st Army finally joined Marshal Rokossovsky's 1st Byelorussian Front during the spring of 1944. Berling had about 100,000 men under arms, comprising five infantry divisions, a tank brigade, four artillery brigades and an air wing. Many recruits, who were former prisoners of war, saw it as a way of getting home, though Stalin kept them under tight control. For his plans to work it was important that Berling liberated Warsaw and no one else.

After Operation Bagration had smashed Hitler's Army Group Centre in spectacular fashion, Rokossovsky's Lublin-Brest Offensive was conducted from 18 July to 2 August 1944 as a follow-on and to support Konev's Lvov-Sandomierz offensive by tying down German forces in central-eastern Poland and culminated in the Battle of Radzymin. To the north of Konev's 1st Ukrainian Front, Rokossovsky's 8th Guards, 47th and 69th Armies, supported by the 2nd Tank Army and the Polish 1st Army, struck from the Kovel area towards Lublin and Warsaw, thereby making Army Group North Ukraine's position untenable.

Berling was instructed to cross the Vistula at Pulawy on 31 July on a wide front in order to support other elements of the Soviet 69th and 8th Guards Armies crossing near Magnuszew. The Polish 1st and 2nd Infantry Divisions gained the west bank on 1 and 2 August, but by the 4th had suffered 1,000 casualties and were ordered to withdraw. They were then assigned to protect the northern part of the Magnuszew bridgehead.

In five weeks of fighting Rokossovsky covered 453 miles and was within reach of Warsaw. The Polish capital looked a tempting prize as a culmination of Operation Bagration's remarkable success, but Stalin's summer offensive was beginning to lose momentum. Rokossovsky's 1st Byelorussian Front was at the very limit of its supply lines; ammunition and rations were exhausted, as were his men.

In many ways the German defences of Warsaw echoed those of Minsk, the eastern approaches of the Polish capital being protected by a 50-mile ring of strongpoints. The only difference was that this time Field Marshal Model had sufficient mobile reserves with which to parry Rokossovsky's thrusts. He had gathered his wits and more importantly sufficient men with which to thwart the oncoming tide. By this stage the German defences were coalescing around five weak panzer divisions deploying around 450 tanks and self-propelled guns. Over the next week things would start to go badly wrong for Rokossovsky and his Front would experience its first major setback.

North of Warsaw, Model turned to Himmler's Waffen-SS for assistance in stabilizing the front. The remnants of the 1st SS and 2nd SS Panzer Divisions had been shipped west after their mauling in the Kamenets-Podolsk Pocket to re-equip and prepare for the anticipated Anglo-American landings in France. However, the 3rd SS and 5th SS Panzer Divisions remained in Romania and Poland rearming. The 3rd SS was notified to move north as early as 25 June, but the disruption to the rail networks and roads meant that it took two weeks to get to north-eastern Poland. Arriving on 7 July it found the Red Amy was already striking toward the Polish city of Grodno threatening the southern flank of Army Group Centre's 4th Army and the northern flank of 2nd Army.

Deployed to Grodno, the 3rd SS were assigned the task of creating a defensive line for 4th Army to retire behind. Spectacularly the division held off 400 Soviet tanks for eleven days before withdrawing south-west toward Warsaw. Joined by the Hermann Göring Panzer Division at Siedlce 50 miles east of the Polish capital, they held the Soviets for almost a week from 24 July, keeping open an escape corridor for 2nd Army as it fled toward the Vistula. Three days later the Soviets threw almost 500 tanks to the south and by the 29th were at the suburbs of Warsaw. The 5th SS arrived in western Warsaw on 27 July and passed through the city to take up positions to the east. The next day Stalin ordered Rokossovsky to occupy Praga, the suburb of Warsaw on the eastern bank of the Vistula, during 5–8 August and to establish a number of bridgeheads over the river to the south of the city.

At this stage Rokossovsky enjoyed a 3:1 superiority in infantry and 5:1 in tanks and artillery. His Front had at its disposal nine armies: one tank army, two tank corps, three cavalry corps, one motorized corps and two air armies. Against this Model's 2nd Army could muster four understrength panzer divisions and one infantry division, while 9th Army had just two divisions and two brigades of infantry.

The Soviet 2nd Tank Army and 8th Tank Corps attacked westward along the Warsaw-Lublin road toward Praga. About 40 miles south-east of Warsaw in the Garwolin area 2nd Tank Army was opposed by two advanced battalions of General Dr Fritz Franek's 10,800-strong German 73rd Infantry Division. Holding the north bank of the Swidra river, they were backed up by the Hermann Göring Panzer Division 12 miles east of Praga. In addition, four panzer divisions, the 3rd SS, 5th SS, 4th and 19th, poised to counter-attack, now defended the approaches to Warsaw. The men of 19th Panzer were veterans of the Eastern Front, having fought on the central and southern sectors from June 1941 to June 1944 before being shipped to the Netherlands for a refit.

When the 2nd Tank Army's 16th Tank Corps struck toward Otwock along the Lublin road, 19th Panzer counter-attacked with forty panzers and an infantry regiment, but were unable to hold Otwock and by the evening the Soviets were a mere 15 miles from Warsaw, having taken the villages near Milosna Stara. They were now poised to assault the key defences of Okuniew. The 8th Tank Corps opened the attack only to be stalled by determined German air and artillery attacks.

In the meantime, General Nikolai Vedeneev's 3rd Tank Corps bypassed the German positions in the Zielonka district and drove them from Wołomin (also spelt Volomin) and Radzymin, just 12 and 16 miles north-east of Warsaw respectively, where they took up defensive positions along the Dulga River. Having outstretched his supply lines and outrun the rest of the Soviet 2nd Tank Army, Vedeneev was in a dangerously exposed position. The 39th Panzer Corps was in the area and five German panzer divisions were coming together in the direction of Radzymin-Wołomin.

Rokossovsky's forces were quick to react to this threat and attempted to alleviate the pressure on Vedeneev's 3rd Tank Corps with a diversionary attack. At dawn on 31 July, following heavy air and artillery bombardment, the Soviet 8th Tank Corps threw itself at the Germans who fell back toward Okuniew. The 5th SS counter-attacked in a westerly direction from Stanislawow with fifty panzers in an effort to link up with the Hermann Göring and 19th Panzer who were fighting a tank battle with the Soviets at Okuniew and Ossow.

The 5th SS were repulsed and on the evening of 31st the Soviets took Okuniew, but could not budge the Germans from their strongpoint at Ossow. North of the Soviet 8th Tank Corps, the 3rd Tank Corps remained unsupported and like the 16th Corps had endured a day of heavy attacks from German armour, artillery and infantry. The commander of the Soviet 2nd Tank Army was in an impossible position: his units were enduring heavy casualties, he was short of supplies and his rear was under threat.

Model began to probe the weak spot in Rokossovsky's line between Praga and Siedlce. His intention was to hit him in the flank and the rear and soon to the north-east of Warsaw the 39th Panzer Corps was counter-attacking the 3rd Tank Corps and driving it back to Wołomin.

The 3rd SS, Hermann Göring and 4th and 19th Panzer Divisions struck south into the unsupported Soviet columns. The Hermann Göring's 1st Armoured Paratroop Regiment launched the counter-attack from Praga toward Wołomin on the 31st, heralding a much larger effort to halt the Red Army before Warsaw, while from the south-west along the Warsaw-Wyszków road, attacking toward Radzymin, came the 19th Panzer. From Wyszków 4th Panzer acted in support.

The next day the 5th SS pushed toward Wołomin from Wegrow. At the same time the 3rd SS was launched into the fray from Siedlce towards Stanislawow, with the intention of trapping those Soviet forces on the north-eastern bank of the Dluga. Rokossovsky simply could not fulfil his orders to break though the German defences and enter Praga by 8 August: it was simply not possible. At 1610 hours on 1 August he ordered the attack to be broken off just as Model launched his major counter-attack.

General Nikolaus von Vormann, appointed by Guderian to command 9th Army, brought up reinforcements from 2nd Army's reserves and also launched a counter-attack. Using units of the 5th SS and 3rd SS attacking from the forests to the east of Michalow he drove the Soviet 8th Tank Corps from Okuniew at 2100 hours on 1 August and linked up with 39th Panzer Corps from the West.

On 2 August all Soviet forces assaulting Warsaw were redeployed. The 28th, 47th and 65th Armies were sent northwards to seize the undefended town of Wyszków and the Liwiec river line. Crucially this left 2nd Tank Army without infantry support. This situation was compounded when 69th Army was ordered to halt while the 8th Guards Army under Vasily Chuikov ceased the assault to await a German attack from the direction of Garwolin.

By the 2nd the 19th Panzer Division, followed by 4th Panzer, were in Radzymin, north-east of Warsaw, and the Soviet 3rd Tank Corps was thrown back towards Wołomin. The following day the Hermann Göring Panzer Division rolled into Wołomin. Pressed into the area of Wołomin, Vedeneev's corps was trapped. Attempts by the 8th Guards Tank Corps and the 16th Tank Corps to reach them failed, with the 8th Guards suffering serious casualties in the attempt.

After a week of heavy fighting the Soviet 3rd Tank Corps was surrounded by 4th and 19th Panzer, 3,000 troops being killed and another 6,000 captured. The Soviets also lost 425 of the 808 tanks and self-propelled guns they had begun the battle with on 18 July. By noon on 5 August the Germans had ceased their counter-attack and the battle for the Praga approaches had come to an end. Two German divisions had to be transferred south to deal with the Soviet threat there.

The 3rd Tank Corps was destroyed and the 8th Guards Tank Corps and the 16th Tank Corps had taken major losses. The exhausted Soviet 2nd Tank Army handed over it positions to the 47th and 70th Armies and withdrew to lick its wounds. Stalin clearly did not hold Lieutenant General Vedeneev responsible for the encirclement and destruction of his command. He remained in charge and the 3rd Tank Corps was honoured by being designated the 9th Guards Tank Corps in November 1944.

It was not until 25 August that Rokossovsky would inform Stalin that he was ready to have another go at Warsaw. After such heavy fighting north-east of the Polish capital, it is easy to see way Stalin saw the Polish Home Army's Warsaw rising as being of little consequence in the overall strategic scheme of things. After enduring two months of terrible bloodletting, the Poles had to wait another three and a half agonizing months before being finally 'liberated' by the Red Army.

Hitler had five army groups defending the Eastern Front in January 1945. Army Group Centre held East Prussia and northern Poland along the Narew to the junction with the Vistula. Army Group A was deployed along the middle reaches of the Vistula, from the north of Warsaw down to the Carpathian Mountains. Warsaw was the responsibility of the German 9th Army, but holding the city was not a viable option. The garrison comprised just four fortress battalions, one of which was an 'ear battalion' made up of former casualties and invalids, plus some artillery and engineering units. It was supposed to have been of divisional strength, but units had been transferred to the Western Front. Nonetheless, Hitler told General Guderian, the German Chief of the General Staff, 'that Warsaw be held at all costs'.

It seemed inevitable that Stalin would strike along the Warsaw–Berlin axis as this was the most direct route to the German capital. Zhukov's offensive was initially dubbed the 'Warsaw-Poznań' operation. Early in 1945 Stalin's Red Army conducted a two-pronged drive on Berlin. Zhukov was to thrust through Poznań in Poland and Konev through Breslau on the River Oder in Germany. Once German forces in East Prussia had been overwhelmed, the Red Army could then advance on Poznań. It was to bypass the city and race toward the Oder, where Hitler was only belatedly trying to create a coherent defensive line. Once over the river Stalin would be at the very gates of Berlin, the Seelow Heights.

Zhukov launched his offensive on 14 January 1945, a day after Konev's from the Baranów bridgehead. For 25 minutes his guns pulverized German defences before advancing from the Magnuszew and Pulawy bridgeheads. Soviet reporter Vasily Grossman, who was with Zhukov's 1st Belorussian Front, recalled 'Crossing of the Pilica. We blew up the ice and crossed over on the river bed, thus saving two to three hours.'

The Red Army's 26th Rifle Corps gained a foothold near Warka and the German defenders soon retreated towards Warsaw. The following day Zhukov's right flank attacked north of the city, while other forces pressed toward Warsaw from the south-west. The Soviets captured the airfield at Sochaczew, a town west of Warsaw, and within 24 hours the Red Air Force was operating from it.

The Warsaw garrison was cut off from 9th Army. Signals communications were also lost. Hitler designated Warsaw a 'fortress' and demanded that it be held to the last. He also belatedly decided that his forces should go over to the defensive on the Western Front so that reinforcements could be rushed east. However, faced with being trapped, the German garrison commander evacuated the city on 17 January. Before they left he attempted to blow up anything of use or value in a final needless spasm of wanton destruction.

Stalin gave the honour of liberating Warsaw to the communist Polish forces fighting as part of the Red Army. The Polish 1st Army with Zhukov was given the job of getting into the city. Its 6th Division crossed the Vistula near Praga while the Polish 2nd Division attacked from the north. The 6th Division was given covering fire by the Soviet 31st Special Armoured Train Artillery Battalion. Support was also provided by the Soviet 47th and 61st Armies and the Red Air Force.

By midday German troops had been cleared from the city centre. 'When we arrived, liberated Warsaw was looking majestic and sad, even tragic', wrote Vasily Grossman, 'City streets were filled with heaps of broken bricks.' He visited the remains of the ghetto and saw 'the wall, one and a half times the height of a man, made of red bricks, two bricks thick, with broken glass cemented along the top of it'. Inside he witnessed the flattened buildings and noted 'The Beast's anger was terrible'. Amidst the devastation just two Roman Catholic churches had been left standing.

In Berlin, Guderian observed, 'In the late afternoon officers of the Operations Department informed me of the constantly deteriorating situation on the Warsaw front and proposed the establishment of a new defensive line on the premise that Warsaw was already in enemy hands.' He then went to brief Hitler at the Chancellery. During their meeting a message arrived from the Warsaw commandant. According to Guderian it 'stated that the city was still in German hands but would have to be evacuated in the course of the coming night'.

'They could not possibly have held the city', said Guderian 'and would certainly have been taken prisoner if the commandant had obeyed Hitler's orders.' Hitler was furious. Guderian, however, noted that Warsaw was 'only of comparatively minor importance'. For the rest of the conference Hitler remained obsessed with Warsaw and largely ignored all other developments on the Eastern Front. In a fit of petulance, he then sacked the commanders of Army Group A and 9th Army and had three colonels from the General Staff arrested. To the north two Soviet armies overran 50 per cent of East Prussia and reached the Gulf of Danzig.

Losing interest in Poland, Hitler decided to move his SS 6th Panzer Army from the Ardennes to Hungary in a ridiculous effort to hold the oilfields there. He seemed oblivious to the impending destruction of Army Groups A and Centre plus the growing threat to the Oder. Guderian was flabbergasted, 'The efforts made in Hungary would have proved considerably more effective if carried out on Polish territory or in East Prussia ...' Nothing could stop the Red Army's advancing tanks now.

Chapter 17

The Road to Hungary

Hungary was also the scene of massed tank battles, involving this time the newly-formed 6th Guards Tank Army. Work on building up Budapest's defences against the Red Army had started in late September 1944, with the creation to the east of the Attila Line, in the north the Karola Line between the Cserhát, Mátra and Zemplén Hills and in the south-west with the Margit Line between the city and Lake Balaton. The Germans' eastern Pest bridgehead was protected by three semicircular defensive belts consisting of minefields, anti-tank ditches, barbed wire and earth bunkers.

The 2nd Ukrainian Front renewed its attempt on Budapest on 29 October 1944 and secured the southern approaches to the city by 2 November, but could get no further. A frontal attack on the city from the east was also fended off. The Soviets launched a fresh assault on 5 December, aiming to trap the city in a pincer movement. The Soviet 7th Guards and 6th Guards Tank Armies and Pliyev's mechanized cavalry group struck from the north-east, while the 46th Army attacked from the south-west. Four days later they had got as far as Sahy and the Danube to the north of the city. While the 46th Army got across the river it was at great cost and it still could not get through the defences to the south-west.

On 12 December 1944 the 2nd and 3rd Ukrainian Fronts were instructed to take Budapest. The 2nd Ukrainian Front on the left was to attack from Sahy southward to the Danube north of Esztergom, which would cut off any German retreat to the north-west. The 3rd Ukrainian Front was directed to move northward from Lake Velence and link up with the 2nd Ukrainian Front near Esztergom. This offensive commenced on 20 December and within six days the two fronts had met, finally encircling the Hungarian capital.

Budapest was completely cut off by the Red Army once the Budapest–Vienna road was severed. This trapped almost 43,000 German and 37,000 Hungarian troops, along with over 800,000 civilians. Forbidding any withdrawal, Hitler declared Budapest a *Festung* which was to be defended until the last. Hitler persisted until the end of the war with his fortress strategy. His rational was that reinforcements would cut their way through to a designated fortress, which could then be used as a springboard for a counteroffensive

Trapped in the Budapest Pocket was the 9th SS Mountain Corps, comprising the 8th SS Florian Geyer and 22nd SS Maria Theresia Cavalry Divisions, the 13th Panzer Division, the 60th Panzergrenadier Division 'Feldherrnhalle' with a handful of King Tigers and the 271st Volksgrenadier Division. Hungarian forces in the city included the 1st Armoured, 10th Mixed and 12th Reserve Divisions as well as elements of six assault artillery battalions and a number of armoured car units. The assault artillery was equipped with Hungarian-built Zrinyi and German-supplied StuG III assault guns. To the south of Budapest, the 18th SS Panzergrenadier Division Horst Wessel managed to escape.

Florian Geyer had started its career as a brigade conducting anti-partisan operations in the Soviet Union. In the summer of 1942 it was expanded to a division and the following year was deployed to Yugoslavia. Under the command of SS-Brigadeführer Joachim Rumhor, it saw action in Czechoslovakia in 1944 and then moved into Hungary. The Maria Theresia Division was essentially its bastard child, having been raised in Hungary in the spring and summer of 1944 under SS-Brigadeführer Zehender. It was formed around Florian Geyer's 17th SS Cavalry Regiment, supplemented by two regiments of Hungarian ethnic Germans. By the time the division went into action at Debrecen only the 17th and 52nd SS Cavalry Regiments had been assembled. In October they were joined by the 53rd SS Cavalry Regiment and the whole division fought in the Budapest area until encircled. Similarly, the 18th SS Panzergrenadier Division, which had been formed in early 1944, drew its recruits from the ethnic German community in Hungary.

The 13th Panzer Division had formed in Romania in October 1940, where it served as a training unit until June 1941. After fighting on the Eastern Front in Ukraine, the Caucasus and Kuban the division was withdrawn to Germany in September 1944 and sent to Hungary the following month. The three other panzer divisions committed to the Battle of Debrecen had since been redeployed. The 23rd Panzer Division was sent north to the Baranów bridgehead in Poland, and from December 1944 to January 1945 24th Panzer was in Slovakia before being sent to West Prussia. Only 1st Panzer remained in Hungary available to help, but on its own it was very unlikely to cut through to Budapest. Reinforcements were on their way from Poland comprising the 3rd Panzer Division and the 4th SS Panzer Corps with two tough SS panzer divisions.

The garrison commander, General Karl Pfeffer-Wildrenbruch, had started his career as a gunner and then a high-ranking policeman before joining the SS. At the start of the Second World War he had commanded the 4th SS Polizei Division before becoming a corps commander. In Budapest he lacked infantry with which to properly protect the city. Between them the two SS cavalry divisions could muster around 19,000 men with 46 tanks and assault guns. The SS units included a huge array of foreign 'volunteers' of dubious loyalty

By 28 December the Soviets were within 1.25 miles of the city west of the Danube after capturing János Hospital. They were also the same distance north-west of the German and Hungarian headquarters in the Buda Castle tunnel. Also at risk was Városmajor Grange. This was the most sensitive point in Buda because if it was captured the Soviets could reach the Castle Hill District and cut the garrison in half. Defence of the Grange was assigned to the Hungarian Volunteer Vannay Battalion.

The Vannay Battalion numbered 450 men supported by two 40mm guns, six 81mm mortars and two heavy anti-tank guns plus three guns of a Hungarian artillery battalion. The troops were initially deployed in the church within Városmajor Grange while their command was in Csaba Street to the south. The German defences were anchored on three points at the Cogwheel Railway embankment and the second and third within Városmajor Grange along Temes and Szamos Streets. The embankment was protected by machine-gun teams, mines and barbed wire with a lorry blocking the level crossing. The Grange was also mined in case the embankment was overrun. The local school and apartment blocks were turned into strongpoints.

Just before Budapest was cut off, on 24 December 1944 Hitler despatched the tough 4th SS Panzer Corps from the Warsaw area plus the 96th and 711th Infantry Divisions, totalling 60,000 men supported by 200 panzers, to Hungary. SS-Obergruppenführer Otto Grille, who had been decorated for breaking out of the Cherkassy Pocket at the start of the year, was placed in command. This immediately weakened German defences on the Vistula, enabling the Red Army to reach the Oder. Nonetheless this development signalled Hitler was intent on holding Budapest at all costs.

Inside Budapest Pfeffer-Wildrenbruch and the men of his 9th SS Mountain Corps were under siege and getting desperate. The Red Army shelled and bombed their positions and squeezed them into an ever-shrinking pocket. Ammunition, food and medical supplies were running low and they endured a miserable Christmas. The Luftwaffe attempted to airdrop supplies, but in the face of the Red Air Force and heavy flak this became increasingly difficult to accomplish. Their only hope was a New Year's present from the 4th SS Panzer Corps marshalling its forces to the west.

Hitler's intention was not so much to relieve the Budapest garrison but to reinforce it. On the table were two options – Operation Paula, which would strike from Székesfehérvár to the south-west of the city, or Operation Konrad from the north-west. Konrad offered the shortest route and, although the terrain was not ideal, was approved. The Hungarians offered their 1st Hussar Division, 2nd Armoured Division and 23rd Division to support Konrad, but these units were too exhausted to be of any real assistance. Instead just two battalions of the Hungarian Ney SS Combat Group were attached to the two SS panzer divisions. The 4th SS Panzer Corps, plus 1st Panzer Division, did have some opportunity of breaking through as initially they had 70 per cent more troops and 140 per cent more armour than the Soviet 4th Guards Army holding the outer ring, although the Soviets did enjoy a 3:1 superiority in artillery.

Operation Konrad I was launched on 1 January 1945 and saw 4th SS Panzer Corps strike from Tata north of Budapest; attacks were also conducted to the west of the city. Martin Steiger, commander of the 3rd SS Panzer Division's tank regiment, was in the thick of the bitter fighting. 'The attack began on 1 January 1945, at 6pm, without preparatory artillery fire. ...', Steiger recounts, adding, 'Enemy tanks of the type T-34/85 sat in the farms in town [Dunaalmas] and fired at our point vehicles from only five metres away.' Every step of the way his men met determined resistance.

The Soviet 6th Guards Army thwarted the first attempt launched from Komárno which had initially pushed the Soviets back along the right bank of the Danube. The 6th Guards were ordered to march down the left bank to Komárno, thereby compromising the Germans' flank and rear. The Soviets deployed four extra divisions and the German counter-attack was halted on a line Bicske–Mány–Zsámbék and by the 12th they were forced to withdraw, having got to within 15 miles of the city.

Despite Konrad I, the Soviets did not let up their pressure on the German-Hungarian defenders in Budapest. The Soviet 180th Rifle Division attacked Városmajor Grange on 1 January. After a heavy bombardment up to eight Soviet tanks and supporting infantry overran the Hungarian Vannay Battalion's machine guns. The Hungarians knocked out two tanks and retook the Cogwheel railway embankment. This they reinforced by incorporating the wrecked tanks into their defences and digging foxholes underneath them. The embankment remained in Hungarian hands until 19 January.

Determined to stop the German relief effort, Tolbukhin redeployed the 2nd Guards Mechanized Corps, plus the 49th and 86th Guards

Rifle Divisions, from their encirclement in Budapest on 3 January. The Soviet 46th Army was also instructed to halt its attacks and ensure that the garrison did not attempt a break-out. Key to preventing this was possession of Mátyás-hegy Hill, it changed hands seven times on 3 January.

Sashegy and Rózsadomb Hills were also fought over. The loss of the former, which dominated the southern part of the city, would have made Buda untenable. From Sashegy, Soviet spotters could have called down fire to destroy the defenders' artillery between the Citadel on Gellért Hill and Castle Hill and eliminate the emergency airfield on Vérmezo Meadow. On 12 January the Soviets made a dent in the Sashegy defensive line and three days later took the heights, only to be driven off by a counter-attack.

Between 1 and 7 January German and Hungarian losses totalled around 3,500, almost 10 per cent of the 4th SS Panzer Corps' strength, killed, wounded or missing, along with thirty-nine tanks and assault guns destroyed. Tolbukhin meantime had deployed defences blocking both the garrison and the relief force and on 3 January ordered attacks on Buda to stop in order to free up more troops. Three days later seven Soviet divisions were in place to prevent the garrison from breaking out. Despite the hopelessness of the situation, on 11 January 1945 Pfeffer-Wildrenbruch was awarded the Knight's Cross and on 1 February the Oak Leaves to it.

Desperate to open an air bridge to Budapest, the Germans tried to recapture Budapest airport. Konrad II was launched from Esztergom on 7 January, but again was halted just short of its objective at Pilisszentkereszt. Having failed to breach the Soviet lines to the north the Germans fell back on the southern option. Konrad III, the last part of the operation, commenced on 17 January with 4th SS Panzer Corps and 3rd Panzer Corps attacking from the south of Budapest near Székesfehérvár with the aim of trapping ten Soviet divisions against the Danube. Again this operation failed, with the Germans getting no closer than 12 miles from the city. It was brought to a halt at Zámoly north of Székesfehérvár with the loss of fifty-seven panzers.

During the second counter-attack, 100 panzers supported by two regiments of motorized infantry tried to punch through the Soviet 5th Guards Airborne Division. Eighteen panzers broke through only to run into the Soviet 1963rd Anti-Tank Regiment, which accounted for half of them. The Soviet 34th Guards Rifle Division also held fast despite everything that was thrown at it.

Hitler reluctantly agreed on the 17th to abandon low-lying Pest, in order to hold the hills of Buda. The garrison and the civilian population fled across the five Danube bridges, until the Germans brought them down the following day in the face of Hungarian objections. The SS ensconced themselves in the Citadel on Gellért Hill, while other units defended Buda Castle on Castle Hill, the city cemetery and Margaret Island. Soviet plans were distracted by a renewed German relief effort which was attempted on 20 January to the south of the city. General Balck, commander of the 6th Army, seeking to trap the Soviet divisions north of Lake Balaton summoned 4th SS Corps south to his assistance, but stiff Soviet resistance also thwarted this effort. This diversion of effort sealed the fate of Budapest's garrison.

Karl-Heinz Lichte was with the 5th SS Panzer Division Wiking when their attack was thwarted on 20 January 1945. He observed, 'A number of "Josef Stalin" tanks were spotted. The numerically vastly superior enemy bypassed us and attacked our flank. Then, the first of our panzers was knocked out.' Their commander was killed and Lichte ordered a withdrawal. 'At the same time I grasped a smoke grenade', he recalls, 'pulled and threw it to obstruct the enemy field of vision of our withdrawal. That very moment, there was an immense bang. I saw a bright flash, then darkness …'

'Counter-attacks began, and our attack had to be stopped …', continues Steiger of 3rd SS Panzer, 'The expected enemy tank attack deep into our flanks took place on 29 January from Vertes Aska. It started a huge tank battle near Pettend. Some 200 enemy tanks were knocked out. The enemy attacks increased on 30 January. We could no longer hold our positions and withdrew westward on both sides of the Velence Lake.'

This third attack, launched from north of Lake Balaton, proved to be the most threatening. The Germans quickly reached the Danube near Dunapentele on the western bank of the river and cut the 3rd Ukrainian Front in two. To counter this, reinforcements had to be transferred from the 2nd Ukrainian Front. From these two combat groups were formed and they counter-attacked north and south of the German breakthrough on 27 January. Ten days later they had restored the outer ring.

General Gustav Harteneck, commander of the German Army's 1st Cavalry Corps, bitterly recalled their role in the relief effort,

> While the Corps was still in the process of being transferred, we were once again ordered to take up stationary positions, to our great disappointment. The cavalry divisions of the Waffen-SS were fighting in the metropolis of Budapest. Every cavalryman knows that no good could come of that, and, as it turned out, nothing did. The SS divisions were encircled ... My Cavalry Corps launched a night attack in an attempt to relieve them, but it was too late, and the Russian forces were too powerful. Although we managed to fight out way to the city limits, only 100 or so cavalrymen, under the command of the famous rider Staff Colonel von Mitzlaff, were able to break through to us. The subsequent battles, in the course of which my Corps was under the command of 6th SS Panzer Army, might have turned out quite differently had the two SS cavalry divisions been deployed to full advantage as cavalry divisions, instead of being ordered to hold Budapest.

The Konrad operations cost the German and Hungarian relief forces a total of around 35,000 men. This figure comprised around 8,000 dead, 26,000 wounded and about 1,000 captured.

Chapter 18

Tanks in Budapest

After two days, the Red Army captured Budapest's southern railway station on 10 February 1945 and this allowed them to push up toward Castle Hill. The defenders of Gellért Hill, holding the Citadel fortress, successfully repulsed several Soviet attacks until the following day, when a three-pronged assault seized the feature. Soviet artillery was quickly moved on to the hill, which enabled them to dominate the entire city. This made movement for the Germans and Hungarians very dangerous. In Buda Castle and the palace complex the remains of the trapped garrison continued to refuse to surrender.

General Pfeffer-Wildrenbruch gathered his officers on Castle Hill early on 11 February and it was decided they would run the gauntlet of the Soviet tank cordon and try to escape. It was an almost impossible task as Soviet troops were in the area around Széll Kálmán Square and Széna Square. Just before Pfeffer-Wildrenbruch decided to break out the Soviet 180th Guards Rifle Division had deployed to Széll Kálmán and Olasz Avenue supported by T-34 tanks dug in along Bimbó Road and at János Hospital. The road between Tinnye and Perbál was cut by another Soviet tank unit in the Dorog area. In addition, all the civilians living around Széll Kálmán Square and the immediate streets were evacuated ready to meet any anticipated break-out.

Pfeffer-Wildrenbruch's plan was that the first wave comprising the 8th SS on the right and the 13th Panzer on the left would leave at 2000 hours. They were to be divided into groups of thirty each led by a Hungarian guide. The second wave would consist of the 22nd SS and the Feldherrnhalle panzergrenadiers and the Hungarian units. The attack on Széll Kálmán Square and Széna Square was to drive the Soviets from their positions along Margit Boulevard for a distance of 1km. From there they would drive all out for the fork of Hidegkúti Road and Budakeszi Road some 2.5km north-west of Széna Square. From Remete-hegy Hill it was hoped to escape westward into the nearby forests and on to Tinnye. Their Hungarian allies were not to be informed until the last minute for fear of betrayal.

Pfeffer-Wildrenbruch had left it far too late, as the garrison was exhausted, starving and discipline was at breaking point. Morale was understandably at rock bottom. If they had been in the countryside and discipline could have been maintained, they might have fought their way through, but in the confines of the city the men would be quickly divided up as they sought different routes and could therefore be easily picked off. In Széll Kálmán and Széna Squares the fleeing troops were illuminated by Soviet flares and met by machine-gun and mortar fire. Although some broke through the Soviet 180th Guards positions' they were halted with heavy losses 2.5km along Olasz Avenue. Széna Square remained dominated by Soviet machine guns and anti-tank guns and many of those fleeing became casualties or were paralysed by fear.

General Gerhard Schmidhuber, commander of 13th Panzer Division, got across Széna Square only to be killed in Retek Street. SS-Brigadeführer August Zehender, commander of the 22nd SS Cavalry Division, fared no better. A grenade took off his right leg and he promptly committed suicide. The streets became strewn with badly-injured men pleading to be put out of their misery rather than be captured.

Elements of the Soviet 297th Rifle Division, who were deployed in Virányos Road, were confronted early in the morning by an enemy column numbering up to 2,000 men taking up the whole width of the street. The Germans were running and firing into the windows and throwing hand grenades as they went. Soviet troops fired their weapons into this dense mass and a 120cm mortar began to drop bombs into the column, adding to the carnage. In neighbouring Szarvas Gábor Street a German light tank desperately sought cover until a Soviet anti-tank weapon knocked it out. The surviving Germans ran on and straight into Soviet multiple rocket launchers firing at point-blank range. Everywhere the fleeing garrison was massacred.

The Soviet 37th Rifle Corps blocked the escape route towards the western end of the Buda Hills. The Germans desperately tried to break out to the west and north-west towards Zugliget and Nagykovácsi. The Soviets claimed 16,000 German and Hungarian troops broke through the inner encirclement to reach the nearby woods. On the eastern edge of Nagykovácsi the Soviet 19th Rifle Division was redeployed to Heights 262 and 544 to stop the enemy coming out of the woods. The Soviet 11th Cavalry Division then hunted down those hiding amongst the trees.

The Red Army had secured Széll Kálmán Square, which was littered with dead, and parts of the Castle District by the afternoon of 12 February. It took them until noon the following day to move along Olasz Avenue as far as János Hospital. Up to 5,000 men, mainly Hungarians, had been left behind in the Castle District either because they did not get the order to run, or the fight had simply gone out of them. In the tunnels underneath Buda Castle and the vault of the National Bank several thousand wounded had also been left behind.

The few who were fortunate to break through the Soviet cordons had a panic-stricken flight that involved ducking and diving from Red Army units intent on their destruction. All around them their comrades were ambushed and slaughtered. During the night of 12 February the first group reached safety at the Szomor Catholic cemetery. They numbered just twenty-three soldiers, three German officers and a Hungarian officer. SS-Hauptsturmführer Joachim Boosfeld and a companion reached Remete-hegy Hill and joined a group of 100 mainly German soldiers. Early on the 13th they got to the front line. Tantalisingly they could see German positions but were given no covering fire. Just ten to twenty of them crossed over, many of the others being shot by Soviet snipers.

Lieutenant Colonel Helmut Wolff, commander of the Feldherrnhalle Panzergrenadier Division, and Major Wilhelm Schöning, acting commander of the 13th Panzer Division, led the largest group of up to 400 men. On 13 February they got to the forest above Nagykovácsi and fought their way to the German 3rd Cavalry Brigade. They then spilt up into smaller groups to fight through Soviet blocking positions. Wounded in the legs, Schöning called on one of his officers to put him out of his misery. Instead two wounded panzergrenadiers hauled him to the German lines. Wolff also managed to escape. Just 624 men reached their destination by 16 February 1945.

Pfeffer-Wildrenbruch fled through the sewers only to emerge into the midst of the Red Army. He was badly wounded and taken prisoner. Elsewhere his men were mown down and only 800 men ever reached German lines. The vengeful Soviets annihilated both SS divisions in the city. During the break-out General Rumohr, commander of the 8th SS Cavalry Division, was wounded and took his own life rather than face capture; just 170 of his men escaped.

Pfeffer-Wildrenbruch would have been better ordering his garrison to surrender rather than break out as this may have saved more lives. Groups in their hundreds and in some cases in their thousands were cut down by the Soviets as they charged through the shattered city desperately seeking to escape. He had 43,900 men under his command on 11 February; four days later 17,000 had been killed and 22,350 captured. Up to 3,000 tried hiding in the surrounding hills but they had been caught by 17 February. To deal with the dead large pyres were built and mass graves dug. Some Soviet soldiers went on the rampage, looting and raping.

Taking Hungary and Budapest cost the Red Army 70,000 dead and over 200,000 wounded and sick. The German and Hungarian armies lost up to 140,000 killed, wounded and captured, while 40,000 civilian perished. Eighty per cent of the city lay in ruins. The Red Army anticipated a trouble-free push through the rest of Hungary to the Austrian capital Vienna, Hitler planned otherwise.

In late January 1945 SS-Oberstgruppenführer (General) Sepp Dietrich, commander of the 6th SS Panzer Army, was summoned to Berlin, where he saw Army Chief of Staff, General Heinz Guderian. They both agreed that all available troops should be sent immediately to defend the Oder. The Red Army was already over the river at Wriezen near Küstrin, a mere 45 miles from Berlin. They got 100 tanks across before the Germans moved to seal off the developing bridgehead. The anticipated Soviet offensive toward Berlin would not be for another two and half months, giving the defenders a much-needed breathing space. Guderian meantime wanted the occupying divisions redeployed from Kurland, Italy, Yugoslavia, Norway and Denmark to protect Berlin. He also argued that the 6th SS's armour was desperately needed on the Oder. But Hitler had other plans for Dietrich and his panzers in Hungary.

Ten panzer and five infantry divisions were to attack between Lake Balaton and Lake Velence to split Tolbukhin's 3rd Ukrainian Front in two. Dubbed Operation Spring Awakening, Hitler was convinced if the Soviets were caught by surprise it would be their undoing. To this end secrecy was taken to extremes and reconnaissance of the attack routes was forbidden lest it tip the Soviets off. Not only was the offensive relying on surprise, but also the weather to carry it through. It would take a severe frost to ensure the marshy ground around Lake Balaton would take the weight of Dietrich's panzers, especially the massive Tiger II.

Under Army Group South's direction, the 6th SS Panzer Army and 6th Army, supported by the Hungarian 3rd Army, were to strike between the lakes, while the 4th SS Panzer Corps held the Margarethe defences around Balaton. The German 8th Army north of Budapest was to remain on the defensive. At the same time Army Group South's 2nd Panzer Army, equipped only with assault guns, would employ its four infantry divisions to attack in an easterly direction south of Balaton. This was to be coordinated with a supplementary attack by General Lohr's Army Group E in Yugoslavia, which was to launch three divisions from the direction of the Drava to link up with 6th SS Panzer Army.

In total the German-Hungarian forces destined to assault Tolbukhin's troops amounted to about 30 divisions, 12 of them armoured plus other supporting formations, numbering 431,000 men,

5,630 guns and mortars, and 877 tanks and assault guns supported by 850 aircraft. The main strike force numbered almost 150,000 men, 807 tanks and assault guns and over 3,000 guns and mortars. This was a remarkable achievement considering the catalogue of defeats Hitler had suffered since 1943 and that the war would be over within two months.

In theory this pincer offensive was to crush Tolbukhin's 3rd Ukrainian Front. This consisted of five Soviet field armies, 4th Guards, 26th, 27th and 57th plus the 1st Bulgarian Army, supported by 17th Air Army. The 9th Guards Army formed the reserve southeast of Budapest. This had only been formed in January 1945 under the command of General V.V. Glagolev. It comprised three Guards rifle divisions plus supporting units. To the north Marshal Malinovsky's 2nd Ukrainian Front stretched from Zvolen to the river Hron (a northern tributary of the Danube) in Hungary. The Soviets received intelligence from the British Military Mission on 12 February that 6th SS Panzer Army had moved east from the Western Front following the abortive Ardennes offensive.

On 17 February 1945, Malinovsky and Tolbukhin were ordered to prepare their own offensive that would destroy German Army Group South, drive it from Hungary, deprive the Germans of the Nagykanizsa oilfields, occupy Vienna and threaten southern Germany. This move would also threaten German forces operating in Yugoslavia and Italy. The Soviet offensive was to open on 15 March: little did they know that Hitler was about to pre-empt them.

The 6th SS Panzer Army fielded six panzer divisions, two infantry divisions and two cavalry divisions as well as two heavy tank battalions equipped with about sixty Tigers IIs. The 6th Army had five panzer divisions and three infantry divisions, and the 3rd Hungarian Army had one tank division, two infantry divisions and a cavalry division. On paper 6th SS Panzer Army was a formidable formation that included four veteran SS panzer divisions, with the 1st SS and 12th SS grouped into the 1st SS Panzer Corps and the 2nd SS and 9th SS formed the 2nd SS Panzer Corps. In reality these units had been exhausted during the Ardennes offensive. The Hungarian 2nd Armoured Division, equipped with Hungarian-built Turán medium tanks, was considered inadequate for offensive operations and only a single Hungarian infantry division was placed under Dietrich's command.

The Germans enjoyed a local 2:1 superiority in tanks, the Soviet forces in Hungary being weak in armour, which meant anti-tank guns would be their main defence against the 900 panzers and assault guns about to be thrown at them. Soviet anti-tank gunners were particularly contemptuous of the Panzer IV, which they considered antiquated.

Tolbukhin was ordered to hold the Germans while the Red Army prepared its own offensive. His men established three main defensive lines of considerable depth. He had 407,000 men under his command equipped with 407 tanks and self-propelled guns, 7,000 guns and mortars and 965 aircraft. Soviet suspicions regarding the direction of the Hitler's attempts to stop them were confirmed on 2 March, when Hungarian deserters told their captors of a German assault due in three days' time in the Balaton-Velence sector. Fully prepared, Tolbukhin sat back and awaited the enemy offensive.

The 1st SS Panzer Corps struck the 7th Guards holding the Hron bridgehead on 17 February 1945 with up to 150 tanks and assault guns. Seven days later the Soviets were driven back, with the loss of 8,800 men and most of their equipment. However, this victory cost the Germans 3,000 casualties and confirmed to the Soviets that a major counteroffensive was looming. Although 1st SS Panzer Corps' preliminary attack got off to a good start by destroying the Soviet bridgehead around Esztergom, once Tolbukhin had established the attack was being conducted by Hitler's elite it was obvious what was happening. When Hitler's Spring Awakening commenced the Soviets were already very well awake to the threat.

On the morning of 6 March 1945, after a 30-minute artillery bombardment supported by the Luftwaffe, the 6th SS Panzer and 6th Army crashed into Tolbukhin's defences. As planned, the Germans launched a furious three-pronged offensive, with 6th SS Panzer

Army striking in a south-easterly direction between Lakes Velence and Balaton. The 2nd Panzer Army stuck eastward in the direction of Kaposvar while Army Group E attacked north-east from the right bank of the Davra with the aim of uniting with Dietrich.

The Hungarian plain between the northern extremity of Balaton and the Danube was not good tank country, because it was bisected by canals and drainage ditches. Dietrich was furious with General Wohler who had given assurances that the ground in front of his two panzer corps was passable. The mud claimed 132 tanks and 15 Tiger IIs, which sank up to their turrets. To make matters worse 2nd SS Panzer Corps found itself in a sea of mud and penetrated the Soviet defences to a depth of just five miles, although 1st SS Panzer Corps made much better progress with 25 miles.

General N.A. Gagen's 26th Army and elements of the 1st Guards Fortified Area (part of the 4th Guards Army) bore the brunt of the assault. In response a Soviet artillery group of 160 field guns and mortars was established to provide 26th Army with massed covering fire. During the opening day General Sudet's 17th Air Army also flew 358 sorties, of which 227 were directed at the exposed panzers. A huge and furious battle followed as each side brought their well-honed tactics to bear.

The 2nd SS Panzer Division joined the fight with 250 tanks on 8 March, followed by the 9th SS the next day, bringing the total of panzers committed to the battle up to 600. However, Dietrich was rapidly running out of time and resources. On 11 March he contacted Hitler's headquarters, requesting permission to call off Spring Awakening, and repeated his request three days later. His pleas to save his command from complete destruction fell on deaf ears. The 6th Panzer Division, with 200 tanks and self-propelled guns, Spring Awakening's last reserves, were thrown into a desperate push for the Danube on 14 March. They attacked resolutely for two days and almost reached the Soviet's rear defence line, but Tolbukhin's men held fast. Although the 9th Guards Army was moved south-west of Budapest, Tolbukhin was under strict instructions not to employ it in his defensive operations. It was to remain held ready for the deadly counter-blow.

Just as Hitler's Ardennes offensive had expended the last of his military resources on the Western Front, so Spring Awakening exhausted his remaining strength on the Eastern Front. By 15 March 1945 Sepp Dietrich had lost over 500 panzers and assault guns, 300 guns and 40,000 men battering themselves to death against the Soviets' well-prepared defences. Using the excuse of defending Vienna, he tried to save his shattered forces.

Elsewhere Hitler's master plan also come unstuck. The 2nd Panzer Army's attack launched east of Nagykanizsa was broken up by Soviet artillery fire. Similarly, Army Group E, which attacked the 1st Bulgarian Army and 3rd Yugoslav Army on the night of 6 March, was soon driven back across the Drava by massed Soviet artillery.

Soviet intelligence must have known that with the commitment of the 6th Panzer Division the Germans had exhausted their last reserves in Hungary. It had been touch and go, but the Soviet 9th Guards Army had not been needed to plug any holes in the Soviets' final defences. It meant that when Tolbukhin lunched his own offensive the Germans would have nothing left with which to counter-attack.

Whilst Spring Awakening slowed the Soviet attack on Vienna, ultimately it did not greatly affect their plans, although the main axis off their forthcoming offensive was now moved south of the Danube to Tolbukhin's command. He was still weak in tanks, which numbered just 200, while the mauled German panzer units could still scrape together some 270 tanks and self-propelled guns. To bolster Tolbukhin's attack, the 6th Guards Army from Malinovsky's command joined him, bringing with it 406 tanks and self-propelled guns. Their job was the final destruction of the remnants of Dietrich's 6th SS Panzer Army. Two infantry armies, the 9th Guards and 4th Guards, were assigned the task of cutting the German armour off.

The Soviets launched their counterstroke on 16 March along the entire front west of Budapest. The weight of the attack fell on General Balck's 6th Army and the Hungarian 3rd Army north of Lake Velence.

Soviet tanks and motorized infantry poured through the breach, which 12th SS Panzer Division was hastily sent to seal. The Soviets swung in a south-westerly direction toward Lake Balaton.

Instead of throwing the Red Army back in disarray, 6th SS Panzer Army and 6th Army found themselves in danger of being cut off and a huge tank battle ebbed and flowed around Lake Balaton. In a repeat of the disaster at Stalingrad, Hitler's forces were once again let down by their Eastern Front allies. The inadequately-equipped Hungarians on the left flank of 2nd SS Panzer Corps defected, with inevitable results. The skeletal Hungarian 3rd Army withdrew west, losing the 1st Hussar Division near Budapest. Its remaining divisions including the 2nd Armoured eventually surrendered to American forces in Austria.

Under pressure, the 1st SS Panzer Division gave ground, exposing Balck's flank. Six days after the Soviet counteroffensive commenced 6th SS Panzer was faced with complete encirclement south of Székesfehérvár, with just a mile-wide escape corridor that was already under heavy enemy fire. Four panzer divisions and an infantry division fought desperately to keep the Soviet pincers apart and 6th SS Panzer Army only just managed to escape. Against orders Dietrich retreated and when Hitler was informed he flew into a rage.

By 25 March 1945 Malinovsky's offensive had torn a 60-mile wide gap in the German defences and penetrated more than 20 miles. He then prepared to strike toward Bratislava. Hungary was lost. In the meantime, 6th SS Panzer Army and 6th Army attempted to hold the River Raab, south of Vienna, and Lake Neusiedler against Tolbukhin's troops. The Soviets crossed on 28 March and brushed aside the exhausted defenders. By the end of the month up to 45,000 German and Hungarian soldiers had surrendered. Vienna now lay open to the Red Army. Once more Hitler was incensed. Austrian by birth, he knew the implications of his defeat in Hungary.

Chapter 19

Beneath the Brandenburg Gate

All of Stalin's tank armies played a prominent role in the defeat of Nazi Germany in the closing months of the war. Hitler's intelligence was well informed of Stalin's intentions in early 1945. This indicated that his assault would commence on 12 January, with a superiority of 11:1 in infantry and 7:1 in tanks. An evaluation of Stalin's total strength gave him a superiority of approximately 15:1 on the ground and 20:1 in the air. Such forces could only be overwhelming.

Stalin launched his Vistula-Oder Offensive as predicted, which took the Red Army from the Vistula in Poland to the Oder east of Berlin. The two million men of Zhukov's 1st Byelorussian and Konev's 1st Ukrainian Fronts, supported by 4,529 tanks and 2,513 assault guns, simply overpowered the 400,000 troops of Army Group A supported by 1,150 panzers. After 23 days they tore a breach 625 miles wide by 375 miles deep and swept across the Oder.

By the end of the first week of February the Germans' Oder defences in Silesia had collapsed and the Red Army was beyond the left flank of the Upper Silesian front. On the night of 12 February Soviet troops came together in the Tinz-Domslau area, encircling Breslau. The key point in this battle occurred on the 13th, when the 19th Panzer Division in the Kostomloty area held open the autobahn to enable two infantry divisions to escape. That night the 7th Guards Tank Corps succeeded in sealing off the rest of the garrison. By 15 February Soviet forces had surrounded Breslau as the 3rd Guards Tank Army closed the gap to the west.

Striking from Greiffenberg, 8th Panzer made a surprise attack three days later against the southern wing of the Soviets advancing from Löwenberg to Lauban. Although they slowed them, on the 28th

Lauban fell to the 3rd Guards Tank Army, allowing them to prepare to move on Görlitz and Dresden. The Germans counter-attacked with elements of 8th, 16th and 17th Panzer, knocking out 230 Soviet tanks and halting the advance.

It was not until early March that the Germans attempted to relieve Breslau, gathering seven divisions including four panzer divisions in the Gorlitz area. On 3 March they attacked the weak 3rd Guards Tank Army, but after fierce fighting the attack was halted with both sides suffering heavy casualties. Stalin sought to clear the rest of Silesia with the Upper Silesian Offensive conducted from 15 to 31 March 1945. Konev launched his main assault with the 4th Guards Tank Army piercing the German lines west of Oppeln and heading southward for Neustadt. South-east of Oppeln, the Soviets also broke through the German defences, swinging westwards to link up with the 4th Guards Tank Army. By the 22nd the Soviets had crushed the Oppeln 'cauldron', claiming to have killed 15,000 Germans and captured another 15,000.

By early 1945 Hitler's panzer forces were on their last legs, but were determined to put up one last fight against Stalin's coming assault on Berlin. As ever, Hitler remained obsessed with launching counter-attacks using formations that were little more than flags on a map. Zhukov arrived in Moscow on 29 March to discuss his plans. His intelligence indicated that Hitler had four armies in the region with no less than ninety divisions, remarkably including fourteen panzer and motorized divisions. However, from the very beginning the battle was a one-sided affair. In total the Red Army fielded two and half million troops, equipped with some 6,250 tanks. Zhukov was able to hurl almost a million men of the 1st Belorussian Front against Berlin's outer defences anchored on the Seelow Heights.

In his path lay about 100,000 exhausted troops of General Theodor Busse's 9th Army, which formed part of Army Group Vistula. He defended the front which encompassed the Seelow Heights. In total 9th Army had fourteen divisions with 512 panzers, 344 artillery pieces and 300 anti-aircraft guns. Further south the front was held by the exhausted 4th Panzer Army, tasked with fending off the vengeful 1st Ukrainian Front. General Weidling, commanding the 56th Panzer Corps, observed the sheer weight of Zhukov's attack: 'On 16 April, in the first hours of the offensive the Russians broke through on the right flank of the 101st Army Corps on the sector of Division Berlin, thereby threatening the left flank of the 56th Panzer Corps.'

Coordination of the Seelow assault proved chaotic, however. Signals traffic overwhelmed the decoders and Zhukov, desperate for results, continually meddled. He needed to take the heights that morning to allow the breakthrough to encircle Berlin otherwise Konev would get the credit. He soon discovered he had completely underestimated the strength of the defences. General Mikhail Katukov, commander of the Soviet 1st Guards Tank Army, was ordered to bludgeon his way through the Germans on the heights. However, throwing the 1st and 2nd Guards Tank Armies into the fight did not immediately have the desired effect. The original plan was that they would exploit the breakthrough, not achieve it. Lacking space and due to the swampy ground, the tanks had to use the roads which were already packed with infantry. This created major traffic jams and provided the German anti-tank gunners with prime targets. Predictably German artillery caught the Soviet tanks in the open. Even when the tanks did reach the escarpment they found the gradient too steep and were knocked out in great numbers. The 65th Guards Tank Brigade, Katukov's vanguard, found the going tough and the defenders desperately clung onto their positions. South-east of Seelow his armour ran into Tigers of the 502nd SS Heavy Panzer Battalion.

Despite the stubborn resistance Katukov gained a foothold on the heights. The 9th Army weathered three days of preliminary attacks and then spent 24 hours enduring the full force of Zhukov's assault. They knocked out over 150 Soviet tanks but the 1st Belorussian Front smashed through the final defences of the Seelow Heights, leaving little in the way of effective resistance between the Soviets and Berlin. The Germans lost some 11,000 killed while the Red Army suffered

30,000. All that remained to defend Berlin itself were about 45,000 troops.

According to Soviet figures there were just 200 panzers facing the British and American forces in the West, while there were 1,500 protecting Berlin; this estimate was wildly inaccurate. The Red Army assaulted Berlin itself on 21 April 1945. It threw its tanks into a massive assault to encircle the beleaguered Nazi capital; the Germans in stark contrast had fewer than 650 panzers to defend it. Amongst the attacking forces were powerful IS-2 heavy tanks of the 11th Tank Corps, which formed part of the 2nd Guards Tank Army. However, the armour on both the IS-1 and IS-2 was found to be vulnerable at long range because of faulty casting. Even if it withstood the impact of a German round it had a nasty tendency to splinter, wounding the crew.

Units of the 2nd Guards Tank, 3rd Assault and 47th Armies were committed to the attacks on the outskirts of Berlin and four days later the city was assaulted from the south-east by General Berzarin's 5th Shock Army and General Katukov's 1st Guards Tank Army. Along the northern bank of the Teltow Canal facing Rybalko's 3rd Guards Tank Army were some 15,000 men with 130 tanks. Crouching behind their T-34s, ISs and self-propelled guns the Soviets battled their way along Berlin's streets as the final battle was played out.

Despite being on the brink of victory, the T-34s and SU-85/100s did not have it all their own way. On the streets of Berlin, the T-34 crews were not only confronted by panzers and anti-tank weapons, but also mines, petrol bombs and tank-buster teams, often recruited from impressionable Hitler Youth armed with Panzerfausts. The latter made use of the city's tunnels and sewers to pop up and catch unwary tankers. At street junctions T-34 crews were caught by emplaced 75mm and 88mm anti-tanks guns and mines or had petrol bombs dropped on them from the surrounding buildings.

To avoid ambushes, Soviet tanks often shelled or simply drove through buildings, bringing them crashing down along with the defenders and any cowering residents. Also ISU-122 and ISU-152 heavy self-propelled guns were used to blast buildings at point-blank range. Escape for the Germans became almost impossible. During the desperate fighting German troops succeeded in breaking through the Soviet encirclement twice, though on both occasions they were stopped. In the Beelitz area 30,000 German soldiers almost reached General Wenck's 12th Army, which had been sent from the Western Front to help Berlin. Konev claimed only 4,000 men got through, the rest being killed or captured.

On 26 April Chuikov's 8th Guards Army and the 1st Guards Tank Army fought their way through the southern suburbs and attacked Tempelhof Airport, just inside the S-Bahn defensive ring. The Soviets commenced shelling the Reich Chancellery building (Hitler was sheltering in the adjacent bunker built in the gardens), that very night. The Red Army was less than a mile away from its final destination. By the 27th the T-34s and their accompanying infantry were at Potsdamer Platz just a few hundred yards from Hitler's bunker. Inside he was still waiting for General Walther Wenck's 12th Army, which was fighting on the Elbe. to come to the relief of Berlin. With no prospect of help, on 30 April Hitler committed suicide. Shortly after Germany surrendered. The T-34's final moment of triumph came when T-34/85 crews stopped before Berlin's Brandenburg Gate to have their photographs taken.

Hitler's few remaining panzers tried to flee the following day. The Soviets, suspecting they were carrying fleeing Nazi officials, destroyed them 10 miles north-west of the shattered city. At that point the German garrison surrendered. The Red Army claimed it lost 2,156 tanks and self-propelled guns taking Berlin and that it captured over 1,500 panzers and assault guns. During the course of the entire war the Red Army lost a staggering 96,500 tanks and self-propelled guns.

Stalin's very last armoured assault of the war was the Prague Offensive conducted after Berlin had been overwhelmed. Fought from 6 to 11 May 1945, it culminated in the liberation of the Czech capital by the 3rd and 4th Guards Tank Armies. The 1st Ukrainian Front struck west of Dresden and through the Erzeberg mountain passes in south-east Germany. The two tank armies then rolled relentlessly toward Prague, supported by tank offensives conducted by the 2nd and 4th Ukrainian Fronts. Army Group Centre, which had been at the very heart of Operation Barbarossa and Hitler's dream of capturing Moscow, fought to the very last. It did not surrender in Czechoslovakia until nine days after the capture of Berlin and three whole days after Victory in Europe Day. The 4th Guards linked up with the US 3rd Army east of Pilsen on 11 May, finally bringing to an end the Red Army's major field operations.

Chapter 20

Heroes of Socialist Labour

On the eve of Hitler's invasion, Stalin possessed thousands of fast and light tanks that needed replacing by an uparmoured and upgunned tank. At the time there were just two contenders for the crown: in Leningrad, Zhosif Kotin's team were working on the KV heavy tank, while in Kharkov, Mikhail Koshkin and his colleagues were developing the T-34 medium tank. Hitler had no heavy tanks in 1940, which meant that Kotin was offering Stalin a much-needed advantage. He and his supporters argued that their heavy breakthrough tank would slice through the enemy's lines with impunity, meaning that it did not greatly matter what type of tank was exploiting the breakthrough as the hard work had already been done. The reality was that the speed of Hitler's Blitzkrieg almost sealed the KV's fate as it was swiftly outmanoeuvred by the panzers.

What Koshkin did in the late 1930s was to create a good all-rounder that made a heavy tank largely superfluous to requirements. However, in terms of design the T-34/85 was the end of the road for his creation. The SU-100 tank destroyer with its 100mm gun was as far as the T-34 could go with the size of its armament and even this was far from perfect. Kotin very nearly saw his KV consigned to the scrapheap after his tank's poor showing in 1941. The much-maligned KV actually had several things to recommend it, but it only stayed in front-line service until 1943 and very few of the upgunned KV-85 were produced. In contrast the T-34 fought all the way to Berlin.

Nonetheless, it was Kotin who paved the way for the Soviet Union's future main battle tanks with the redesign of his KV chassis. Most notably he produced some of the Second World War's most potent tank killers with his ISU self-propelled guns and the KV-85 and

IS-1/IS-2 Joseph Stalin heavy tanks which were armed with massive 152mm and 122mm guns. These would eventually give rise to the T-54 and T-62, which dominated the Cold War, but Kotin's late-war heavy tanks were never produced in such decisive numbers as the T-34.

The ISU and IS totalled about 8,000 vehicles. Thanks to Armaments Minister Vannikov and his factories some 60,000 T-34s of all types were built. For his part, Vannikov did such a good job for the Soviet war effort that he remained Armaments Minister until 1962. He was awarded the highest civilian honour, Hero of Socialist Labour, three times, as well as the State Stalin Prize First Class twice. In recognition of his contribution, Mikhail Koshkin was posthumously awarded the State Stalin Prize in 1942 and the Order of the Red Star. Just before the collapse of the Soviet Union in 1990 he was posthumously made a Hero of Socialist Labour.

The summer of 1941 was a complete disaster for Stalin's armoured and mechanized forces. Hitler's highly experienced panzertruppen ran circles round Stalin's bewildered tankers. His massive tank force, albeit most of them obsolete, just vanished from the Red Army's order of battle and were knocked out, abandoned or trapped in the vast pockets created by the Wehrmacht's highly effective blitzkrieg. They knew the T-34 was too few in numbers and its crews too inexperienced to make any difference to the overall outcome of the battle. Engine and transmission problems and a lack of ammunition also compounded their woes. The Germans photographed T-34s overturned, driven into each other, into rivers and into marshes after the novice crews had desperately sought to escape the attentions of the Luftwaffe, German artillery and the panzers.

Equally shaming for the Red Army was the fact that some of these mishaps had occurred as the crews, with no understanding of the T-34's capabilities, attempted to move into position to counter-attack. There was a no more humiliating sight than the Soviet Union's latest battle tank needlessly up to its hull in water the engine flooded. Some might have argued that this was a criminal waste and indeed some generals paid for their ineptitude in front of a firing squad.

The one thing the Soviets learned from the disastrous tank battles fought in 1941 was the imperative of having well-trained tank crews. The tank units' fighting capabilities were a combination of the quality of the tank, crew training as well as tactical training, and logistical support. While the workers in the Soviet Union's tank factories strove to keep increasing their output, the tank training schools had to keep up with the demand for new crews.

After the Soviet Union's tank factories had been relocated out of reach of the enemy, tank training regiments were co-located at Chelyabinsk, Nizhniy Tagil and Sverdlovsk. Tank schools were also located at Kurgan, Ufa, Ulyanovsk and Saratov. Soviet crews normally spent up to eight weeks receiving basic training with a tank training battalion. They were then sent to a tank training regiment near one of the factories. These regiments could produce about 2,000 crew a month, but many of the men were often diverted to the factories, which were constantly short of labour. Once issued with their tanks a march company of about ten vehicles conducted firing trials and then proceeded to the nearest railhead. The company was then shipped to the front to join its assigned tank battalion.

During the battles of 1941–2 the inexperienced tank crews paid a heavy price. Those who survived the fierce winter battles of 1942–3 formed an important battle-hardened cadre who would make all the difference at Kursk. One man who acted as an inspiration and a shining light in those dark days was Senior Lieutenant Dimitry Fyodorovich Lavrinenko serving with the 1st Guards Tank Brigade, 15th Tank Division. During 1941 he showed just what could be achieved with the T-34/76 if used properly and he became the highest-scoring Allied tank ace of the war. Reportedly of Kuban Cossack stock, Lavrinenko completed his crew training in May 1938 at the Ulyanovsk Tank Academy. He subsequently took part in the invasions of eastern Poland in 1939 and Bessarabia the following year. This gave him and his comrades some idea of the capabilities of the T-26 and BT-7.

At the time of Barbarossa, Lavrinenko's unit had been equipped with the T-34/76. He managed to employ the tank to its full potential and in the space of two and a half months of fighting the Nazi invaders he destroyed fifty-two panzers. Lavrinenko's mounting tally was only curtailed when he was killed on 18 December 1941 at the age of 27. While his victories were actually small compared to German tank aces, such as Michael Wittmann who managed 138 tanks and self-propelled guns, Lavrinenko's total was not surpassed by any other Allied tanker. For his achievements he was posthumously awarded the title of Hero of the Soviet Union on 5 May 1990. Even if Soviet propagandists had inflated Lavrinenko's success, he had shown the way with the T-34 – in the right hands it was a panzer killer.

The sheer number of T-34s produced inevitably meant that were a very large number of other tanks aces. Lavrinenko's nearest rivals were half a dozen T-34 commanders who included First Lieutenant Vladimir Alexeyevich Bochkovsky who also fought with the 1st Guards Tank Brigade and chalked up thirty-six kills, which included other armoured fighting vehicles. He achieved this first with the T-34/76 and then the T-34/85. Just behind Bochkovsky were Captain N. Dyachenko with thirty-one kills, Colonel Alexander Fyodorovich Burda with thirty-one, eight of which were achieved on 4 October 1941 (he fought in both the T-28 and the T-34/76), Lieutenant M. Kuchenkov with thirty-two, Lieutenant N. Moiseyev with thirty-one, Captain Konstantin Mihaylovich Samohin with thirty-plus, Master Sergeant N. Novitsky with twenty-nine and Major Vasiliy Yakovelich Storozhenko also with twenty-nine (these were achieved fighting in the T-28, T-34/76 and the T-34/85). Another twenty or so Red Army tank aces scored over twenty tanks and other armoured fighting vehicles apiece.

Although much maligned, a number of Red Army tanks aces started their careers in the T-28 medium tank. As well as Burda and Storozhenko, these included Sergeant Makagon who reportedly scored six kills on 22 June 1941 with his T-28 while serving with the 9th Tank Regiment. T-28 tanker Yevgenny A. Luppov of the 1st Guards Tank Brigade went on to score half a dozen kills in the T-34/76. Likewise, Nikolay P. Kapatov started with the T-28 and then converted to the T-34/76, claiming half a dozen enemy vehicles on 6 October 1941.

Tanker Nikolai Zheleznov recalled:

In essence, until we got the 85mm gun we had to run from Tigers like rabbits, and look for an opportunity to turn back and get at their flanks. It was difficult. If you saw a Tiger 800–1,000 metres away and it started 'crossing' you, while it moved its gun horizontally you could stay in your tank, but once it started moving it vertically you'd better jump out, or you could get burned! It never happened to me, but other guys bailed out. But when the T-34/85 entered service, we could stand up against enemy tanks one on one.

Despite their obvious shortcomings the T-34 self-propelled gun and tank destroyer platforms also produced a number of aces who managed to get the best out of their equipment. This was no easy feat as these guns were really only effective when the enemy was coming directly at them – otherwise aiming the hull-mounted gun required a lot of clutch and brake work to swing the barrel round. The 1454th Self-propelled Artillery Regiment, equipped with the SU-85 tank destroyer, produced at least three aces who managed to knock out about half a dozen enemy tanks and self-propelled guns apiece. First Sergeant Alexander Nikolayevich Kibizov, serving with the same regiment but in the newer SU-100, managed to knock out twenty-four armoured fighting vehicles and countless guns.

Vasiliy Semyonovich Krysov fought first with a KV-1, assigned to the 4580th Separate Heavy Tank Battalion, and then with the SU-122 and the SU-85, with the 1435th and 1454th Self-propelled Artillery Regiments during which time he clocked up nineteen enemy vehicles. Sergeant Nurtynov achieved fifteen kills which included armoured fighting vehicles and some guns with his SU-122. As the commander of a heavy tank, a self-propelled gun, a tank destroyer and a T-34, Krysov fought his way westward across Russia, Ukraine and Poland against a determined enemy and lived to tell the tale. He wrote of his experiences after the war and these were eventually published in English.

The very day after Krysov completed tank school, Hitler attacked the Soviet Union, but his first battle experience was not until July 1942 when his KV-1 regiment was deployed to the important city of Kalach, west of Stalingrad on the great bend of the Don River to prevent the German 6th Army crossing. Having fought during Operation Uranus as a KV-1 tank commander, he was transferred to tank destroyers, commanding SU-122s and later SU-85s, fighting at Kursk, in the central Ukraine and finishing the war as a T-34 commander in Germany.

Krysov recalled that he regularly came up against the Waffen-SS, such as the 1st SS Panzer Division Leibstandarte Adolf Hitler in the Bruilov-Fastov area in 1943, and the 5th SS Panzer Division Wiking in Poland in 1944. The 1454th Self-propelled Artillery Regiment fought with the 1st Guards Tank Army during the battle for Lvov in the summer of 1944. At Kursk the previous year Krysov recalled coming up against the Panther and Tiger and participated in the counter-attack at Ponyri. His claims to have knocked out eight Tigers in one engagement seem rather fanciful, but reflect a tendency of all Allied tank crews to term any type of panzer a Tiger. Like all tank aces these men became consummate professionals with a fatalistic outlook on life. Nonetheless, like the Red Air Force aces they were feted as heroes of the Motherland and for good reason.

It is important to remember that the T-34 did not have it all its own way, far from it – this is clearly evidenced by the enormous tanks losses that the Red Army suffered throughout the Second World War. Although the Red Army resurrected Marshal Tukhachevsky's concepts of Deep Battle and Deep Operation as well as learning from the Nazi Blitzkrieg, their tactics, strategy and technology also evolved as the war progressed. Following the Nazi defeats at Stalingrad and Kursk the war on the Eastern Front became one of attrition.

Initially Nikolai Kucherenko's T-34 hull design was protected by 45mm of armour at the front, 40mm at the rear and 20mm on top. While the welding was often bad it did not cause weld failures. At the front the glacis plate was set at 60 degrees and was free of openings apart from the driver's hatch and the ball-mounted machine gun. As a result, this gave ballistic protection of 75mm, which made the T-34 almost invulnerable in 1941, but this superiority was very short lived.

The appearance of the T-34 and the KV-1 came as a rude awakening for the panzer and anti-tank crews who found their standard 37mm and 50mm guns could only penetrate Soviet armour at close range. The early Panzer III Ausf C–Fs were only armed with a 37mm gun, while the follow-on models had a 50mm gun. The final version the Ausf N was armed with the short 75mm KwK L/24 support gun. This is why Panzer III chassis production was eventually switched to assault guns armed with the 75mm StuK40 L/48 anti-tank gun. Likewise, the Panzer IV only really held its own with the advent of the Ausf F2.

Once the German Army introduced the Panzer IV F2 armed with the 75mm KwK 40 L/43 in May 1942, the panzers could destroy the T-34 at 1,000m rather than at point-blank range. While the Germans developed ever more deadly anti-tank weapons, the T-34's armour was only doubled during 1940–3 whereas 90mm of frontal armour was needed to offer any protection from the KwK 40. To add to the T-34 tank crews' woes the nickel content used to harden the steel plate was very low. This meant that even if an enemy anti-tank gun did not penetrate the armour of the T-34, the violent impact could break off splinters, showering the crew.

From the very start of the war the Germans possessed a weapon that was greatly feared by all Allied tankers – this was commonly known simply as the 'Eighty-Eight'. Initially designed as an anti-aircraft gun it was soon redesigned for an anti-tank role or as a vehicle weapon. Fortunately for the German forces on the Eastern Front in 1941 they found that the '88' Flak gun was capable of penetrating 84mm of armour at 2,000m. In fact this anti-aircraft gun, particularly the Flak 36, in this dual role proved so successful against tanks it became the basis for the 88mm KwK 36 used to arm the Tiger I, while the Flak 41 became the 88mm KwK 43 in the Tiger II and the 88mm PaK

43 which was installed in the Ferdinand/Elefant, Hornisse/Nashorn (Hornet/Rhinoceros) and Jagdpanther.

The standard Germany Army anti-tank gun was the PaK 39 which was only a 50mm gun and the scaled-up 75mm PaK 40 – the later introduced in 1941 became the standard anti-tank weapon for the rest of the war. The follow-on PaK 41 could penetrate 150mm armour at 2,000m, but the squeeze-bore barrel meant it wore out quickly and a growing shortage of tungsten required for its special ammunition ensured only 150 were built. Another T-34 killer produced in relatively small numbers was the 88mm PaK 43/41. This was dubbed the *Scheunentor* or 'barn door' by its crews because it was so heavy and difficult to manoeuvre into position. One such gun was reported to have destroyed six T-34s at a range of 3,500m, while another blew the engine out and the turret off a T-34 at a range of 500m.

Up until September 1942 anti-tank guns up to and including 50mm accounted for over 75 per cent of T-34 losses, usually at very close range. In sharp contrast the 88mm only accounted for 3.4 per cent. By the summer of 1944 the 75mm and 88mm were both claiming around 40 per cent each (i.e. a total of 80 per cent) of T-34s knocked out. During the first quarter of 1945 the 88mm was claiming up to 70 per cent. Clearly the Germans simply did not catch up with their larger calibre anti-tank guns fast enough.

The real T-34 killer was the Tiger I armed with the 88mm KwK 36, which had roughly a 50 per cent chance of penetrating 110mm of armour at 2,000m, while at half this range it could penetrate 138mm of armour with a 95 per cent chance of a hit. At 500m the hit probability was 100 per cent. Luckily for the T-34 crews the Tiger I was never produced in great numbers, as it was complicated and time-consuming to build. The follow-on Tiger II with the KwK 43 was equally deadly and at 1,500m had a 60 per cent chance of hitting and penetrating 148mm of armour, although again it only appeared in very small numbers.

The German Panther was intended as the panzertruppens' answer to the T-34. It was designed to withstand the T-34's 76.2mm gun.

The Germans knew that the F-34 gun could penetrate up to 63mm of armour at 1,000m. Unfortunately, while the Panther's frontal armour was as good as the Tiger's, its side armour was little better than the Panzer IV. This meant that the Panther Ausf D and Ausf A models committed to the battles in Ukraine in 1943 were too lightly armoured. While the Ausf D had better frontal armour than the T-34/76 Model 1943, the level of protection was still inadequate. The early Panthers also suffered mechanical problems which greatly reduced their combat availability.

While the Panther was essentially a rushed design that entered combat far too quickly, its armament still made it a very good T-34 killer. The 75mm KwK 40 L/43 gun on the Panzer IV F2 fired an armour-piercing round that at 1,000m could penetrate 87mm of armour, therefore easily overcoming the T-34. The gun developed for the Panther, the 75mm KwK 42 L/70, was even more powerful and could blast its way through 111mm of armour at 1,000m. This bigger gun came at a cost though, namely a bigger turret, requiring a wider hull in resulting a heavier and slower tank than was hoped for.

Hitler's 'zoo' was a range of armoured fighting vehicles and tanks equipped with various models of the 88mm – all of which could chew through the T-34. The Soviets knew that the Germans had put their faith in Hitler's 'zoo' to secure victory in 1943. Nikita Khrushchev saw captured panzer orders that confirmed as much:

It contained a message addressed to the German troops which went something like this: 'You are now waging an offensive with tanks far superior to the Russian T-34s. Until now the T-34 has been the best tank in the world, better even than our own. But now you have our new Tiger tanks. There is no equal to them. With such a weapon you warriors of the German Army cannot fail to crush the enemy.'

'Their new tanks were very menacing indeed', acknowledged Khrushchev, 'but our troops learned quickly how to deal with them.

At Kursk we won a battle which tipped the balance of the war in our favour.'

From the air, like all tanks, the T-34 was vulnerable to attack by bombers and dive-bombers. In particular, the late model Junkers Ju 87 known as the Ju 87-G1 was a conversion of the Ju 87D-5 to a dedicated tank-busting role. This was armed with a 37mm cannon beneath each wing which was more than capable of cutting through the upper hull of the T-34. For a period, the Ju 87G-1 enjoyed some success on the Eastern Front. At Kursk the attack of 2nd SS Panzer Corps was aided by the Luftwaffe's Schlachtfieger and the Panzerjäger-Staffeln and the G-1s caused havoc amongst the Soviet tanks. Tactics developed by Hans-Ulrich Rudel, one of the top Stuka pilots, involved attacking the T-34 from behind and hitting the engine which would explode, destroying the tank. However, by 1943 the Stuka was increasingly being mauled by Soviet fighters that were being produced in ever-growing numbers. Only during the opening stages of Kursk did the Germans enjoy air superiority.

Similarly, the Henschel Hs 129B-2/R2 ground attack/anti-tank aircraft carried 20mm cannon in the nose and a 30mm cannon mounted in a gondola beneath the fuselage. This too was employed to support the German attack at Kursk and was used to crush a T-34 attack on the flank of the 4th Panzer Army on 8 July 1943. The Luftwaffe claimed to have destroyed 1,100 Soviet tanks at Kursk, but not all these were as a result of the tank-buster attacks. The problem faced by the Luftwaffe was that they never had enough G-1s or R2s available to overcome the T-34 on anything other than a local level. In the face of superior Red Air Force numbers any advantages these aircraft offered soon vanished.

On the ground and in the air Hitler's designers came up with some extremely deadly T-34 killers, but they were simply never produced in decisive numbers. Furthermore, the lack of standardization greatly hampered panzer production and inevitably impacted on both maintenance and tactics. While Stalin's designers also dabbled with various stopgaps and successor tanks, Soviet factories stuck with what they knew best – namely the T-34.

While the Germans produced some excellent anti-tank guns, tanks and self-propelled guns that were more than capable of tackling the T-34, in the summer of 1943 that proved the turning point in the war on the Eastern Front they were simply not available in sufficient numbers. For example, 1,750 Panther tanks were built in 1943, though only 1,071 reached the front. Just 647 Tiger Is were built in 1943 along with 345 Rhinoceros and 90 Ferdinand self-propelled guns. Just over 3,000 Panzer IVs and 3,000 StuG IIIs armed with the L/43 or L/48 were produced. Compare to this the 15,812 T-34s built in 1943, which included 283 T-34/85s (plus another 4,047 assault guns, 3,463 light tanks and 684 heavy tanks) – the previous year they had managed 12,553 T-34/76s.

In 1943 Soviet tanks losses of all types outstripped 1941 at 22,400, while the Germans lost 6,362 on all fronts. The following year the Red Army lost another 16,900 tanks compared to panzer losses of 6,434 (German losses for the two years look suspiciously similar). This did not matter because Soviet tank production peaked at 28,983, including 14,773 T-34s. Faced by this crude arithmetic the T-34 carried all before it.

By 1943 the Germans were being outproduced by almost 3:1. Rather than disrupt tank production the Soviet High Command put off introducing a T-34/76 successor until really necessary. In contrast the Germans diverted 41 per cent of tank-production resources to the Tiger and the Panther at the expense of the Panzer IV, which remained the backbone of the panzer units. As a result, not enough tanks reached the depleted panzer units. It proved to be a strategic gamble that Stalin won. Even in 1944 when the panzer factories pulled out all the stops they were still outproduced by 2:1, and the following year was even worse at 4:1. For Stalin victory was assured.

Appendices

Appendix A

Red Army Tank Units 1941–1945

Initially the Red Army's principal armoured formations were tank and motorized units. At the start of the war the Red Army had sixty-one tank and thirty-one motorized divisions, the bulk of which were very belatedly grouped into twenty to thirty mechanized corps. These were swiftly destroyed during Hitler's invasion. Constant reorganization subsequently led to new tank and mechanized corps that were grouped into armies. In total the Red Army raised about thirty tank corps and thirty mechanized corps, some of which were destroyed, disbanded or resurrected as Guards units. In mid-1942 the Red Army began the process of creating five dedicated tank armies, with a sixth being formed in 1944. Some of these were soon lost in combat and then recreated with the designation Guards Tank Army. These tank armies consisted of two tank corps and one mechanized corps, which numerically were roughly equivalent to three divisions. The mechanized corps had more infantry but the same number of tanks, i.e. 200. This gave a total force, including supporting arms, of about 50,000 men and 600 tanks. Not all corps had enough T-34 medium tanks and had to also deploy the T-70 light tank. The Red Army formed a huge number of other tank, mechanized, self-propelled artillery and tank destroyer units. For the sake of brevity and space only dedicated tank forces are listed below.

Mechanized Corps – 1941

1st Mechanized Corps:	2nd Mechanized Corps:
1st Tank Division	11th Tank Division
3rd Tank Division	16th Tank Division
163rd Motorized Division	15th Mechanized Division

3rd Mechanized Corps:
2nd Tank Division
5th Tank Division
84th Motorized Division

4th Mechanized Corps:
8th Tank Division
32nd Tank Division
81st Motorized Division

5th Mechanized Corps:
13th Tank Division
17th Tank Division
109th Motorized Division

6th Mechanized Corps:
4th Tank Division
7th Tank Division
29th Motorized Division

7th Mechanized Corps:
14th Tank Division
18th Tank Division
1st Mechanized Division

8th Mechanized Corps:
12th Tank Division
34th Tank Division
7th Motorized Division

9th Mechanized Corps:
20th Tank Division
35th Tank Division
131st Motorized Division

10th Mechanized Corps:
21st Tank Division
24th Tank Division
198th Motorized Division

11th Mechanized Corps:
29th Tank Division
33rd Tank Division
204th Motorized Division

12th Mechanized Corps:
23rd Tank Division
28th Tank Division
202nd Motorized Division

13th Mechanized Corps:
25th Tank Division
31st Tank Division
208th Motorized Division

14th Mechanized Corps:
22nd Tank Division
30th Tank Division
205th Motorized Division

15th Mechanized Corps:
10th Tank Division
37th Tank Division
212th Motorized Division

16th Mechanized Corps:
15th Tank Division
39th Tank Division
240th Motorized Division

17th Mechanized Corps:
27th Tank Division
36th Tank Division
209th Motorized Division

18th Mechanized Corps:
44th Tank Division
47th Tank Division
218th Motorized Division

19th Mechanized Corps:
40th Tank Division
43rd Tank Division
213th Motorized Division

20th Mechanized Corps:
26th Tank Division
38th Tank Division
210th Motorized Division

21st Mechanized Corps:
42nd Tank Division

46th Tank Division
185th Motorized Division

22nd Mechanized Corps:
19th Tank Division
41st Tank Division
215th Motorized Division

24th Mechanized Corps:
45th Tank Division
49th Tank Division
216th Motorized Division

25th Mechanized Corps:
50th Tank Division
55th Tank Division
219th Motorized Division

26th Mechanized Corps:
52nd Tank Division
56th Tank Division
103rd Mechanized Division

A further five mechanized corps were formed in March 1941, the 23rd, 27th, 28th, 29th and 30th, but their component divisions are unknown.

Mechanized Corps' Deployment in June 1941
Northern Front (formed 24 June 1941):
1st Mechanized Corps (23rd Army)
10th Mechanized Corps (Reserve)

Northwestern Front:
3rd Mechanized Corps (11th Army)
12th Mechanized Corps (8th Army)

Western Front:
6th Mechanized Corps (10th Army)
11th Mechanized Corps (3rd Army)
13th Mechanized Corps (10th Army)
14th Mechanized Corps (4th Army)
17th Mechanized Corps (13th Army)
20th Mechanized Corps (13th Army)

Southwestern Front:
4th Mechanized Corps (6th Army)
8th Mechanized Corps (26th Army)
9th Mechanized Corps (5th Army)
15th Mechanized Corps (6th Army)
16th Mechanized Corps (12th Army)
19th Mechanized Corps (Reserve)
24th Mechanized Corps (Reserve)
22nd Mechanized Corps (5th Army)

Southern Front (formed 25 June 1941):
2nd Mechanized Corps (9th Army)
18th Mechanized Corps (9th Army)

Stavka Reserve:
5th Mechanized Corps (16th Army)
7th Mechanized Corps (20th Army)
21st Mechanized Corps (Unassigned)
25th Mechanized Corps (21st Army)
26th Mechanized Corps (19th Army)

Central Asian Military District:
27th Mechanized Corps

Orel Military District:
23rd Mechanized Corps

Transcaucasus Military District:
28th Mechanized Corps

Tank Armies, Brigades and Corps – 1942

1st Tank Army:
13th Tank Corps
28th Tank Corps
158th Tank Brigade

3rd Tank Army:
12th Tank Corps
15th Tank Corps

4th Tank Army:
22nd Tank Corps
23rd Tank Corps

5th Tank Army:
2nd Tank Corps
7th Tank Corps
11th Tank Corps

Other Corps:
1st Guards Tank Corps (formerly 26th Tank Corps)
2nd Guards Tank Corps (formerly 24th Tank Corps)

Other Units:
9th Army
51st Tank Brigade
121st Tank Brigade

6th Army:
5th Guards Tank Brigade
37th Tank Brigade
38th Tank Brigade
48th Tank Brigade

Plus:
21st Tank Corps
64th Tank Brigade
198th Tank Brigade
199th Tank Brigade

23rd Tank Corps:
6th Tank Brigade
130th Tank Brigade
131st Tank Brigade

9th Army:
51st Tank Brigade
121st Tank Brigade

21st Army:
10th Tank Brigade

28th Army:
6th Guards Tank Brigade
57th Tank Brigade
84th Tank Brigade
90th Tank Brigade

38th Army:
13th Tank Brigade
36th Tank Brigade
133rd Tank Brigade

Army Group Bobkin:
7th Tank Brigade

Tank Armies, Brigades and Corps – 1943

1st Guards Tank Army:
6th Tank Corps
31st Tank Corps
112th Tank Brigade
3rd Mechanized Corps

2nd Tank Army:
11th Tank Corps
16th Tank Corps
11th Guards Tank Brigade

3rd Guards Tank Army:
6th Guards Tank Corps
7th Guards Tank Corps

4th Guards Tank Army:
11th Tank Corps
30th Urals Volunteer Tank Corps
6th Guards Mechanized Corps

5th Guards Tank Army:
3rd Guards Tank Corps
29th Tank Corps
5th Guards Mechanized Corps

Steppe Front Assets:
4th Guards Tank Corps
10th Tank Corps
18th Tank Corps

Other Corps:
5th Guards Tank Corps (formerly 4th Tank Corps)
6th Guards Tank Corps (formerly 12th Tank Corps)
7th Guards Tank Corps (formerly 15th Tank Corps)
10th Guards Tank Corps (formerly 30th Urals Volunteer Tank Corps)
11th Guards Tank Corps (formerly 6th Tank Corps)

Other Units:
1st Guards Heavy Tank Breakthrough Regiment
34th Guards Heavy Tank Breakthrough Regiment

Tank Armies, Brigades and Corps – 1944

2nd Guards Tank Army:
3rd Tank Corps

5th Guards Tank Army:
3rd Guards Tank Corps
3rd Guards Tank Brigade
18th Guards Tank Brigade
19th Guards Tank Brigade
35th Guards Tank Brigade
3rd Mechanized Corps

6th Guards Tank Army:
5th Guards Tank Corps
5th Guards Mechanized Corps

3rd Army:
9th Tank Corps
23rd Tank Brigade
95th Tank Brigade
109th Tank Brigade

5th Army:
2nd Tank Brigade
153rd Tank Brigade

11th Guards Army:
2nd Tank Corps
4th Tank Brigade

25th Guards Tank Brigade
26th Guards Tank Brigade

31st Army:
213th Tank Brigade

39th Army:
28th Tank Brigade

43rd Army:
1st Tank Corps
89th Tank Brigade
117th Tank Brigade
159th Tank Brigade

49th Army:
42nd Guards Tank Brigade
43rd Guards Tank Brigade

65th Army:
1st Guards Tank Corps
15th Guards Tank Brigade
16th Guards Tank Brigade
17th Guards Tank Brigade
219th Tank Brigade
1st Mechanized Corps

Other Corps:
9th Guards Tank Corps (formerly 3rd Tank Corps)

Other Units:
1st Czechoslovak Tank Brigade
36th Guards Tank Brigade

71st Independent Heavy Tank Regiment
72nd Independent Guards Tank Regiment

Tank Armies, Brigades and Corps – 1945

1st Guards Tank Army:	2nd Guards Tank Army
11th Guards Tank Corps	3rd Guards Tank Army
1st Tank Brigade	4th Guards Tank Army
40th Guards Tank Brigade	5th Guards Tank Army
44th Guards Tank Brigade	6th Guards Tank Army
45th Guards Tank Brigade	
8th Guards Mechanized Corps	

Soviet Tanks and Tracked Armoured Fighting Vehicles 1941–1945

BT Fast Tanks

BT-1

After the T-26 light tank the mainstay of the Red Army's tank fleet in 1941 was the *Bistrokhodny Tank* (or BT fast tank). It was known to the crew's as *Betka* (Beetle) or *Tri-Tankista* (three tank men). The idea behind a fast tank, as opposed to a light tank, was that it would have a mechanized cavalry role, with the T-28 medium tank in an infantry-support role. However, because of the Red Army's continually evolving and changing attitude toward the use of tanks, by the late 1930s they were all seen as infantry-support weapons.

Ironically the BT family of tanks came about thanks to an American design. During the 1900s the Christie motor company had built civilian vehicles, but in 1919 constructed its first tank. Thanks to the lure of a potentially lucrative domestic and export market, in 1928 J.W. Christie came up with a new tank. Despite its shortcomings the US Army ordered seven Medium Tank T3 or Combat Car T1 in mid-1931. The resulting improved T3E2 had a new two-man turret, thicker armour and five machine guns.

What made this design innovative was its simple solution to unreliable narrow tracks, which invariably had very short service lives. On the Christie tank the suspension used a track and wheel system. This meant it could drive without tracks using just wheels to the front by road, then in about 15–30 minutes the tracks could be fitted to facilitate off-road combat.

This innovation came to the notice of Innokenti Andreyevich Khalepsky, who was in charge of the Red Army Military Technical

Board. Moscow had systematically set up organizations in both the UK and US to acquire new military technology. In Britain the drawback was that the War Department only allowed the export of vehicles not being used by the British Army – hence the T-26. In America the Soviet Amtorg Trading Company began looking at getting hold of the Christie tank.

On 29 April 1930 the vice-president of Amtorg, A.V. Petrov, signed a contract with Christie for two improved models of their tank. Amtorg negotiated a tough deal essentially demanding exclusive rights to the tank for ten years, access to the technical drawings and the appointment of a Soviet engineer to work at the US Wheel Track Layer Corporation. Preparations were then made to ship two Christie Model 1930 T3s to the Soviet Union.

Christie was not permitted by US law to export tanks to the Soviet Union, as since the Russian Revolution it was a country that America did not officially recognize. When the US State Department and the War Department got wind of the deal they attempted to stop it, but Christie found an easy way round the problem. Since the Soviets were only interested in the suspension system the two vehicles had their turrets and main armament removed. On 24 December 1930 the two 'agricultural tractors' were shipped on their way.

Christie had no intention of being restricted by any exclusivity clauses and sold the design to Britain, France and Poland. Use of his suspension in the UK was to result in the poorly-armed and armoured, but fast, family of cruiser tanks, the most famous being the Crusader that saw extensive action in North Africa. When Christie died during the Second World War his company was tangled in lawsuits brought by the US government and was facing bankruptcy.

Back in the Soviet Union the Kharkov Locomotive Works quickly set about building its own 10-ton version for evaluation designated the BT-1, armed with machine guns in a small turret. This differed from the Christie design as it replaced the four solid twin-disc road wheels with spoked wheels. Notably the first wheel was of a different style to the other three, featuring round holes between the spokes rather than the triangular gaps on the others.

Nonetheless, the BT-1 retained the narrow tracks, characteristic American pointed nose or 'prow' at the front of the hull and general layout. The driver was seated in the middle at the front and was served by a central visor or hatch. The other two crew members consisted of the commander and gunner. Ironically the Soviets seemed to ignore the fact that the Soviet Union's road network was extremely undeveloped, which largely negated the benefits of the track and wheel system. In addition, they must have known that ultimately narrow tracks were simply not suited to Russia's harsh winter conditions or the muddy spring and autumn.

BT-2

The BT-2, armed with a 37mm gun or three machine guns, entered service in 1932 and some were still active nine years later. This had a flat nose on the prow. It had the same road wheels as the BT-1 and the small one-man turret lacking a rear stowage bustle or bin. The machine-gun variant lacked firepower and proved unpopular with the crews and so it was dropped.

BT-3

Improving on the BT-1 resulted in the BT-3 armed with a 45mm gun and solid disc road wheels. Not many of these were built and they ended up as bridgelayers or flamethrower tanks.

BT-4

The BT-4, with a twin machine-gun turret, was only developed as an unwanted prototype.

BT-5

The BT-5, that went into mass production in late 1932, was essentially an upgunned BT-2 armed with a 45mm M1932 gun mounted in the larger cylindrical T-26-style turret. The initial production run featured a very small rear turret bustle, but subsequently the model had a much larger one. Its V–12 petrol M–5 aero engine generated 350bhp and running on its tracks the BT–5 could manage 65km/h and on just wheels was even faster at 112km/h. It saw service in Spain, Finland and Mongolia.

BT-7

Experience fighting the Japanese in Mongolia led to the BT–7 in 1935, which had thicker armour, increased fuel and ammunition storage and the T–26-style conical turret with a ball-mounted machine gun. The BT–7's main armament was the 45mm M1935 gun and it could carry 146 rounds for it, which was much better than the BT–5 that carried anything from 72 to 115 rounds. It was powered by the new M-17-TV-12 petrol engine that developed 500bhp. This gave a road speed of 72km/h and a cross-country one of 50km/h, with a road range of 430km. This was a copy of a German BMW engine that had been developed for use in aircraft. On the BT–7 the maximum hull armour was increased from the 13mm on the BT–5 to 22mm, though the minimum remained the same at just 6mm.

The easiest way to tell the BT–7 and BT–5 apart was that the former had a rounded prow, rather than the tapered flat nose of the latter. In 1937 the BT–7 was produced with a cylindrical turret similar to that on the later T–26. However, it had two round hatches rather than one round and one square as on the T–26. This version was followed two years later by the BT-7-2, which featured minor technical modifications. By 1939 the BT–7 was the main Soviet combat tank.

Due to the numbers built, totalling about 7,000 BT-5/7s, like the T–26 the BT series became one of the most photographed tanks following the German victories in 1941 and 1942. BT tanks were photographed in all sorts of predicaments: some were plainly abandoned, some burnt out, others crashed into each other or stuck in swamps. Often, as with the T–26, it was the BT driver who failed to escape when the vehicle was hit.

BT-7A Close Support Tank

A number of support and special-purpose variants were also produced. These included a close support tank armed with a 76.2mm regimental howitzer, which required a larger turret, known as the BT-7A.

BT-7M/BT-8

Just before Operation Barbarossa the Soviets produced a transitional tank that essentially paved the way for the war-winning T-34 medium tank design. This consisted of a much-modified BT-7 known as the BT-7M and BT-8 or Model 1938. At 14 tons it was almost a ton heavier. The key change was that it had a sloping glacis plate rather than the rounded prow and a diesel engine. However, the armour was the same as the BT-7.

Importantly the diesel engine reduced the risk of fire and increased the tank's range by over 30 per cent for the same volume of fuel. It was also simpler to produce and maintain. The V–12 liquid-cooled engine was again courtesy of a foreign supplier and was based on the Hispano-Suiza 12Y designed for aircraft. This gave a top speed of 86km/h on the road and 50km/h cross-country.

The BT-8 was armed with the newer M1938 45mm gun with 146 rounds, plus 2,394 rounds for its two machine guns. Between 1939 and 1940 about 700 BT-7M/BT-8 were produced. These helped Zhukov secure a decisive victory over the Japanese at Khalkhin-Gol in 1939. Nonetheless, BT-7 production ceased in 1940 with the introduction of the T-34.

Tank designer Mikhail Koshkin at Kharkov was not a fan of the wheel and track system, which he argued offered no real benefits for the added weight. As a result, he worked hard to ensure that his new T-34 was not lumbered with it. He was also able to draw on the experimental BT-IS that had sloping side armour as well as a sloping glacis. Both features were to be incorporated into the T-34.

BT-7V Command Tank

The commander's model was known as the BT-7(V) or BT-7TU, utilizing the BT-5(V) turret with the radio frame antenna, although later models had the much less obvious whip or aerial antenna.

BT OP-7 Flamethrower

A flamethrower version, which carried the flame fuel on the right-hand side of the hull in an armoured pannier, was called the OP-7.

IS Heavy Tanks

IS-1/2

The Soviets introduced new upgunned tanks in 1944 that finally gave them parity with the best of the German heavy and medium tanks, namely the T-34/85 and the IS-1 and IS-2 (i.e. Iosif Stalin, the Cyrillic alphabet not having the Western J for Joseph). Although classed as a heavy tank, the IS was actually roughly the same weight as the German Panther medium tank. Initially equipped with the 85mm gun, this was replaced with a 122mm, enabling Soviet tank crews to engage any German tank at extremely long ranges. This capability was a deathblow to the panzers already struggling to fend off superior Soviet tank numbers.

The IS-1 went into production in 1943, though only just over 100 were produced; the following year Soviet factories churned out 2,252 of the upgunned model. The IS-2 had an improved hull, with contour castings and armed with a 122mm proved to be one of the most powerful tanks to go into service with any army during the Second World War. However, the IS suffered from a slow rate of fire (just two or three rounds per minute) and could only carry twenty-eight tank gun rounds. The IS-1 was issued to the 1st Guards Heavy Breakthrough Regiment. Its successor equipped the Guards Heavy Tank Regiments including the 71st and 72nd. The IS-2 first went into action with the 11th Guards Independent Tank Brigade in April 1944.

IS-3

The IS-3, with a much flatter and rounder 'frying pan' turret, appeared in the closing months of the war. A few reportedly saw combat in Berlin and some were photographed during the Red Army's victory parade through the city.

IS-85

At the same time as the development of the KV-85 heavy tank, work commenced on the KV-13, which featured a redesigned KV chassis and hull, re-designated the IS-85. This had better protection and mobility than the KV-85 and eventually became the IS-1.

ISU-122/152 Self-Propelled Guns

The IS chassis also provided the basis for the ISU-122 and ISU-152 self-propelled guns, which both entered service in 1944, superseding the SU-122 and SU-152 based on the earlier KV chassis. Their commonality proved useful as they were mainly employed with the heavy tank regiments equipped with the IS tanks.

KV Heavy Tanks

KV-1

The KV-1 heavy tank was just coming into service in 1941. Armed with a 76.2mm gun it was both better armed and armoured than its predecessors, but was neither manoeuvrable nor reliable enough. About 5,200 KVs of different variants were produced and it remained in production until 1943. Its swansong was at the Battle of Kursk.

Experience in Spain showed the Soviets that the basic requirement of making tanks able to withstand machine-gun fire and artillery shrapnel was no longer sufficient. Although tank losses to direct fire were minimal, the emergence of new 37mm anti-tank guns and large-calibre field guns showed the way things were going. In response, in 1937 the Directorate of Armed Forces issued specifications for a new heavy tank. This would be able to act as a breakthrough weapon and engage enemy armour at the same time. It was to be able to resist up to 76.2mm guns out to 1,200m and be powered by a less-flammable diesel engine.

Initially drawing on the multi-turreted T-35 heavy tank, it was proposed that this new tank would have five turrets. In light of the difficulties in coordinating the gunners, the designer got the number reduced to three, with the main one armed with a 76.2mm gun and the two subsidiary ones armed with 45mm guns. The Kharkov Locomotive Factory responsible for building the T-35 seemed the logical home for a new heavy tank, but Stalin's purges had led to a shortage of engineers and the work was passed over to the Experimental Design Mechanical Section (OKMO) at the Bolshevik Factory in Leningrad under N. Barykov and the Zirovskiy Factory led by Lieutenant Colonel Zhosif Kotin. The latter was to prove particularly able and ultimately was to be responsible for the powerful late-war IS tanks.

In the spring of 1939 Barykov's team presented their ideas for the T-100 and Kotin's the SMK (named after the late Bolshevik leader S.M. Kirov). Both designs featured three turrets, and rather than use the T-35's dated and less effective spring suspension, they used the new torsion bar suspension. They also had wide tracks to lower ground pressure and improve cross-country performance.

When Kotin argued with 'The Boss' over the futility of having three turrets, Stalin broke a turret off the presentation model saying, 'Why make a tank into a department store?' Both teams were then sent away to work on two-turret prototypes. These were ready by the summer of 1939 and sent to the testing grounds at Kubinka outside Moscow. Kotin would not let the turret issue rest and in February started designing a single-turret version of the SMK. In August the plans were shown to Stalin and permission was granted for a third heavy tank prototype known as the KV (named after Marshal Klimenti Voroshilov – though it had been planned to call it the KS or Kotin-Stalin).

During the prototype trials held in front of Voroshilov, the tank bearing his initials performed the best. All three were then packed off to take part in the Russo-Finnish War of 1939–40 with the 91st Tank Battalion, part of the 20th Heavy Tank Brigade. This seemed foolish as it exposed them to the risk of capture. They saw action between 17 and 19 December 1939 near Summa, supported by T-28s. The SMK was disabled after running over a mine, but after its crew repaired the damaged track they could not get the engine started. Attempts to tow it with the T-100 failed. The SMK had to be abandoned and was not recovered until February 1940. In the meantime, on 19 December 1939 it was decided to put the KV-1 Model 1939 into production, of which just 141 were built.

It had been hope to arm the tank with the F-32 76.2mm gun, but problems ensured the turret was fitted with the much less effective short L-11 instead. The T-34 was to suffer exactly the same problem thanks to the obstinacy of Marshal Grigory Ivanovich Kulik, head of the Main Artillery Directorate responsible for the gun factories. He was not a fan of tanks and refused to step up production of the F-32 or the newer F-34. His actions also ensured that there was a shortage of 76.2mm ammunition. Bizarrely the T-34 medium tank would end up with a more powerful gun than the KV-1 heavy tank.

Use of the L-11 meant it had a distinctive gun mantlet, due to the location of a recuperator above the barrel. Close protection on the KV-1 was supplied by three machine guns; one coaxial, one in the rear of the turret and the other in the front of the hull (the M1939 does not seem to have had a hull machine gun, but was fitted with a pistol port). The turret and hull front were protected by 90mm and 75mm of armour respectively, making it impervious to most weapons except at point-blank range. The KV-1 took a crew of five.

Although weighing in at 43 tons, it could still achieve 35km/h on roads and 13km/h cross-country. By road it could manage a range of 160km and across country 100km. This was thanks to revising the SMK suspension, that employed six wheels either side mounted independently on torsion bars with three return rollers plus wide tracks. The KV-1 was powered by a model V-2K V-12 diesel engine generating 500bhp.

The KV-1's combination of firepower, armour and mobility made it one of the most powerful tanks of its day and was only rivalled by the T-34, which was under development. It seemed as if that, along with the latter, the KV-1 would give the Red Army the tools it needed to implement its theories of Deep Operation. However, while the KV-1 was very impressive in appearance and on paper, it paid a heavy price thanks to its weight. Therefore it went into production despite a series of very serious problems that would be highly detrimental to its combat performance.

Key amongst these was its antiquated transmission, and also the clutch was difficult to operate. Alarmingly the driver had to bring his vehicle to a halt to change gear, which prevented changing up through the gearbox whilst on the move to achieve any sensible acceleration. Likewise, it meant it was inadvisable to change gear whilst in combat as a stationary tank always offers a ready target. Engine efficiency was affected by poor air filters. All this meant that the tank was difficult and exhausting to steer. In practice the mighty KV-1 breakthrough tank was impeded by poor mobility.

Visibility was not good either. With the tank closed up the commander and driver had limited vision. The design of the driver's periscope was poor as it only had limited traverse. Similarly, the quality of the laminated glass in the driver's forward slit visor was such that it was hard to see through. This often left the driver reliant on directions from the commander for the simplest of manoeuvres. In contrast, the commander had two reasonably good periscopes in the turret roof, but as well as coordinating the driver, gunner and radio operator he had to double up as the loader.

KV-1A

Until production ended in 1943, the KV tank was subject to constant fine tuning. Notably the Model 1940 (German designation KV-1A), the main production model by the time of Hitler's invasion, was given a more powerful engine and the higher velocity F-32 gun as originally intended. The latter had a new-style mantlet. Kulik convinced himself and Stalin that the panzers were armed with very large calibre guns and that Soviet tanks should be uparmoured. As a result, 35mm armour plates were bolted onto the turret and hull. These were eventually superseded by stronger welded turrets. The bolt heads were very prominent on the turret sides. The M1940 with additional bolt-on appliqué armour was also known as the KV-1E.

KV-1B

KV-1 production was carried out at the Kirov Factory in Leningrad, but once the city came under siege it was transferred to the Chelyabinsk Tractor Factory. There the design was simplified in the same way as was done with the T-34. Hull appliqué armour was standardized. A cast turret was introduced that was easier to produce than the welded design and the road wheels were simplified. This resulted in the KV-1B with a distinctive curved bustle that was cast as part of the turret. The shot trap created by the turret's rear overhang was also eliminated. Introduced in late 1941, it had its armament supplemented by a hull machine gun. The Model 1941 (KV-1B) was armed with the longer-barrelled ZiS-5 76.2mm gun, which was very similar to the F-34 used in the T-34/76 medium tank. It was much more powerful than the F-32 and ended the illogical disparity between the Red Army's heavy and medium tanks.

KV-1C

The uparmouring of the Model 1942 (KV-1C) was carried out by Kotin's TsKB-2 (Central Design Bureau). The hull protection was increased from 75mm to 90mm, plus a new thicker cast turret, with 120mm at the front, was produced. This process of adding yet more weight caused additional problems with the engine and transmission and the crews found the Model 1942 a mixed blessing. Also by this stage the 76.2mm gun in both the KV-1 and T-34 was no longer really adequate. The steady uparmouring of the KV-1 between 1941 and 1942 meant that it was simply not mobile enough to operate alongside the faster T-34. While the KV-1s were gathered into assault brigades to support the infantry, a heavy tank was still needed to support the mobile units. This problem was not really resolved until the introduction of the T-34 armed with an 85mm gun and the heavy IS tank.

KV-1E

Uparmoured Model 1940 – see KV-1A entry.

KV-1-S Fast Tank

Efforts to produce a lighter and therefore faster version led to the KV-1-S (S: *skorostnoy*, or speed) with a smaller and thinner turret as well as lighter road wheels. Overall the armour was reduced, with the front given just 60mm. A much-needed improved clutch and gearbox was installed, as were improvements to engine lubrication and cooling. This gave the KV-1-S a road speed of 40km/h. It went into production in August 1943, but as it was no better armed than the T-34/76 only 1,379 were built before production was terminated in late 1943.

KV-2 Heavy Assault Tank

The KV-2 heavy assault tank, or artillery tank, was armed with a massive 152mm howitzer. Due to the size of its gun, once again this tank was not agile enough and was regularly photographed by the Germans having been abandoned. Thanks to the Russo-Finnish War it was decided to develop an artillery support variant of the KV-1. The Finns well dug in along the Mannerheim Line had shown that Soviet tanks were not suited for bunker busting. General Meretskov, commanding the Soviet 7th Army in Finland, requested a heavy tank mounting a large-calibre gun to deal with enemy fortifications as soon as possible.

Using its T-100 heavy tank hull, the OKMO team sought to arm it with a 130mm B-13 naval gun. This was quickly rejected because of difficulties accessing the navy's heavy weaponry and ammunition, which included semi-armour-piercing rounds. Besides, using Kotin's KV chassis seemed a far more logical step from a production point of view.

The first attempts employing a lengthened KV hull to carry a 152mm BR-2 and a 203mm B-4 howitzer were not successful. The third design envisaged mounting a standard 152mm M1938/1940 L20 howitzer on an unmodified chassis. It was this that became the KV-2. The first trials took place on 10 February 1940 and thereafter two prototypes were hurriedly despatched to Finland's Karelian Isthmus. It is not clear if they were used in active operations or simply tested on captured positions.

The most immediate drawback with the KV-2 was very self-evident. The turret required to house the large 152mm gun was simply enormous and weighed some 12 tons. This meant that the KV-2 had a towering height of 4.9m compared to the KV-1's 3.1m. To protect this very exposed turret it was given 110mm frontal and 75mm side armour. This resulted in an overall weight of 53 tons compared to the 43 tons of the KV-1. This made the tank impervious to direct fire except at very close range by high-velocity weapons. The size and the shape of the turret inevitably led to its six-man crew dubbing it the 'Dreadnought'.

The clutch and transmission problems suffered by the KV-1 were greatly magnified with the much heavier KV-2, which used an unimproved 500bhp V-2 diesel engine. On a good day it could manage 25km/h on the roads and half that cross-country. The enormous weight of the turret and the poorly-designed turret bearings meant the tank had to be on flat ground in order to traverse the main gun. Nor could the gun be fired whilst on the move. These limitations were not conducive to mobile warfare and confined the KV-2 to operating on the roads. By the time of the German invasion its original purpose as a bunker-buster had become an irrelevance. Essentially the KV-2 was consigned to the role of a mobile pillbox in the face of Operation Barbarossa.

In October 1941 production of the KV-2 was stopped when Stalin's weapons factories were evacuated eastward. By that stage only 334 had been produced. Subsequently a few were used in the defence of Moscow and Stalingrad. The 152mm gun was not abandoned, however. It was married to a turretless KV chassis to produce the ISU-152 assault gun, which appeared in the summer of 1943.

KV-3 Support Tank

It was planned to create a KV-3 at Kirov, armed with a 107mm gun using a longer hull and larger turret, but this was shelved in favour of using the prototype chassis armed with an 85mm naval gun for the defence of Leningrad. There had been some discussion by Kulik of arming the T-34 with a 107mm gun, but such a tank gun did not exist (other than as an obsolete First World War howitzer) and would have required a very large turret. Kotin developed two KV-3 prototypes, the second keeping the basic KV-1 design but with an improved turret layout. The need for a new engine that was unavailable led to the cancellation of both designs.

KV-8 Flamethrower

There were a number of other KV variants, most noteworthy being the KV-8 heavy flamethrower. The Russo-Finnish War highlighted the vulnerability of light tanks converted to a flamethrower role. In order to make space for the ATO-41 flamethrower (which was also installed in the T-34 to create the OT-34), the 76.2mm gun was replaced by the smaller 45mm. To conceal the barrel of the flame gun it was camouflaged with a gun jacket. The KV-8 had enough flame fuel for 107 shots and could fire 3 shots every 10 seconds. These tanks were organized into flamethrower battalions, comprising two companies of KV-8s and one company of OT-34s. Some KV-1-S were converted into flamethrowers using the ATO-42, becoming the KV-8S. Two prototypes of an upgraded KV-8S, known as the KV-8M, were produced equipped with two flamethrowers. Once all the KV-8s were lost in action they were phased out

KV-85

To counter the German Tiger tank, which first appeared on the Eastern Front in 1942, the Soviets adapted their 85mm Model 1939 anti–aircraft gun for anti–tank use. Once modified this had an effective range of 1,000m and could penetrate 100mm of armour, so constituted a very real threat to the Panther and Tiger, although it was far from accurate at long range. At the end of the summer of 1943 the gun was installed into a heavy cast turret and fitted to the KV-1 chassis, creating the KV-85. This was produced as a stopgap until the IS heavy tank was ready for production and just 148 were built. These were issued to the 34th Guards Heavy Tank Breakthrough Regiment.

SU-152 Self-Propelled Gun

At the end of 1943 the SU-152 known as the 'Animal Hunter', based on the KV-1 heavy tank chassis, was produced armed with a 152mm howitzer. This was intended for a dual role, as an anti-tank gun and heavy assault gun. While an effective weapon, its lack of storage restricted its ammunition load and therefore its tactical flexibility as it was reliant on ammunition carriers.

T-20 Armoured Artillery Tractor

The T-20 Komsomolets armoured artillery tractor was designed in 1936 at the Ordzhonikidze Moscow Plant No. 37 to tow light support weapons such as the 45mm anti-tank gun and the 120mm heavy mortar. It was also built at the STZ and GAZ factories during 1937–41. The T-20 was wholly unsuitable as a weapons or troop carrier. While it had an armoured, enclosed driver and machine-gunner compartment at the front, the six seats on the back were highly exposed. Nonetheless, it was used offensively with predictably fatal results for the crew and passengers.

ZiS-30 Self-Propelled Anti-Tank Gun

In response to the German invasion the T-20 artillery tractor chassis was used to create the ZiS-30, a self-propelled anti-tank gun using the 57mm ZIS-2 gun. This combination was rare, only about 100 ever being produced.

T-26 Light Tank

In early 1931 the Revolutionary War Council took the decision to mass produce the T-27 tankette, signalling the Red Army's commitment to developing its armoured and mechanized units. At the same time, it was decided to build the T-26 light tank. While the tiny two-man T-27 was intended for reconnaissance work, the T-26 was to support the infantry divisions during the breakthrough of enemy lines. This formed part of the Red Army's developing concept of Deep Battle, which envisaged enveloping an enemy over a very wide area.

The T-26 light tank constituted Stalin's most numerous tank type in 1941. It first entered service a decade earlier and by the time of the Second World War some 12,000 had been built. Essentially there were four models of the T-26, the M1931, M1933, M1938 and M1939. The T-26 first saw combat in the Spanish Civil War, the Russo-Japanese border conflicts and the Russo-Finnish War. The Red Army was also equipped with smaller numbers of the T-37, T-38 and T-40 light reconnaissance tanks.

The T-26 was based on the British Vickers-Armstrong 6-ton Mk E light tank built for the export market. This came in two versions, the Type A and B, one with twin turrets side by side and the other with a large single turret. The first examples of these had arrived from Britain in 1930, but before they were put into production the Soviets built competing prototypes known as the TMM-1 and TMM-2 with American engines and the driver to the left. The superior British design was then put into production under a licence agreement as the T-26 Model 1931. It first appeared in large numbers at the Red Square Parade on 7 November 1931.

The tank was powered by an 8-cylinder Armstrong Siddeley petrol engine (known as the GAZ T-26), also produced under licence. This provided a road speed of 32km/h and a road range of 140km. The engine was located at the rear of the hull with the transmission being sent forwards to the front drive sprockets. The gearbox located by the driver's feet had five forward speeds, and steering was of the clutch and brake type. The Soviet version retained the simple and robust

Vickers suspension, which comprised two groups of four bogie wheels each side sprung on quarter-elliptic leaf springs. The crew or fighting compartment was in the middle with the driver seated to the right of the turret.

The T-26 was initially armed with two DT 7.62mm machine guns mounted in individual turrets, though the T-26TU commander's variant was produced with a 37mm gun in the right-hand turret and a hand-rail frame antenna on the hull. It carried 180 rounds of main armament ammunition, had three crew and was normally issued to the platoon and company commanders. The Model 1932 also had a 37mm gun.

The initial double-turret configuration proved far from ideal. The gunners' seats did not automatically rotate with the turret mechanism, but had to be traversed manually, which was far from helpful in combat. In addition, to stop the turrets jamming each other, locks had to be fitted to restrict traverse to 265 degrees. As a result of these limitations the twin turrets were soon abandoned in favour of a single one. To start this was achieved by removing the right-hand turret and installing the gun in the remaining left-hand one. However, the German Rheinmetall 37mm gun chosen to upgun the T-26 proved difficult to mount in the restricted space on the left. Firing this much more powerful gun generated a recoil that had a tendency to crack the turret ring.

The Bolshevik Leningrad Factory and the KhPZ Kharkov works were tasked to develop a larger central cylindrical turret that could house the new 45mm Model 1932 gun. This became standard on the T-26 Model 1933 and on the BT-7 and T-35 tanks. Similarly, it was intended that all T-26s would have radios, which required a distinctive horseshoe-shaped frame antenna being fitted to the top of the turret. In reality those tanks with radios were reserved for the platoon and company commanders. The horseshoe radio antenna soon proved vulnerable to artillery fire and was eventually discontinued.

The Model 1933 became the most numerous type of T-26 with over 5,000 being built by 1937. In service the crews soon developed an understandable dislike for the poor armour and the underpowered engine. Following the border clashes with the Japanese between 1934 and 1935, the T-26's riveted armour was dropped in favour of welded armour. This was after it was found that machine-gun fire split the rivets which then sprayed around the crew compartment. Attempts to improve the engine only managed to increase its 90bhp to 97bhp. The last of the Model 1933 built in 1936 were armed with two additional machine guns, one to go on the top of the turret for anti-aircraft use and another one in the rear of the turret. It was followed by the Model 1938 and Model 1939 with a new conical turret.

The T-26 was blooded in the Spanish Civil War of 1936–9, the Russo-Japanese border war of 1938–9 and the Russo-Finnish War of 1939–40. The vast variety of geography and climate conditions meant that the T-26 was thoroughly tested. In Spain Republican crews often lacked coordination with the infantry, leaving the T-26s vulnerable to counter-attacks and artillery fire. Spanish Nationalist armour suffered from the same problem. However, throughout the war the T-26's 45mm gun gave it an advantage over Franco's Nationalist tanks and those of his German and Italian allies. The Nationalists were not averse to press-ganging the T-26 into their own service and offered 500 pesetas for every one captured.

On 29 October 1936 Republican T-26s broke through Nationalist defences at Sesena, overrunning an artillery battery and destroying two tankettes. During the Red Army's fighting against the Japanese in the late 1930s the T-26 proved superior. In these campaigns the T-26 was deployed en masse with supporting arms such as infantry, artillery and bombers. Nonetheless, the T-26's greatest weakness was its 15mm frontal and 6mm side armour. The use of new anti-tank weapons and indirect artillery fire during all three conflicts led to heavy losses. In Finland the lack of artillery and infantry support contributed to heavy casualties. It was clear that the T-26's days as an assault tank were limited.

As a result of these hard-won lessons the T-26 was redesigned, leading to the final standard version, the T-26S Model 1939, which was known as the T-26C outside the Soviet Union. This had 25mm frontal armour and a new conical turret with thicker sloping armour. The hull armour was also sloped and extra plates added. This made the tank heavier. Around 2,000 M1938/29s were produced.

Despite this, by the time of Hitler's invasion of the Soviet Union in June 1941 the T-26 was obsolete when pitted against modern anti-tank guns. Production was stopped in 1940 with the view to replacing it with the T-34 that was just entering service. Although the 45mm gun could handle all German armour expect for the Panzer IV, many T-26s proved mechanically unreliable. Most notably there were clutch and gearbox failures during the height of the fighting.

A number of specialized variants of the T-26 were also produced as bridgelayers and flamethrowers.

OT-26 Flamethrower
Most notable of the T-26 variants was the OT-26 flamethrower. This was based on the Model 1931 T-26 and had a flame gun with a range of 25m mounted in the right-hand turret. To increase space for the fuel tanks the left-hand turret was omitted on the later versions.

OT-130 Flamethrower
The turret was really too small for the flame gun on the OT-26, so the larger Model 1932 turret was also used, resulting in the OT-130.

OT-133 Flamethrower
The OT-130 was followed by the OT-133 based on the more reliable and uparmoured T-26S. The OT-130 and the OT-133 both saw combat during the Russo-Finnish War, but their limited range made then vulnerable to enemy fire and mines. They lacked a close defence weapon as neither version featured a machine gun. These experiences led to the development of the KV and T-34 flamethrower tanks, although the OT tanks were still in service in the summer of 1941.

ST-26 Bridgelayer

The Red Army also pioneered bridgelaying tanks with the ST-26 seeing service between 1934 and 1938. It was fitted with a 7m bridge that could cross narrow gaps. Other variants included observation and towing vehicles.

T-27 Armoured Gun Tractor

The machine-gun armed T-27 tankette produced in the late 1920s was based on the British tracked Vickers Carden-Loyd Mk VI tankette. Used for training and internal security purposes, its lack of a turret and amphibious capability led to the development of the T-37 amphibious light tank. Although production stopped in 1933, some were still in service when the war broke out. By that stage they were not used as weapons carriers, but rather as tractors to tow 37mm and 45mm anti-tank guns.

T-28 Medium Tank

The T-28 medium and T-35 heavy tanks were only built in limited numbers but like the T-26 and BT-7 proved a source of endless fascination for the German victors. The T-28 was one of the world's very first medium tanks: about 500 of these and just 60 T-35s were ever built. Due to its imposing size the T-35 was regularly captured on film. The T-28 for some reason is much rarer.

During the 1930s multi-turret tank designs were popular in Britain, France, Germany and the Soviet Union. While the idea of land-based battleships had its merits, only the Soviet Union saw such tanks go into action and they proved far from successful against the agile panzers with their better command and control.

Although designated a medium tank, the T-28 with three turrets looked more like a heavy tank and could be easily mistaken for the very similar-looking T-35. It was developed as a breakthrough weapon at the Leningrad Kirov or Bolshevik Factory in 1932. It may have taken its inspiration from the British A6 medium and German Grosstraktor designs. The latter had been seen at Kazan when Stalin allowed the

Germans to conduct secret tank training in the Soviet Union. Both countries though abandoned the multi-turret type tank as impractical. The British only built three A6s and the Germans produced just six prototypes of the Grosstraktor.

The T-28A was armed with a 76.2mm Model 27/32 gun as its main armament but this was later replaced by the 76.2mm (L/16.5) gun. It was accepted as the Red Army's very first Soviet-built medium tank on 11 August 1933. It required a crew of six who manned the central turret with the main gun, plus three machine guns: a coaxial DT and two in forward-mounted turrets. It carried 70 rounds of main-armament ammunition and 7,938 machine-gun rounds. In 1938 the L/16.5 calibre gun was upgraded to a 26-calibre L-10 and the version with this was known as the T-28 Ob.1938 or T-28B.

Maximum armour was 80mm while the minimum was 20mm. Although it was bulky and at 31.5 tons was three times the weight of the T-26 and BT-7, it was fast for the period, managing 37km/h on roads. However, cross-country it was only capable of 20km/h. The T-28 was powered by a M-17L V-12 372kW (500bhp) petrol engine which produced 1,400rpm (this was a Soviet version of the American Liberty aero engine). The tank had a multi-wheel suspension with twelve wheels mounted in pairs either side. The drive sprockets were to the rear and the idlers at the front. Four return rollers were also fitted either side. Most of the suspension was protected by skirting plates that featured mud chutes to prevent clogging.

When the T-28 went into production it was built by the Red Putilov Factory in Leningrad as the Bolshevik Factory was busy producing the T-26. The first ten were ready to take part in the Moscow May Day Parade in 1933. During its production run to 1940 the tank underwent four main modifications. The T-28A Model 1934 had a modified suspension that consisted of twelve bogie rollers with four return rollers, plus increased frontal armour. The Germans dubbed it the T-28V, while the B version or Model 1938 was known as the T-28M. The main difference with the latter was that the main gun was uprated and a ball-mounted machine gun was installed in the rear of the turret.

When the Russo-Finnish or Winter War broke out, the Red Army had available the 10th and 20th Tank Brigades equipped with the T-28. The Finns soon nicknamed it 'The Mail Train' and although they had few anti-tank guns they were still able to inflict heavy losses. The Red Army's response was to order the T-28C modification. The frontal armour on the hull and turret was boosted from 50mm to 80mm and the rear and side to 40mm with the use of additional 'screened armour'. Thanks to this increased protection the T-28 served in the breakthrough attacks against the Finns' Mannerheim Line in 1940.

The T-28 was intended for frontal assaults and as a breakthrough tank, hence the three turrets which could pour fire onto anything in its path. In 1941 when it came up against the panzers its auxiliary turrets were all but useless in open tank warfare. In addition, the tank's relatively thin rear and side armour plus its high profile made it an easy prey to enemy anti-tank guns, artillery, dive-bombers and tanks. In anticipation of the T-34, production of the T-28 ceased.

T-34 Medium Tank

T-34/76

By 1941 the Red Army had in its possession a tank that was vastly superior to all its other designs with the partial exception of the KV-1. It first appeared the year before and was technically more advanced than Hitler's panzers. The only drawback for the Red Army was that when the war commenced it did not have many of them, and those it did have were suffering teething problems and needed time to be fine-tuned, which was a luxury they did not have.

This meant that the world-famous T-34 medium tank, along with the T-26 and BT-7, became one of the most photographed tank wrecks on the Eastern Front. While the latter two types were photographed largely out of contempt and the T-28 and T-35 as lumbering novelties, the Germans must have taken their photos of the T-34 with a mixed sense of relief and amazement at how incompetently the Soviets had handled this modern-looking tank.

Like the other Soviet tank types, the T-34 was found abandoned in the most ridiculous of places, stranded in the middle of swamps, piled into each other, rear-ended and even upside down. It was self-evident from these situations that the crews had little idea of what they were doing. This would change as the war progressed and the T-34's problems were ironed out, but in the meantime growing numbers of T-34s joined all the other tank wrecks on the Eastern Front.

During the 1930s tank designer Mikhail Koshkin began work on a new tank to replace the T-26 and BT. He suggested to Defence Commissar Voroshilov that it be dubbed the T-34 to mark the 1934 state decree that had authorized the major expansion of the Red Army's armoured forces. Although working on a number of other designs, he envisaged a medium tank that would only run on tracks.

Two prototypes were completed by January 1940 and, determined to prove the robustness of his design, Koshkin drove them all the way from Kharkov to present them to Red Army officials in Moscow. They were then sent to Finland to test the 76.2mm gun on captured Finnish bunkers. Additional firing tests were conducted in Minsk and the prototypes were then sent back to Kharkov via Kiev. During February and March 1940 the T-34 prototypes covered a round trip of 2,280 miles.

The production T-34 Model 1940 came off the Kharkov factory floor in September 1940. Tragically, after his winter test drive Koshkin developed pneumonia and died at the end of the month. His colleague Alexander Morozov took over. Unfortunately, due to problems with gun manufacture, the M1940 was armed with the inadequate short 76.2mm L-11 Model 1938 rifled gun with a length of 30.5 calibres. The T-34 carried 77 main gun rounds, though this was increased to 100 on the Model 1943. This was a disaster because it meant the bulk of the T-34s started the war on the Eastern Front with a less effective gun, with predictable results. The following year a few were fitted with the 57mm ZiS-4 long-barrelled high-velocity gun, which could engage lightly-armoured targets at a longer range.

The 76.2mm F-32 used to arm the KV-1 had better armour-piercing qualities than the L-11 because of its longer barrel. By the end of 1940 the former had been improved without authorization to create the F-34 of 42 calibres, which was vastly superior to the L-11. The first T-34s armed with the F-34 and known as the Model 1941 appeared at Kharkov in February 1941. These were issued to company and platoon commanders and their enhanced hitting power was confirmed resisting the German invasion.

As word spread that the tankers did not want any more T-34s armed with the L-11, the Main Defence Committee officially authorized the F-34 as the standard T-34 tank weapon in August 1941. Firing the BT-350A, the standard Soviet armour-piercing round, at the beginning of the war it could penetrate the Panzer III and cope with the Panzer IV Ausf F with its 50mm of frontal armour at most ranges. With the introduction of the Tiger and Panther tanks the balance shifted because the F-34 could not penetrate their frontal armour at regular combat ranges. This was only remedied with the appearance of the T-34/85 armed with an 85mm gun in mid-1944.

The T-34 chassis utilized the Christie system, but instead of four pairs of road wheels it had five (with a gap between the second and third) either side. Each was independently mounted and transversely swung on an interior vertical coil spring. Like the Christie M1928 and the BT tanks, the T-34 did not have return rollers. The drive sprockets were mounted at the back, driving round the skeleton-type manganese steel tracks, employing central guide horns that engaged alternate track links.

The most notable innovation on the T-34 was undoubtedly its wide tracks which measured 483mm. This spread the ground pressure meaning that the T-34 did not exceed 0.7kg–0.75kg per cm^2. In contrast American, British and German tanks exerted some 0.95kg–1kg per cm^2. The tracks were held together by dry track pins which were pushed back into place by a curved wiper plate welded on either side of the hull to the rear facing the upper track run. This system facilitated the swift removal of damaged track links, or shoes, and made life a lot easier for crews in combat when time was of the essence.

Unlike the Soviets' earlier tanks, the T-34's hull had sloped sides that overhung the upper track run. It was manufactured from homogeneous rolled-steel plate and electro-welded together. The armour was 45mm at the front and sides and 20mm on the top. The glacis plate was set at a 60-degree angle with just two openings, one for the driver's hatch and once for the ball-mounted hull machine gun. The angle of the T-34's frontal armour gave it the equivalent protection of 75mm of vertical armour. This made the T-34 almost invulnerable in 1941.

The power-to-weight ratio on the 28-ton tank was first class, thanks to the V-type four-stroke 12-cylinder water-cooled diesel engine, which generated 493bhp at 1,800rpm. This gave the T-34 a top road speed of 54km/h and 10km/h cross-country. The less flammable diesel engine also increased the combat range to 464km compared to those tanks with petrol engines.

While the T-34 was a first-class design, it started the war with transmission problems, an inadequate gun, shortages of ammunition and fuel plus very poor crew training. The result was that most of the early production T-34s were swiftly lost during the German invasion.

T-34/85 Medium Tank

During the summer of 1943 Morozov, who had taken over as chief designer from the late Koshkin, redesigned the T-34 to take a new turret armed with an 85mm gun on par with the KV-85 and SU-85. Adapting the cast turret designed for the KV-85 introduced standardization between the two classes of tank. Later the turret was redesigned and a second model of T-34/85 was produced. The Model 1943 turret displayed a unique style of bolted collar and was armed with the shorter D-5T 85mm gun which was capable of penetrating the frontal armour of the German Tiger at 1,000m, although accuracy remained a problem. This interim model also featured a rounded front-hull join, rounded front fenders and no turret fillet

The T-34/85's larger turret allowed for a five-man crew instead of four, which freed up the commander who had previously fired the main gun as well as directing the tank. Also the frontal armour was increased to a maximum of 75mm. Despite the numerous improvements and refinements that had been introduced since 1940, the T-34 remained the same simple and rugged design that was well suited to mass production. The basic T-34 chassis still included the 500hp V-12 cylinder diesel engine, driving the rear sprockets and the Christie-style suspension of large road wheels on pivot arms controlled by long coil springs.

The larger-calibre armament provided greater range and combat parity with the Germans' heavy tanks; this, combined with ever growing numbers, was a war-winning combination. The T-34/85 was approved for mass production on 15 December 1943. By the end of the year 283 had been produced and during the following year a further 11,000 were built. Approximately 800 T-34/85 Model 1943s were produced at Gorkiy early in 1944.

The T-34/85 had three distinctive wartime production models. These comprised the Model 1943 (which had a short production run with the D-5T 85mm gun). This was followed by the Model 1944 that was produced from March 1944 through to the end of that year, featuring the simpler ZiS-S-53 85mm gun, a new gunner's sight, improved internal layout and the radio moved from the hull into the turret. Finally, the Model 1945 was confusingly manufactured from 1944 to 1945, with an electrically-powered turret traverse motor, an enlarged commander's cupola with a one-piece hatch, and the TDP (*tankovoy dimoviy pribor*) smoke system with electrically-detonated MDSh canisters. This remained in production until the mid-1950s when the T-54 tank was adopted. After the war there was a Model 1946, plus there were refurbishment programmes in 1960 and in 1969.

The T-34/85 Model 1945 differed from the Model 1944 in that it featured a larger cupola, which extended close to the port edge of the turret, requiring a tiny lip underneath on the turret side. Although the Red Army did not differentiate between the variants, the Model 1946 entered service during late 1945 and saw front-line action in the closing days of 'The Great Patriotic War'. It could be distinguished from the Model 1945 by its fuller lower turret sides and the new configuration of ventilator domes. Another improved variant was developed that year known as the T-44, but it did not see service until the early post-war years.

Nearly a dozen uses were found for the robust T-34 chassis, key amongst them being the self-propelled gun and tank destroyer roles. Following the German invasion, the Soviets sought to outgun German armour; the challenge for the designers was to marry the gun to the mount, which was easier said than done. The Red Army had been particularly impressed by the German Sturmgeschütz assault gun and sought to emulate it.

OT-34 Flamethrower

The OT-34 and OT-34-85 flamethrower tanks had an internally-mounted ATO-41 (Model 1941) or ATO-42 (Model 1942) flame gun with the nozzle replacing the hull machine gun. The fuel for the flamethrower was carried in an armoured tank on the back of the vehicle. The OT-34 equipped with the ATO-42 carried 44 gallons (200 litres) of fuel and was powered by compressed air. It had a range of up to 90m with unthickened fuel or 110m with thickened fuel. The ATO-42 was operated by an electrical pump that was started by a 20mm cartridge. The OT-34 was capable of six bursts each of about two seconds' duration. The flamethrower tanks were organized into battalions consisting of one company of eleven OT-34 medium flamethrowers and two companies of KV-8 heavy flamethrowers with ten tanks. As the heavy KV-8s were lost, the flamethrower battalions were reorganized in 1943 consisting of two companies of OT-34 supported by a company of standard T-34 gun tanks.

PT-34 Mine Clearer

For mine-clearing operations there were roller-equipped variants both with the T-34/76 and the T-34/85 that were dubbed the PT-34. The rollers were propelled on arms in front of the tank. A variant was also produced using chain flails similar to the British Scorpion and Crab. Finnish minefields caused the Red Army major problems during the Winter War – in fact it lost several thousand armoured fighting vehicles to various causes. As a result, P.M. Mugalev at the Dormashina Factory in Nikolaev was instructed to design a mine-clearing vehicle that could sweep a path for the assault tanks following up behind. In 1940 prototypes were tested employing the cumbersome T-28 medium tank, but these trials were interrupted by the German invasion and were not resumed until 1942, by which time the T-28 had been thoroughly discredited, so the T-60 light tank and KV heavy tank chassis were tested instead. Ultimately only the transmission and clutch on the T-34 was found to be up to the job.

The plough, normally fitted to the T-34/76D, consisted of a steel fork girder frame fixed to the front of the tank. Attached at the front of the frame were two sets of steel rollers consisting of five spiked discs (each spike was actually a steel triangle with the base of the triangle facing out from the disc which pressed into the ground as the tank rolled forward to detonate mines). The drawback with this design was the gap between the two sets of rollers, which only covered the width of each track, so the tank could miss a mine and pass right over it. While the roller fork was semi-permanently mounted on the T-34/76 or T-34/85, the rollers were normally removed when the tank was in transit. This meant that the rollers had to be installed near the front just before commencing operations. The rollers could withstand a maximum of ten detonations of up to 10kg anti-tank mines, after which they had to be replaced.

Once the design was greenlighted in May 1942, trial detachments of PT-34s were created. That August two experimental PT-34s saw combat at Voronezh with the 223rd Tank Battalion, 86th Tank Brigade. Some were also used during the Battle of Stalingrad, notably spearheading the assault on Kanteirovets airfield by the 16th Guards Tank Battalion during the Soviet counter-attack that encircled the Germans. It was not until October the following year that an initial independent engineer tank regiment with eighteen PT-34s was established – by the end of the war there were some five such regiments. The PT-34 played a leading role in Operation Bagration during the summer of 1944 and in the Vistula-Oder offensive when two regiments of mine rollers were deployed with the advancing Red Army.

SKP-5 Armoured Recovery Vehicle
The first specialized recovery vehicle was the SKP-5, comprising a T-34 chassis carrying a 360-degree traverse crane with a 5-ton capacity.

SU-85 Tank Destroyer
Once the Soviets had phased out most of their old light and medium tanks, only the T-34 and KV chassis remained in production to provide an upgunned platform. By the autumn of 1942 the Red Army was encountering the German Tiger tank that had armour too thick to be penetrated by the T-34 and KV-1's 76.2mm guns at a safe range. The following summer they also had to contend with the Panther, which meant the Red Army needed a more powerful main armament.

In order to provide a tank that was roughly equivalent to the Tiger, during the summer of 1943 the Soviets worked to upgrade the KV-1 by fitting a new turret armed with an 85mm gun. Similarly, a tank destroyer or tank hunter variant of the T-34 was supplied to the Red Army in August 1943, by fitting the D-5T high-velocity 85mm anti-tank gun into the limited-traverse mount of the SU-122 self-propelled gun superstructure (SU stands for *Samokhodnaya Ustanovka* or self-propelled carriage). This new armoured fighting vehicle presented a low profile to enemy tanks and enjoyed the same mobility as the T-34, but the trade-off with the hull-mounted gun, as with the SU-122, was relatively thin armour.

Around 100 had been built by the end of 1943 and the following year production was continued to replace the SU-76 self-propelled gun, which was relegated to an infantry support role. Two versions appeared, the basic one that had a fixed commander's cupola with a rotating periscope and three vision blocks, and the SU-85M, which had the same casemate as the follow-on SU-100 and the T-34/85 commander's cupola.

The SU-85 was designed to stand off and destroy enemy armoured vehicles and bunkers. As a consequence, it lacked a self-defence machine gun and like the German Ferdinand/Elefant was very vulnerable to enemy infantry at close quarters. The SU-85 first saw combat along the Dnieper River in August 1943 and was initially popular as it was one of the few tanks that could take on the Tiger and the Panther.

The SU-85s were issued to two types of unit. Firstly, there were the self-propelled gun battalions equipped with twelve SU-85s at army and corps level. Then there were the larger regiments each with four batteries of sixteen SU-85s. The SU-85 was swiftly superseded by the T-34/85 so production was halted in late 1944 by which time 2,050 had been built. The production lines were switched to the SU-100 instead and the remaining SU-85s were withdrawn after the war ended.

SU-100 Tank Destroyer

As the SU-85 offered no advantages over the T-34/85, it was decided to develop an upgunned version. The SU-100 appeared in September 1944 and was essentially the same vehicle as the SU-85, but armed with a 100mm Model 1944 high-velocity gun fitted in a larger mantlet. This made it one of the best self-propelled anti-tank guns of the war as it could penetrate 125mm of vertical armour out to 2,000m and the German Panther's sloped 85mm frontal armour at a range of 1,500 metres. Its hull also had major improvements over its predecessor with the frontal armour increased from 45mm to 75mm and the commander's area expanded by a sponson on the right-hand side of the hull. Combined with the commander's cupola, this made him more effective in directing his crew.

The only real drawback with this vehicle was the length of the gun barrel, which greatly reduced manoeuvrability. The SU-100 was not suited to fighting in forests or urban warfare. Likewise, it would have struggled on some country roads, particularly in the Carpathian Mountains where negotiating hairpin bends would have been completely out of the question. This tank destroyer saw widespread service during 1945 and was used to help defeat Hitler's ill-fated spring offensive in Hungary. By July that year Soviet tank factories had produced 2,335 SU-100s. It was much more successful than its predecessor and remained in service well into the late 1950s

SU-122 Self-Propelled Gun

The SU-122 was the first of several self-propelled guns based on the T-34 put into series production. This design involved removing the turret and installing a Model 1938 122mm field howitzer in the hull, using a limited-traverse mount at the front of the vehicle. A simple box superstructure was created following the existing slope of the T-34 front armour. The gun was held in an enormous mantlet, with a fabricated armoured cover for the very prominent recoil system.

Doing away with the turret allowed for a larger fighting compartment to house the gun breech and made it cheaper and easier to manufacture than a regular tank. However, aiming the gun required manoeuvring the entire vehicle. This rather cumbersome-looking vehicle was designed in 1942 with the first production vehicles coming into service in January 1943, initially as the SU-35. This was a combination of work carried out on the SG-122 based on the German StuG III and the U-34 (armed with the standard 76.2mm tank gun), neither of which went into production.

In late 1942 the first self-propelled regiments equipped with the SU-122 were formed. They consisted of two batteries of SU-122s with some eight vehicles and four batteries of the lighter SU-76 assault guns with a total of seventeen vehicles. The SU-122 was deployed in platoons of three, providing close fire support for the tank divisions. They were first used to equip the 1433rd and 1434th Self-propelled

Artillery Regiments. These joined the 54th Army on the Volkhov Front near Leningrad, which had been commanded by former head of the Artillery Directorate General Kulik, until he was court-martialled for incompetence in March 1942.

The combination of the SU-76 and the SU-122 was not ideal, especially as the former had an open fighting compartment. This meant the SU-122s were organized into separate units. The massive gun proved effective providing direct fire against enemy strongpoints and the concussion from the high-explosive round could take the turret off a Tiger tank at close range. The SU-122 was phased out in late 1943 and replaced by the SU-152 based on the robust KV chassis. However, production continued into the summer of 1944 by which time around 1,150 had been completed.

TT-34 Armoured Recovery Vehicle

Some battle-damaged T-34s were converted to T-34T or TT-34 (*tyagach* or tractor) armoured recovery role, with the removal of the turret and the turret ring was either plated over or a superstructure added for the crew. They were used in a towing role.

T-34/MTU Bridgelayer

There were at least three models of bridgelayer based on the T-34 designated the T-34/MTU. These included an 'ARK' type bridge fitted to the vehicle, another was a rigid arm-launched bridge (the MTU) as well as a Czech-designed folding scissor bridge, although these were post-war designs. The ARK featured an adjustable platform instead of the turret and the bridge could not be removed from the tank. The driver simply drove the tank into the gap that needed bridging and the bridge was then adjusted to the required height.

T-34-T Crane

A number of T-34s were fitted with specialized engineering equipment but this was not until after the Second World War had ended. In the early 1950s the T-34-T appeared which included a rigging assembly, a loading platform and jib crane. The rear deck was reinforced so that the cargo platform had a weight capacity of 2.5 tons

T-34/STU Dozer
Some T-34s were fitted with dozer blades and designated the T-34/STU.

T-34/57 Tank Hunter
As a stopgap some T-34s were fitted in 1941 and 1943 with the ZiS-2, ZiS-4 or the ZIS-4M high-velocity 57mm gun to be used as tank hunters. This gun actually had better penetration than the 76.2mm F-34, but its small bore meant its high-explosive shell was ineffective against unarmoured targets. Around 324 T-34s are believed to have been converted to this role.

T-35 Heavy Tank
During the interwar years the Soviets had designed a series of Direct Infantry Support (NPP) and Distant Remote (DPP) heavy tanks which were underpinned by the Red Army's Field Regulations of 1929. Only the Soviet Union's massive industrialization made this possible thanks to the provision of new factories capable of such an undertaking.

In December 1930 the Soviet Directorate of Mechanization and Motorization, in cooperation with the General Design Bureau of the Artillery Department, initiated the first heavy tank. The T-30 was envisaged as a 50-ton tank armed with a 76.2mm gun and five machine guns. A prototype appeared in 1932, but problems with the running gear led to the project being cancelled.

With the assistance of German designers, the Bolshevik Factory in Leningrad came up with the 30-ton T-22 and T-29 armed with 76.2mm and 37mm guns. They also conceived the T-42, that would have weighed 100 tons and been armed with a 107mm howitzer. However, none of these ideas got any further than the drawing board. These efforts may have been informed by German work on the

Grosstraktor and the subsequent Neubaufahrzeug, though both these were medium tanks in the 20-ton range.

At the same time a second team was working on the T-35 and two prototypes were completed between 1932 and 1933. The T-35-1 weighed 50 tons and was armed with a 76.2mm gun based on the Model 27/32 howitzer, surrounded by four smaller auxiliary turrets, two with 37mm guns and two with machine guns. The front right and rear left ones mounted the heavier guns. It soon became apparent that this prototype was not suitable for mass production.

The T-35-2 had a more powerful M-17 engine with a rebuilt suspension, fewer turrets and a crew of seven rather than ten. The armour was slightly thicker, with 35mm on the front and 25mm on the sides, which could withstand shell splinters and small-arms fire. The Work Defence Council on 11 August 1933 authorized production of the T-35A at the Kharkov Locomotive Factory that required eleven crew.

The T-35 was undoubtedly influenced by British and German designs, particularly the British Vickers A-6 Independent tank. Whatever its origins, the size and complexity of the T-35 resulted in only about sixty ever being built between 1933 and 1939. Like most early Soviet tanks, it suffered from poor quality control and assembly. It also had inadequate steering which made it hard to manoeuvre. The Red Army needed large numbers of tanks quickly so the T-35 suffered due to BT fast tank production.

Like all tanks the T-35 went through endless fine tuning. The 1935 model was longer and fitted with the turret designed for the T-28 armed with the L-10 76.2mm gun. The 45mm gun intended for the T-26 and BT-5 tanks replaced the 37mm guns in the two sub-turrets. A final batch of six tanks had turrets with sloped armour.

The T-35 was issued to just three battalions of the 5th Separate Heavy Tank Brigade, which came under the Supreme Command Reserve. A few were used in Finland to little effect. In the run-up to the Second World War it saw little active service and in 1940, during of a conference of Red Army tank specialists, it was recommended that the T-35 be relegated to training duties. Up to that point it only ever appeared during Moscow's May Day and November parades, where to the general public it looked a very formidable beast. Instead it was decided to keep them in service until they wore out.

When Hitler invaded many of the operational T-35s were simply overrun by the panzers. Those serving with the 67th and 68th Tank Regiments forming the 34th Tank Division, assigned to the 8th Mechanized Corps, quickly broke down during the battles that summer. Under noisy combat conditions with the engine running, trying to coordinate the actions of the dozen crew proved almost impossible. A few remaining T-35s took part in the defence of Moscow acting as fixed strongpoints.

T-37 Amphibious Light Tank
The Red Army had thousands of small light tanks, including the tiny two-man amphibious T-37/38 armed with a 7.62mm machine gun. Some 1,200 T-37s were built between 1933 and 1936. These replaced the T-27 tankette and served with the Red Army tank, mechanized and cavalry units in a reconnaissance role until 1942. Both types only had 10mm of armour.

T-38 Amphibious Light Tank
The T-38 was essentially a redesigned T-37, which had better manoeuvrability and swimming capabilities. The armament remained the same. About 1,300 were produced between 1937 and 1939.

T-40 Amphibious Tank
The larger T-40 came into service in early 1941 and was armed with one 12.7mm machine gun and one 7.62mm machine gun, or a 20mm cannon and 7.62mm machine gun. If it had been restricted to reconnaissance, as intended, it could have played a useful role against the Nazi invasion, but instead Soviet commanders threw them away by deploying them as regular tanks.

T-43 Medium Tank

In 1943 a small number of T-34s were manufactured with much thicker armour and designated the T-43. These sported 110mm frontal armour and 75mm on the sides, a new five-speed gearbox and the late-pattern turret. It was still armed with the 76.2mm gun that was not powerful enough in the face of the new German 75mm and 88mm high-velocity tank and anti-tank guns, which were appearing in greater numbers. The T-43 was not very successful as the increase in weight greatly reduced the tank's performance and it was swiftly superseded by the KV-85 and T-34/85.

T-44 Medium Tank

Towards the end of the Second World War the Soviets decided that rather than maintaining large fleets of dedicated light, medium and heavy tanks they needed a good all-rounder – this resulted in the main battle tank concept. A 'one size fits all' solution. Soviet tank designers began to look at developing a successor for the T-34/85 medium tank and the IS heavy tank. Drawing on their experiences with the T-34/76, T-34/85, KV-85 and IS-1/2, in 1944 they came up with the T-44, which bore a striking resemblance to the late-war T-34/85 and was armed with the same 85mm gun. It was essentially the same tank with a number of modifications. The main improvements to the rugged T-34/85 design were a similar-shaped turret but without the characteristic thick turret neck, plus a better-shaped hull. Other improvements included a transverse-mounted engine and transmission and torsion bar suspension. The crew was reduced from five in the T-34/85 to four in the T-44.

One of the designers' tasks was to lower the height of the T-34/85. Upgunning the T-34/76 had resulted in a much bigger turret, which increased the T-34's height from around 2.4m to over 2.7m. While the improvement from the 76.2mm gun to the 85mm gun was very welcome, it made the T-34/85's bulky turret a much more promising target. Similarly, the IS heavy tank was almost 3m high.

On the T-44 one way to achieve a lower silhouette was to eliminate the prominent collar at the turret base. The hull side armour, which on the T-34 was sloped, was vertical and thicker. This was to permit a wider turret ring because the turret's armour was more slanted than that on the T-34/85. Another way that the height was reduced was by installing the diesel engine transversely. Also the Christie spring suspension was replaced with a torsion bar suspension. The result was that the T-44 had a height of just under 2.5m.

Improving on the T-34/85's main armament was unsuccessful. Attempts were made to upgun the T-44 with a 122mm, but the turret was too small. Although experiments with a 100mm gun were slightly more promising, only a few prototypes were ever built and the production T-44 retained the 85mm gun. The only way to get round this problem was to design a new tank with a larger turret.

While the T-44 was very similar to the T-34, the glacis plate at the front was much steeper which meant it had to be thicker. The driver was only provided with a very narrow vision port in the glacis and his hatch, located next to the hull machine gun on the glacis on the T-34, was repositioned to the hull roof. The hull gunner was dispensed with in line with the existing trend with Soviet heavy tanks. Protection against infantry was provided by a 7.62mm machine gun mounted in a fixed position next to the driver, which was fired through an opening in the glacis plate. This was a feature later retained in the T-54.

The successful T-34 five twin-road wheel running gear was largely unchanged, although the T-44 had a wider gap between the first and second pairs of road wheels instead of the second and third on the T-34. One of the drawbacks of the later was that it employed the American Christie-style suspension. This meant that bulky springs took up a large amount of space within the tank. Efforts to remedy this with the T-34M in 1941 had to be abandoned because of the outbreak of war. The T-43 partially remedied this, but was swiftly superseded by the need for a larger gun and the T-34/85 which used the existing T-34 hull.

The T-44 proved problematic, especially where its weight was concerned. It was supposed to be the same as the T-34/85 at some 31.5 tons, but in light of the thicker armour and lengthening of the hull, it is hard to see what the lowering of the height achieved other than to reduce the tank's silhouette. It is suspected that the T-44 was heavier than its predecessor and suffered from problems with its running gear and transmission.

In the event only a few thousand T-44s were ever built at Kharkov and it did not see much, if any, combat at the end of the war. It was allegedly deployed briefly during the Hungarian uprising of 1956. After proving unreliable in front-line service the tank was rebuilt as the T-44M and continued to be used into the 1970s – largely in a tank driver training role. From all its design faults and teething problems it is evident that the T-44 was very much an interim design and served as a testbed for features that were incorporated in the vastly more successful Cold War T-54.

T-60 Light Tank

The T-60 was similar in appearance to the T-40, but was armed with a 20mm cannon. The outbreak of war disrupted production and subsequent enhancements to its armour meant that it could not keep up with the T-34. Various upgrades failed to remedy this. Nonetheless, by the time it was superseded by the T-70 in early 1943 over 6,000 had been built.

T-70 Light Tank

Armed with an improved 45mm gun, the T-70 light tank went into production in March 1942, with 8,226 having been built by the end of the following year. Although the hull armour was given better angles of protection and the driver had an armoured visor, modifications to the armament and armour of the Panzer III and IV easily cancelled out such improvements. The Red Army deployed 261 T-70s at Kursk where they proved unsuitable in a tank-to-tank combat role.

SU-76 Light Self-Propelled Gun

After the T-34, the SU-76 light self-propelled gun was the most widely produced Soviet armoured vehicle of the Second World War. Using the T-70 light tank chassis as a mount for the 76.2mm anti-tank gun, it appeared in 1943. Intended to provide the infantry with direct artillery fire support, it had a secondary anti-tank role. While the gun was more than adequate for such duties, crew protection was not. The crews hated the SU-76 because of its open fighting compartment and thin armour, which gained it the nickname *Suka*, or bitch. It was later replaced by the SU-85 tank destroyer as an anti-tank platform and switched to a purely self-propelled gun support role.

Bibliography

This work draws on a number of previous Pen & Sword books, all of which are listed below.

Abdulin, Mansur, *Red Road from Stalingrad: Recollections of a Soviet Infantryman* (Barnsley: Pen & Sword, 2004)

Adair, Paul, *Hitler's Greatest Defeat* (London: Rigel, 2004)

Ailsby, Christopher, *Barbarossa: The German Invasion of Russia, 1941* (Hoo: Grange, 2005)

Allen W.E.D. & Muratoff, Paul, *The Russian Campaigns of 1944-45* (Harmondsworth: Penguin, 1946)

Armstrong, Colonel R.N., *Soviet Operational Deception: The Red Cloak* (Fort Leavenworth: Kansas Combat Studies Institute, 1989)

Axell, Albert, *Russia's Heroes* (London: Constable, 2001)

Bailer, Seweryn (ed.), *Stalin & His Generals: Soviet Military Memoirs of World War II* (London: Souvenir, 1970)

Baxter, Ian, *Operation Bagration: The Destruction of Army Group Centre June–July 1942 – A Photographic History* (Solihull: Helion, 2007)

Bean, Tim & Fowler, Will, *Russian Tanks of World War II: Stalin's Armoured Might* (Hersham: Ian Allan, 2002)

Beevor, Antony, *Berlin: The Downfall 1945* (London: Viking, 2002)

Beevor, Antony, *Stalingrad* (London: Penguin, 1999)

Bellamy, Chris, *Absolute War: Soviet Russia in the Second World War* (London: Pan, 2008)

Bessonov, Evgeni, *Tank Rider: Into the Reich with the Red Army* (London: Greenhill, 2003)

Bonn, Keith E. (ed.), *Slaughterhouse: The Handbook of the Eastern Front* (Bedford, PA: Aberjona Press, 2005)

Braithwaite, Roderic, *Moscow 1941: A City and Its People at War* (London: Profile, 2006)

Bryukhov, Vasiliy, *Red Army Tank Commander: At War in a T-34 on the Eastern Front* (Barnsley: Pen & Sword, 2013)

Chaney, Otto Preston, *Zhukov* (Newton Abbot: David & Charles, 1972)

Clark, Alan, *Barbarossa: The Russian German Conflict 1941-1945* (London: Cassell, 2001)

Clark, Lloyd, *Kursk: The Greatest Battle: Eastern Front 1943* (London: Headline Review, 2012)

Collier, Richard, *The War that Stalin Won* (London: Hamish Hamilton, 1983)

Connor, Lieutenant Colonel W., *Analysis of Deep Attack Operations: Operation Bagration, Belorussia, 22 June – 29 August 1944* (Fort Leavenworth, Kansas: Combat Studies Institute, 1987)

Cornish, Nik, *Hitler Versus Stalin: The Eastern Front 1943-1944: Kursk to Bagration* (Barnsley: Pen & Sword, 2017)

Cornish, Nik, *Images of Kursk: History's Greatest Tank Battle July 1943* (Staplehurst: Spellmount, 2002)

Craig, William, *Enemy at the Gates: The Battle for Stalingrad* (London: Hodder and Stoughton, 1973)

Davies, Norman, *Rising '44: 'The Battle for Warsaw'*. (London: Macmillan, 2003)

Ellis, Chris, *Tanks of World War II* (London: Chancellor Press, 1997)

Ellis, Chris & Chamberlain, Peter, *The Great Tanks* (London: Hamlyn, 1975)

Erickson, John, *The Road to Berlin* (London: Weidenfeld and Nicolson, 1983)

Fey, Will, *Armor Battles of the Waffen-SS 1943-45* (Mechanicsburg, PA: Stackpole, 2003)

Forczyk, Robert, *Panther vs T-34: Ukraine 1943* (Oxford: Osprey, 2007)

Forty, George, *Tank Action: From the Great War to the Gulf* (Stroud: Alan Sutton, 1995)

Forty, George & Livesey, Jack, *The Complete Guide to Tanks & Armoured Fighting Vehicles* (London: Hermes House, 2006)

Glantz, David M., *Barbarossa: Hitler's Invasion of Russia 1941* (Stroud: Tempus, 2001)

Glantz, David M., *Kharkov 1942: Anatomy of a Military Disaster Through Soviet Eyes* (Shepperton: Ian Allan, 1998)

Glantz, David M., *The Siege of Leningrad 1941-1944: 900 Days of Terror* (London: Cassell, 2004)

Haupt, Werner, *Army Group Center: The Wehrmacht in Russia 1941-1945* (Atglen, PA: Schiffer Publishing, 1977)

Healy, Mark, *Kursk 1943: The tide turns in the East* (Oxford: Osprey, 1993)

Healy, Mark, *Zitadelle: The German Offensive Against the Kursk Salient 4-17 July 1943* (Stroud: The History Press, 2008)

Hughes, Dr Matthew & Mann, Dr Chris *The T-34 Tank* (Staplehurst: Spellmount, 1999)

Jukes, Geoffrey, *The Defence of Moscow* (London: Macdonald, 1970)

Jukes, Geoffrey, *The Second World War (5): The Eastern Front 1941-1945* (Oxford: Osprey, 2002)

Keegan, John, *Barbarossa: Invasion of Russia 1941* (London: Macdonald, 1971)

Kerr, Walter, *The Russian Army: Its Men, Its Leaders and Its Battles* (London: Victor Gollancz, 1944)

Kerr, Walter, *The Secret of Stalingrad* (London: Macdonald and Jane's, 1979)

Kershaw, Robert, *War Without Garlands: Operation Barbarossa 1941-1942* (Hersham: Ian Allan, 2008)

Khrushchev, Nikita, *Khrushchev Remembers* (London: Andre Deutsch, 1971)

Kirchubel, Robert, *Operation Barbarossa 1941 (3): Army Group Centre* (Oxford: Osprey, 2007)

Kurowski, Franz, *Deadlock Before Moscow: Army Group Center 1942/1943* (West Chester, PA: Schiffer Publishing, 1992)

Lucas, James, *War on the Eastern Front 1941-1945: The German Soldier in Russia* (London: Jane's, 1979)

Mackintosh, Malcolm, *Juggernaut: A History of the Soviet Armed Forces* (London: Secker & Warburg, 1967)

Merridale, Catherine, *Ivan's War: The Red Army 1939-1945* (London: Faber and Faber, 2005)

Messenger, Charles, *The Art of Blitzkrieg* (Shepperton: Ian Allan, 1991)

Miller, David, *The Illustrated Directory of Tanks of the World: From World War I to the Present Day* (London: Greenwich, 2004)

Milsom, John & Zaloga, Steven, *Russian Tanks of World War 2* (Cambridge: Patrick Stephens, 1977)

Morris, Eric, *Tanks* (London: Octopus, 1975)

Moynahan, Brian, *The Claws of the Bear: A History of the Soviet Armed Forces from 1917 to the Present* (London: Hutchinson, 1989)

Nagorski, Andrew, *The Greatest Battle: The Fight for Moscow 1941-42* (London: Aurum Press, 2008)

O'Ballance, Edgar, *The Red Army* (London: Faber and Faber, 1964)

Rayfield, Donald, *Stalin and His Hangmen: An Authoritative Portrait of a Tyrant and those who Served Him* (London: Viking, 2004)

Rees, Laurence, *World War Two Behind Closed Doors: Stalin, the Nazis and the West* (London: BBC, 2008)

Riasanovsky, Nicholas V., *A History of Russia* (New York: Oxford University Press, 1993)

Ripley, Tim, *Steel Storm: Waffen-SS Panzer Battles on the Eastern Front 1943-1945* (Stroud: Sutton, 2000)

Roberts, Geoffrey, *Stalin's General: The Life of Georgy Zhukov* (London: Icon, 2013)

Rogers, Duncan & Williams, Sarah (eds), *On the Bloody Road to Berlin: Frontline Accounts from North-West Europe and the Eastern Front 1944-45* (Solihull: Helion, 2005)

Ryan, Cornelius, *The Last Battle* (London: Collins, 1966)

Seaton, Albert, *Stalin as Warlord* (London: B.T. Batsford, 1976)

Seaton, Albert, *The Fall of Fortress Europe 1943-1945* (London: B.T. Batsford, 1981)

Sebag Montefiore, Simon, *Stalin: The Court of the Red Tsar* (London: Weidenfeld & Nicolson, 2003)

Service, Robert, *Stalin: A Biography* (London: Pan, 2005)

Shtemenko, General of the Soviet Army S.M., *The Last Six Months: Russia's Final Battles with Hitler's Armies in World War II* (London: William Kimber, 1978)

Tucker-Jones, Anthony, *Armoured Warfare on the Eastern Front* (Barnsley: Pen & Sword, 2011)

Tucker-Jones, Anthony, *Armoured Warfare and Hitler's Allies 1941-1945* (Barnsley: Pen & Sword, 2013)

Tucker-Jones, Anthony, *Armoured Warfare and the Waffen-SS 1944-1945* (Barnsley: Pen & Sword, 2017)

Tucker-Jones, Anthony, *Kursk 1943: Hitler's Bitter Harvest* (Stroud: The History Press, 2018)

Tucker-Jones, Anthony, *Slaughter on the Eastern Front: Hitler and Stalin's War 1941-1945* (Stroud: The History Press, 2017)

Tucker-Jones, Anthony, *Stalin's Revenge: Operation Bagration and the Annihilation of Army Group Centre* (Barnsley: Pen & Sword, 2009)

Tucker-Jones, Anthony, *Tank Wrecks of the Eastern Front 1941-1945* (Barnsley: Pen & Sword, 2018)

Tucker-Jones, Anthony, *The Battle for Budapest 1944-1945* (Barnsley: Pen & Sword, 2016)

Tucker-Jones, Anthony, *The Battle for Kharkov 1941-1943* (Barnsley: Pen & Sword, 2016)

Tucker-Jones, Anthony, *The Battle for the Caucasus 1942-1943* (Barnsley: Pen & Sword, 2018)

Tucker-Jones, Anthony, *The Battle for Warsaw 1939-1945* (Barnsley: Pen & Sword, 2020)

Tucker-Jones, Anthony, *Tiger I & Tiger II* (Barnsley: Pen & Sword, 2012)

Tucker-Jones, Anthony, *T-34: The Red Army's Legendary Medium Tank* (Barnsley: Pen & Sword, 2015)

Tucker-Jones, Anthony, *T-54/55: The Soviet Army's Cold War Main Battle Tank* (Barnsley: Pen & Sword, 2017)

Ungváry, Krisztián, *The Battle for Budapest: 100 Days in World War II* (London: I.B. Taurus, 2003)

Vanderveen, Bart, *Historic Military Vehicles Directory* (London: Battle of Britain Prints, 1989)

Vanderveen, Bart, *The Observer's Fighting Vehicles Directory World War II* (London: Frederick Warne, 1969)

Werth, Alexander, *Russia at War 1941-1945* (London: Pan, 1965)

White, B.T., *Tanks and other Armoured Fighting Vehicles of the Blitzkrieg Era 1939-41* (London: Blandford Press, 1972)

White, B.T., *Tanks and other Armoured Fighting Vehicles 1942-45* (Poole: Blandford Press, 1975)

Willoughby, Major General Charles A., *Sorge: Soviet Master Spy* (London: William Kimber, 1952)

Winchester, Charles, *Ostfront: Hitler's War on Russia 1941-45* (Oxford: Osprey, 1998)

Wray, Major T.A., *Standing Fast: German Defensive Doctrine on the Russian Front during World War II – Pre-war to March 1943* (Fort Leavenworth, Kansas: Combat Studies Institute, 1985)

Zaloga, Steven, *Bagration 1944: The Destruction of Army Group Centre* (Oxford: Osprey, 1996)

Zhukov, Georgi K., *Marshal Zhukov's Greatest Battles* (London: Macdonald, 1969)

Index